Many thanks for the generous support of our sponsors:

Chuck and Linda Barbo

Ron and Wanda Crockett

Neal and Jan Dempsey

Tom and Dixie Porter

Michael and Susan Rouleau

Jon and Judy Runstad

Coldstream Holdings Inc.

This book is dedicated to the coaches and players whose performances led to numerous conference championships, many postseason bowl victories, and two national championships. Your commitment, team unity, and resolve have forged one of the greatest football traditions in the nation.

Library of Congress Cataloging-in-Publication Data

Porter, W. Thomas.
 Go Huskies! : celebrating Washington's football tradition / W. Thomas Porter.
    pages cm
 Includes bibliographical references.
 ISBN 978-1-60078-827-7
 1. University of Washington—Football—History. 2. Washington Huskies (Football team)—History. I. Title.
 GV958.U5865P67 2013
 796.332'6309797772—dc23
                          2013012453

This book is available in quantity at special discounts for your group or organization. For further information, contact:

Triumph Books LLC
814 North Franklin Street
Chicago, Illinois 60610
(312) 337–0747
www.triumphbooks.com

Printed in China
ISBN: 978-1-60078-827-7
Design by Patricia Frey

GO HUSKIES!

Celebrating Washington's Football Tradition

W. Thomas Porter

TRIUMPH
BOOKS

Contents

Don James,
UW's winningest
football coach.

On Husky Stadium

There are numerous things that make Washington football special. I can think of none greater than Husky Stadium. Every morning, as I drove to work from my home in Bellevue, it rose magnificently from the horizon as a monument to the Husky program. Now, with its extensive renovation completed, the stadium will continue to provide a beautiful setting and a much more fan-friendly venue.

I think Husky football has different meanings to different people. It means something different to each fan, player, and coach. In my 18 seasons of coaching at the University of Washington, I was associated with some of the greatest teams and players in college football history. Washington is truly one of the finest academic institutions in the world and provides an outstanding environment in which to learn, grow, and mature as an individual.

I have been greatly impressed with the commitment, the determination, and the pride of the men who wear the purple and gold. They are very tough competitors, and they play at the very highest level in collegiate football. A classic matchup with a big opponent on a Saturday afternoon in Husky Stadium is one of the best in all of sports.

Husky Stadium is an incredible place to play a football game. Its adjacency to the water and the mountains, its upper decks rising to the sky, the walk down the tunnel and onto the field, and the passion of the Husky fans combine to make it one of the greatest venues in college football.

Husky football excites, inspires, and rallies students, faculty, alumni, and the community around the program. All of them are proud of the Huskies tradition. *Go Huskies!: Celebrating Washington's Football Tradition* is a complete chronicle of the history of Husky football. The book focuses on the major eras in Husky football history. It also spotlights the best teams, the greatest games, the biggest comebacks, and the greatest players—unsung heroes and fan favorites—in Husky history.

Go Huskies! helps all of us to relive the big games and big seasons and rekindles our memories of Husky legends.

—Coach Don James

Current Husky head coach Steve Sarkisian.

Husky Tradition

Before I became the Huskies' head football coach in 2009, I had great respect for the University of Washington's storied football tradition, as well as its outstanding academic reputation.

My most memorable experience in Husky Stadium was playing the Huskies on September 14, 1996, as the starting quarterback for BYU. I remember how loud the fans were, causing us to jump offside a number of times and preventing us from making audible corrections at the line of scrimmage. From the fans in the stands to the players on the field, you could sense their passion and enthusiasm for Husky football. It is something I will never forget.

Upon my appointment as Washington's head coach, I was eager to turn the football program around and get it back to the high level of success that UW football had enjoyed in much of its history. I am very proud of the improvements we have made in almost every phase of the game, and I strongly believe we will soon be among one of the best football programs in the nation.

Go Huskies!: Celebrating Washington's Football Tradition has captured that history and the success of UW football. The book weaves a complete history of Husky football—its humble beginnings, its major eras, the players and teams that forged the Huskies' greatest victories, its greatest seasons and bowl triumphs, and the national championships and rankings.

Go Huskies! will help all of us to relive the greatest games, the thrilling comeback victories, the greatest players, and all of those athletes who wore the purple and gold and raised their helmets with pride and purpose.

—Coach Steve Sarkisian

Bob Rondeau,
Voice of the Huskies.

Witness to History

The long-awaited renovation of Husky Stadium will certainly put a fresh face on the place, setting a framework of promise for years to come. It will be a new chapter in a football history that rubs elbows with many of the finest programs in America.

As the radio "voice of the Huskies" for more than 30 years, I've been fortunate to observe and chronicle a good chunk of that history. The stadium is a tactile reminder of the evolution of Washington football through the years, a fortress of sorts anchored in the most beautiful setting the college game has ever known. In the concrete, wood, and steel, we can touch and feel what Husky football is all about. It is an intimate relationship and will be even more so with the track removed, bringing the fans even closer to the field and their favorite team, their clamoring making it an even tougher environment for visiting squads.

For a moment, imagine you are one of those visiting players, playing in Husky Stadium for the first time. You're ready to go out for pregame warm-ups—about an hour and a half before kickoff. After dressing in the (temporary) comfort of the visitors' locker room in the southeast corner of the stadium, you're ready to take the field.

There might be rays of sunshine dancing across the artificial turf or a chill rain pounding like a snare drum to welcome you to the Pacific Northwest. On a clear day, the majesty of the place is in full view as you look to the east and the snowcapped Cascade Mountains that slope down to sea level—or in this case, lake level. You marvel that Dawg fans can actually take their boats to the game, mooring just outside the stadium complex. A huge American flag flaps gently, just beyond the end zone. It might be pointing stiffly one way or another by game's end as the gentle breeze gives way to the swirling gale that has gotten under the skin of so many Husky opponents through the years.

While you can process all that you see, you cannot know the legends, the passion, and the spirits that inhabit the place. You won't hear the crushing impact of Elmer Tesreau and George Wilson hitting Ernie Nevers, the great Stanford All-American fullback in 1925, lifting him off the ground and knocking him flat, preserving a Washington win and securing its second Rose Bowl trip. You won't see the spot where, in 1951, Hugh McElhenny caught a punt at his goal line, sidestepped the first tackle, shook off another, and began to dance up the north sideline. After a sudden burst of speed and Husky blockers upending USC defenders all over the field, a clear path opened to the Trojans goal line. The King hit the gas pedal and didn't let off until he scored a touchdown, capping off a 100-yard return. Nor will you see Don McKeta's touchdown run in 1960, which completed a 47-yard pass play on a fourth-and-6 situation with just more than two minutes in the game against Oregon. McKeta caught Bob Hivner's short pass near the sideline at the Ducks 37-yard line. Oregon's great defensive back Dave Grayson was moving in on him. Instead of going out of bounds to stop the clock, McKeta put an incredible move on the surprised Grayson and sped into the end zone to tie the score. George Fleming kicked the winning point after with about two minutes to go, sending coach Jim Owens and the Huskies toward a second-straight Rose Bowl victory and a national championship.

And what about the comeback win over Washington State in 1975? You won't see Al Burleson, with about three minutes left in the game, race 93 yards to bring the Huskies within six. Washington forced the Cougars to punt on WSU's next possession and took over on their own 22-yard line. On the next play, Warren Moon threw a pass for the ages, the rain-slicked ball slipping through a Cougars defender's hands, popping into the air and into the arms of Spider Gaines, who used his sprinter's speed to fly into the end zone for a Husky win.

How could you imagine what it was like in 1981, when Washington was hosting third-ranked USC in a howling wind that pushed a steady rain sideways? I can instantly recall how the press box shook with the weather, then rattled with the foot-stomping that accompanied the Dawgs' 13–3 upset of the Trojans on the way to another Rose Bowl.

Perhaps you can sense the electricity that will soon become a full-scale power surge, much like that weekend in 1990 when the Huskies celebrated their 100th year of football with another top-five USC team in town. The night before the game, I was honored to emcee a function honoring members of the Huskies' All-Centennial Team. It was tremendously exciting to see and talk with a number of those players who shaped Washington's football history. They left some big footprints on the Huskies' turf.

The next day, the Huskies left some big footprints on SC, blanking the Trojans 31–0 and serving notice of great glories to come. This was the day Trojans quarterback Todd Marinovich would say, "All I saw was purple." Saw it and heard it, too! Husky Stadium was absolutely on fire that day.

Much like it was in 1992, when mighty Nebraska came to the stadium for the first night game in Husky history, nationally broadcast on ESPN. Or in 2000, when the Huskies humbled highly ranked Miami with the deafening noise, unsettling the Hurricanes' sophomore quarterback from start to finish.

As you prepare to play Washington on this day, not only will you be confronted by a hungry bunch of current Huskies, but also by the great legacy of those who've gone before them—players and fans alike. This is the experience that is Husky football, the character that is Washington.

For me, that experience began in 1977 when I first set foot in Husky Stadium to report on a Husky team that would start the season slowly but finish with a flourish—a victory over heavily favored Michigan in the Rose Bowl.

That year, my employer, KOMO Radio, acquired the broadcast rights for Husky athletics, providing me with a job that has taken me on a remarkable journey that is now extending into a fifth decade.

As much as I've enjoyed the great games and incredible moments along the way, I've enjoyed the great people I've been fortunate enough to meet and work with even more. I will always be indebted to the coaches who've graciously educated me through the years on the finer points of their sport. I'm proud to call men like Don James, Jim Lambright, and Keith Gilbertson not just mentors but friends as well. Working with Steve Sarkisian has been similarly rewarding.

I've always thought one of the great beauties of the college game is the constantly changing cast of players. It keeps the game young and does the same for those of us who love it. My list of favorites grows larger with each passing season. It's gratifying to watch them mature in their college years and to follow their progress after they leave the university. I treasure the relationships I've been able to establish and maintain with many of them.

The feeling that young opponent is feeling as he beholds Washington football for the first time is one I've been able to enjoy for a good, long time now. Talk about "touchdown Washington!"

I'm very pleased to write this introduction to *Go Huskies!: Celebrating Washington's Football Tradition*. This book will help us all rekindle our memories of big games and big seasons, as well as of the players who earned the right to don the purple and gold and the right to be called Huskies.

—Bob Rondeau

Arthur Denny, founder of the University of Washington.

CHAPTER 1

The Seattle Fire of 1889 Ignites the Husky Football Tradition

Soaring with cathedral grandeur from the shore of Lake Washington, with sweeping views of the Cascade foothills and the snowcapped, majestic Mount Rainier, the newly renovated Husky Stadium stands 16 stories high above an emerald field. With its cantilevered roofs—north and south—two new decks on the south side, a completely new west-side complex for the student cheering section, and an enlarged scoreboard seemingly atop the new small stand on the east side, the stadium is one of the most imposing football venues in the nation. With the track in the old stadium removed and the fans now closer to the field, the legendary crowd noise will stun opposing players and make the new Husky Stadium an even more difficult place for opponents to play.

Over the years, there have been so many remarkable plays in this stadium, so many events of athletic and nonathletic import, it would be impossible not to sense the history of the place. But where did Washington's great football tradition begin? Not in Husky Stadium; not even on the present campus of the University of Washington. It started 28 years after the Territorial University opened on September 16, 1861.

Reverend Daniel Bagley moved from Oregon to Seattle in 1860. Working with Arthur Denny and other territorial legislators, he persuaded them to locate a new university in Seattle—the Territorial University.

It was the first public university on the West Coast. Classes began on November 4, 1861, in a stately two-storied structure. Asa Mercer was the temporary president and the school's only faculty member. Two additional structures were built: a two-story president's house with 10 rooms and a "plain box" boarding house for boys. Girls lived in the president's house under the supervision of Mercer's wife. The institution became the University of Washington in November 1889, when Washington officially became a state.

College life at the University of Washington was more than books, classes, and acquiring a formal education. Students had many diversions and experiences that were not to be found in books and classrooms, and they had become aware of football games played by East Coast schools.

The history of American college football can be traced to a version of rugby football in which an oval-like ball was kicked at a goal and/or run over a line. The first recorded football game was played at Rutgers University on November 6, 1869, between Princeton and Rutgers. Two teams of 25 players attempted to score by kicking

The Boarding House

The President's House

Asa Shinn Mercer

The Territorial University

Mrs. Lucie W. Carr

The Territorial University in the late 19th century.

the ball into the opposing team's goal, and the first team to six goals won. Throwing or carrying the ball was not allowed, but there was plenty of physical contact between the players. Rutgers won that first matchup 6–4. Within a few years, several other eastern schools fielded intercollegiate teams.

The nature of those first games was altered by rule changes proposed by Walter Camp, widely considered to be the most important figure in the development of American football. An 1882 graduate of Yale, where he earned varsity honors in every sport the school offered, his

proposals included reducing the number of players to 11, the establishment of the line of scrimmage, the snap from the center to the quarterback, and completely revamped scoring rules—four points for a touchdown, two points for kicks after touchdowns, two points for safeties, and five for field goals.

In 1880 only eight universities fielded intercollegiate football teams; by 1900, the number had expanded to 43. The nation's first college football league, the Intercollegiate Conference of Faculty Representatives, a precursor to the Big Ten Conference, was founded in 1895.

1889: The Seattle Fire and Washington Football

The new campus had few students and no athletic fields. In June 1889 it was a fire that launched what might have been the first football game played in the West. After the fire, which leveled about 60 acres on the waterfront south of University Street, many stories circulated nationally heralding the rebuilding of Seattle and its "boomtown" nature. Many young graduates of leading eastern colleges came to Seattle seeking adventure and perhaps fortune out West. Some of them had played football in college. A few of them instructed some Washington students how to play football.

On Thanksgiving Day, November 28, 1889, the Eastern Colleges Alumni team played against a Washington squad. It was not an official game; in fact, the university cast a severe institutional frown on the whole affair. The *Seattle Post-Intelligencer* announced the game would be played at 2:30 PM and that it would be over by 4:00 PM, so the game would not delay Thanksgiving dinner. The field of play was located south of Jackson Street in a large, open area bound by 16th Avenue to the west and Florence to the east. It was reported that the field was littered with rocks and that there was only one goal post, and that post was crooked. There were no yard lines, but then football playing surfaces were not yet measured in such increments.

The Washington players had no uniforms; they could not afford them. They wore woolen undershirts and baggy pants made of tent canvas. No players wore helmets because they had not been invented. After the game, which the Easterners won 20–0, the newspaper accounts of the game failed to report that Washington might have given a better showing if Frank Griffiths, Washington's captain, had played the entire match. Unfortunately, he departed with 15 minutes left, a sartorial wreck with nothing to wear. An eastern brute had torn Mr. Griffiths' clothes clean off.

Frank Griffiths (sometimes called Griffith) was Washington's first captain, serving in both 1889 and 1890. He had read about Yale's athletic exploits in Seattle newspapers. He sent away to Philadelphia for a rule book and an "oval pigskin." He recounted that it was "some time before we received our purchase... It was in 1889 before we got a team together with which we dared play a match game. We had no coach. We had to coach each other with only the rules for our guide... The difficulties encountered in creating interest, finding material for a team, and getting any kind of equipment were most discouraging."

The second Washington football game was played in Tacoma on November 27, 1890, against the Washington College of Tacoma. It ended in a scoreless tie. There were few West Coast colleges that played football in the 1890s. Typically, students and alumni ran the team; the faculty had no interest in the operation or governance of the sport. Head coaches were part-timers who showed up for the season and often did not show up again. Washington had five coaches in its first 10 seasons, none of whom received pay. Player-captains often trained the team, and student managers took care of the scheduling. Athletic directors did not exist.

With no victories in two years, football was curtailed at Washington when only eight men turned out for practice in 1891. Meanwhile, momentum was building for a much greater venue for all university activities—a new campus. Edmond Meany was the principal leader in establishing the university's new campus. A 6'6" hustling journalist and promoter, he was elected to the state legislature in 1891. He had graduated from the university in 1885 and was an ardent advocate for his alma mater. He sponsored a bill that authorized the purchase of the entire 580 acres of the Interlaken site—an area between Lake Union and Lake Washington—for $28,313.75, backed by a $150,000 construction appropriation.

The major building on the new campus was the Administration Building. The building was renamed Denny Hall in 1910, in memory of university founder Arthur Denny. It featured circular towers and bays that softened the lines of a double-rectangular structure in the style of the French Renaissance. Its exterior was light-colored sandstone and pressed brick trimmed with terra cotta and surmounted by a belfry. To accommodate most of the activities of the university, it had 20,000 square feet of floor space (for up to 800 students) and included several laboratories, rooms for the president and the board of regents, several faculty rooms, 10 small classrooms, a

The main building on the new campus, where most campus activities were conducted in UW's earliest days.

lecture hall, and a large assembly hall for more than 700 people. For all intents and purposes, it *was* the university.

Before the new campus became a reality, Washington won its first game on December 17, 1892, beating the Seattle Athletic Club 14–0, at Madison Street Athletic Park. William "Billy" Goodwin also arrived that year as Washington's first football coach. He had been the captain of the Eastern Alumni team that beat Washington in its first game in 1889. Frank Atkins, who had also played in Washington's first game as a preparatory (precollegiate) student, scored the school's first touchdown on a five-yard run up the center in the first half. After the game, students

paraded the streets. At the *Post-Intelligencer* office, the score was chalked up on a chalkboard. The parade was followed by a banquet at the Rainier Hotel, on Fifth Avenue between Marion and Columbia. It ended with three cheers, first for hotel manager Lee Willard, then for Washington's captain, Otto Collings, and finally for the team.

In 1892, Washington students agitated for organizations and symbols to promote "college spirit." An athletic association was formed. Then a student assembly was called to adopt school colors. A group called "the dormitory gang" made a determined bid to adopt the nation's colors. They reasoned that since the school was named after the

A major catalyst for the new campus, Edmond Meany was a beloved faculty member.

"father of our country," it was obvious that red, white, and blue were the logical choices. Another group, "the townies," protested that it was improper to adopt the national colors for another purpose. After a spirited debate, Miss Louise Frazyer, a faculty member in English, Rhetoric, and Elocution, asked for quiet. She opened a book and recited from Lord Byron's "The Destruction of Sennacherib." The first stanza of the poem reads:

> *The Assyrian came down like the wolf on the fold,*
> *And his cohorts were gleaming in purple and gold;*
> *And the sheen of their spears was like stars in the sea,*
> *When the blue wave rolls nightly on deep Galilee.*

Miss Frazyer did it. She silenced the dormitory gang and rallied the assembly around purple and gold.

Football in the 1890s was very different from today's game. The field was 110 yards long and had no end zones. (The field was not reduced to 100 yards until 1912.) A team received four points for a touchdown from 1883 to 1897 and five points from 1898 to 1911. Starting in 1912, a touchdown earned six points. A team secured five points for field goals from 1883 to 1903, four points from 1904 to 1908, and three points beginning in 1909. A conversion after a touchdown garnered two points from 1888 to 1897 and one point until the 1958 season. Then the two-point option came into effect. A safety has been worth two points since 1884. In 1906 the yardage required for a first down was lengthened to 10 yards from five. Seven men were required on the line of scrimmage.

The flying wedge was a formation used by many teams in the early years of football. A very formidable weapon, the wedge was taught to Washington players in 1892 by the legendary Walter Camp, then Stanford's head coach. Apparently, Washington was very interested in improving its football fortunes, because it hired Camp as a consultant. The wedge was in the form of a *V*, with the ball carrier tucked neatly inside it. The defense had limited options in grappling with the formation, none very pleasing to the point man in the *V*. One defensive tactic was for a defender to punch the point man in the face; another was to render a quick knee to the point man's nose. A third option was for the defender to dive under the wedge and pile it up. With this option, the defender risked getting trampled as the wedge moved forward. The wedge was abolished with an extensive revision of football rules in 1905, a season of record roughness and injuries throughout the nation.

In 1906, a number of other rules were instituted. Among them was the legalization of the forward pass. However, a straight downfield pass was not allowed. The ball had to be passed at a diagonal to the line of scrimmage and had to be thrown at a spot at least five yards on either side of the center. To help officials keep track of this distance, the coaches specified that football fields have both vertical and horizontal lines set five yards apart. This created a checkerboard pattern that resembled those in gridirons, metal racks on which meat was broiled. Thus, football fields came to be called "gridirons." The rules were changed in 1910 to eliminate the vertical lines, but the term "gridiron" lives on today.

Washington played five games in 1893, including against its first intercollegiate foe. On December 29, 1893, Stanford whitewashed Washington 40–0 in front of 600 spectators in West Seattle. Stanford's road trip to play four Pacific Northwest opponents was very successful. They won all four games by an aggregate score of 156–0. With an 8–0–1 record, Stanford made its claim as the Pacific Coast champion. Among the Stanford travel party was a manager named Herbert Hoover, who became the nation's 31st president (1929–33).

In 1893, various colleges with football teams formed the Western Washington Intercollegiate Athletic Conference. Its members included the College of Puget Sound, Whitworth College (then in Tacoma), Washington Agriculture College (now WSU), and Vashon College, a small military school on Vashon Island. The 1894 team recorded Washington's first shutout victory, a 46–0 defeat of Whitman College, and claimed the state championship.

New Campus

In 1895, the university moved to its new campus. Students, in the midst of a natural wonderland for athletic activities, clamored for a gymnasium and a playing field. Washington's football teams practiced and scrimmaged on a field on the north part of the campus, subsequently named Denny Field. From 1889 until October 27, 1906, Washington played most of its home games on three fields, all of them away from the campus. One was the Madison Street Athletic Park at the east end of the Madison Street cable-car line near Lake Washington and what is now Madison Park. Another was the YMCA Park (subsequently called the Athletic Park) located between 12th and 14th Avenues and East Jefferson and Cherry. It is now occupied by Seattle University's Connolly Center and other campus buildings. The third site was Recreation Park located between Fifth and Sixth Avenues and Republican and Mercer.

The Purple and Gold recorded its first unbeaten season in 1895. Two victories were lopsided home wins (44–4 and 34–0) over Vashon College. In the first game, played at YMCA Park, Washington did not have enough players because of injuries, so Vashon loaned Washington a player. Apparently they loaned the wrong man. K.C. Nieman ran for seven touchdowns. Martin Harrais captained the UW team that outscored its opponents 98–8.

All athletic programs were severely restricted during the 1898–99 academic year because of the Spanish-American War and inadequate financial support. Ralph Nichols organized a pickup football team of Washington seniors late in the fall of 1898. After limited practice

University Field was initially a practice field. Starting in 1906, and until Washington Stadium opened, it was the Huskies' home field.

sessions, the team played two games against the Puyallup Indian Reservation squad. The first game against Puyallup was played in Tacoma on December 17, and the Indians won 18–11. A week later, Washington shut out Puyallup in Seattle 13–0. With the score 6–0 and only two minutes left, Sterling Hill broke through the left tackle and guard, and with great downfield blocking, he raced 94 yards for a touchdown, the second-longest run from scrimmage in Husky history. Sterling was one of four Hill brothers to play for Washington in the years from 1896 to 1903. Their father, Eugene Hill, was the fifth president of the University of Washington (1872–74).

Washington closed out the century with a very solid football season. With a 4–1–1 record, they outscored

The 1895 squad was the first unbeaten team in Washington's football history.

their opponents 71–21. A.S. Jeffs coached the team. At YMCA Park on Thanksgiving Day, November 25, Washington hosted Whitman College for the Washington-Idaho Championship. In a heavy wind- and rainstorm, Washington won 6–5 behind the leadership of Hill and the outstanding play of Clarence Larson.

With only a handful of West Coast colleges fielding teams and with funds for travel to out-of-town schools limited, Washington's first decade of football was played primarily against Seattle athletic clubs, YMCA teams, and small local colleges. That changed in 1900 when Idaho, Washington State, and Oregon first appeared on the schedule.

At the turn of the 20th century, the Washington football program was much more organized. It had a practice field on campus, games were played against mostly collegiate opponents, and more fans were attracted to its games. From 1902 to 1903, attendance increased from 3,650 to 9,200; by 1919, it was 37,500. In 1900, Washington hired J. Sayre Dodge, a former end and captain of the University of Indiana football team, as its first paid head coach. He received $500 for the season. In the same year, Washington's greatest rivalry got its start when unbeaten Washington Agricultural College came to town on November 30, 1900, to face Washington at Athletic Park. The game ended in a 5–5 tie. In 1901, Washington beat Idaho 10–0 for the first time before a then-record attendance of 2,000 fans.

In Charles Gates' book, *The First Century at the University of Washington,* Gates states that a Student Assembly was formed, with the purpose of creating a body that could sponsor activities that were outside of the sphere of official university responsibilities. At first, funds were raised by individual subscriptions and targeted money-raising ventures. In 1900, the students secured approval for a registration fee of 50 cents to be assessed to every student. This action produced a stable fund to be used for the support of student enterprises. Gates remarks that perhaps no single innovation did more to give life to student activities.

A new constitution was adopted for the Student Assembly, and in 1901 the Associated Students of the University of Washington (ASUW) was established "for the control of all matters of general student concern." All student activities and all intercollegiate student relations were put under the control of the ASUW, and committees were established to coordinate student organizations. Students were asked to pay a $3.00 registration fee. The

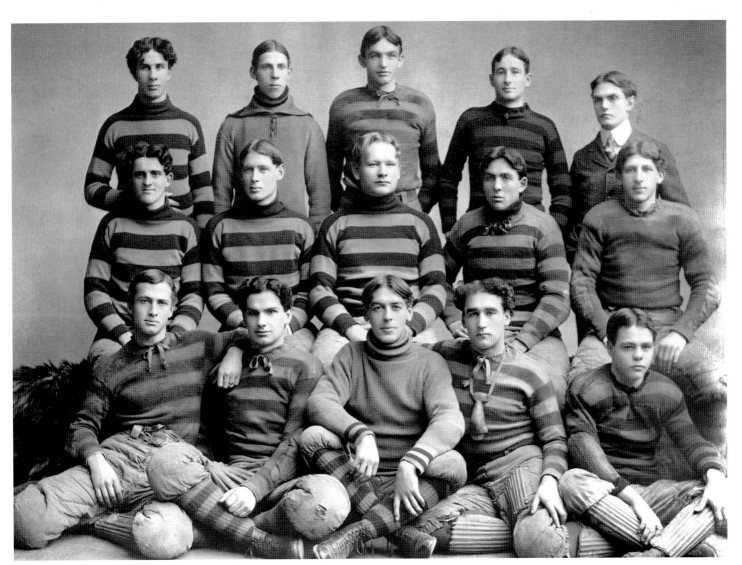

The 1898 squad thrived with help from standout Sterling Hill (bottom row, second from right).

ASUW, under the direction of its board of control and a graduate manager, would be involved in intercollegiate athletic activities until the mid-1950s, when such activities became much broader in scope and required an experienced athletic director to manage operations.

Pacific Coast Champions

James Knight was hired in June 1902 as the football coach. He coached football for three seasons—1902 to 1904—compiling the second-best winning percentage (.775) in Washington history. A football player and gymnast as a Princeton undergraduate, he later became a member of the Detroit Rowing Club and rowed in regattas in Canada and in the United States. In the fall of 1901, he entered Michigan Law School and played end on the football team and was also the assistant coach. While at Washington, he initiated the school's first rowing competition in 1903, also serving as the crew and track coach.

In 1902 and 1903, his football coaching record of 11–0 in collegiate competition was the best in the nation. His 1903 team was crowned Pacific Coast champions after defeating Nevada 2–0 at Athletic Park on November 20. The game was billed as the championship game because Washington had defeated all Northwest schools and Nevada had been victorious over California and Stanford. The game was a defensive struggle; the only score was a safety early in the game.

Two European immigrants played key roles in the victory. One was Alfred Strauss, a senior halfback from Hardheim, Germany. Strauss would become a leading surgeon and cancer researcher and a significant Washington recruiter in the Midwest. The other player was Enoch Bagshaw from Flint, Wales. He made a game-saving tackle near the end of regulation when a Nevada halfback broke clear for a 30-yard run. Bagshaw was the only man left to beat in the secondary. The Welshman would go on to earn a civil engineering degree and later became the first Washington coach to lead a team to the Rose Bowl.

Bill Speidel was Washington's quarterback in 1902 and 1903. He was selected by the *Portland Oregonian* to the first ever All-Northwest team. He was an outstanding

Coach Jim Knight had an 11–0 record in 1902 and 1903, the best in the nation. His 1903 team was crowned Pacific Coast champion.

field captain, calling both offensive and defensive plays. A punishing blocker, he toppled many opponents in the secondary during long runs by Washington running backs. He was probably best known for his punting and kicking. He boomed many long punts to pin the opposition deep in its own territory. In 1903, he kicked five field goals out of eight attempts, netting 25 of Washington's 63 points for the season.

Speidel went on to attend medical school at the University of Chicago, where Hiram Conibear had been the

trainer of track and football at Chicago. In 1906, Speidel met Conibear, then trainer for the Chicago White Sox. Speidel contacted Loren Grinstead, the graduate athletic manager at Washington, and suggested he offer Conibear the position as Washington's athletic trainer. After Conibear moved to Washington, Grinstead said that he was desperately in need of a crew coach and asked Conibear to take on the task. Over the next 10 years, Conibear brought the Washington crew program to national prominence. He died tragically in a fall from a tree while harvesting fruit in his yard on September 10, 1917. He was a charter member of the Husky Hall of Fame opened in 1979, and the Washington crew facility is named after him.

Longest Touchdown Run in Husky History

In 1904, Coach Knight's final season, Washington won four games, lost two, and tied a heavily favored California team on Thanksgiving Day. The most exciting win was over Idaho, on November 5, at Madison Park. Outplayed in every phase of the game, Washington mounted one of the biggest comebacks in its history. Ten minutes before the end of the game, Idaho led 10–0. Washington had just held Idaho on its 5-yard line, so it had 105 yards to go for a Washington touchdown. (The field was 110 yards long then.) On first down, Royal Shaw got the call from Washington's quarterback, Dode Brinker. Big Tom McDonald and Herb Ziebarth opened the hole, and Shaw darted through the line behind Brinker's blocking in the Idaho secondary. He headed straight toward the Idaho safety. The safety's flying tackle staggered Shaw, but buoyed by the wild cheers of the Washington rooters, he fought to stay up with an open field in front of him and the Idaho team in pursuit.

Shaw flung his headgear to the ground and raced toward the goal line. The towheaded sophomore from Yakima fell between the goal posts dragging two Idaho players with him. It was a 105-yard touchdown run, the longest in Husky history. It seemed the Washington crowd's demonstration would never end. Then a hush and another roar as Brinker's kick went right between the uprights. Idaho 10, Washington 6. When Washington got the ball back, Shaw broke another long gainer—40 yards—to

Idaho's 30-yard line. With 30 seconds left, Washington had reached the 15-yard mark. Brinker sent Homer Dean, the right halfback, wide to the right. As Idaho's defense shifted left on the snap of the ball, Dean countered back to Idaho's defensive right side, broke several tackles, and lunged into the end zone to put Washington ahead. Brinker's kick was again good, giving Washington the victory, 12–10. The season ended with a 6–6 tie against heavily favored Cal. Shaw was the hero with a 25-yard run to tie the game. He was also the first Husky to play Major League Baseball, a member of the Pittsburgh Pirates in 1908 who played with Hall of Famer Honus Wagner.

In April 1906, board of regents records indicate that the Associated Students of the University of Washington (ASUW) recommended bleachers be erected at the University Athletic Field (later renamed Denny Field) to encourage the holding of university athletic events on campus rather than in downtown. By Friday, October 26, 1906, the *Pacific Wave*, the student weekly newspaper, reported that every carpenter available had helped to complete covered grandstands with seats for 1,200 people, all sheltered from the rain and sleet by a roof of "good and fat boards." It also noted: "For the benefit of the players, it would be best to add that little stones which are now so much in evidence on the field will be removed, so there will be no danger of one of the contestants falling thereon and thereby breeding a scab on the end of the nose or marring his beauty in any manner." A large grandstand was built on the south side of the field in 1911. In 1916, Denny Field was regraded and the south grandstand was moved about 90 feet. A new larger north grandstand was also built on a slightly different site. All home games from October 27, 1906, through November 5, 1920, were played at Denny Field. On November 27, 1920, Washington Field was opened with Dartmouth as the opponent. In time, the field would be called Husky Stadium.

On Thanksgiving Day, November 28, 1907, Washington played a scoreless tie with Idaho to start a 64-game unbeaten streak. From the last game of the 1907 season until the second game of the 1917 season, Washington never lost a game—winning 60 and tying four.

Head football coach from 1908 to 1916, Gil Dobie had the longest unbeaten record of any coach in American football.

CHAPTER 2

The Greatest Record in Collegiate Football History

The major architect of Washington's greatest unbeaten streak was Robert Gilmour "Gil" Dobie. It is unimaginable that someone who spent his childhood going in an out of orphanages would become one of the greatest coaches in collegiate football history. In the most comprehensive and extensively researched book on Gil Dobie's life, *Gilmour Dobie: Pursuit of Perfection*, author Lynn Borland describes in great detail Dobie's coaching career at Washington.

From 1908 to 1916, Dobie's teams went 59–0–3. His teams also recorded a 40-game winning streak from November 14, 1908, through October 24, 1914. Only Oklahoma's 47-game winning streak (1953–57) is better.

Dobie entered the University of Minnesota in the fall of 1899 and graduated in the spring of 1904 with a Bachelor of Laws degree. He was an end on the varsity football team in 1899 and quarterback on the 1900 and 1901 teams. In 1900 he led the Gophers to a 10–0–2 record and its first Western Conference (later to become the Big Ten) title. He was selected to the 1900 All-Western Conference team and received honorable mention on Walter Camp's All-America squad.

Dobie began his coaching career as an assistant at Minnesota from 1903 to 1905. During that time, he also was the head coach at Minneapolis South High School and led them to two undefeated seasons and one state championship. His college head-coaching career began at North Dakota Agricultural College (now North Dakota State). His 1906 and 1907 teams were undefeated. At North Dakota, he started to relate his coaching to what he had learned as a child—that one must fight hard for what one wants out of life. He always required his players to approach every game by practicing for hours, focusing on running plays over and over. As a law student, he had honed his attention to detail; that perfectionism carried into his coaching techniques and the way he got his team psychologically and physically ready for the next opponent. Dobie believed in power football, focusing on the off-tackle smash. He also perfected the passing game once the rules changed to open up that part of the offense.

Dobie Comes to Washington

Dobie's success started getting noticed by other university programs. Loren Grinstead, Washington's graduate athletic manager, who was then in charge of the football program, offered the Husky head-coaching job to Dobie beginning in the 1908 season.

During his tenure at Washington, he was not able to schedule collegiate teams exclusively, so the first games of each season were played against noncollegiate teams—high schools and athletic clubs—and were sometimes called preseason games. This type of scheduling was typical of many schools at the time, because college football in the early 1900s was simply not that popular and the challenges of long-distance travel made it difficult to schedule games against college teams exclusively. In fact, Cal-Stanford abandoned its nascent football programs for rugby for a time; UCLA didn't even field a team until 1919. Primarily, Washington played collegiate opponents from the Pacific Northwest Intercollegiate Conference (PNWIC)—Idaho, Oregon, Oregon State, Washington State, and Whitman, among others.

Teams in the Dobie days were composed of the 11-man varsity that played offense, defense, and special teams; about four to six substitutes; and 10 to 15 others who practiced with the team but seldom saw actual game time. Each player soon learned about Dobie's insistence on hard work, determination, attention to detail, and game preparation, as well as his gloomy disposition and the reverse psychology he employed to motivate them. He stuck to basic football and was biased to the running game, although his teams often used the forward pass to their advantage.

Five Perfect Seasons

In 1908, Dobie's first season, Washington went 6-0-1. Only a 6-6 tie with Washington State, on November 7, kept the season from being perfect. On November 14, 1908, Washington beat Oregon 15-0, beginning the 40-game winning streak that did not end until 1914, when Oregon State and Washington played to a scoreless tie.

The results of the games of the perfect seasons from 1909 to 1913 were quite lopsided. In a 1911 matchup, Washington beat Fort Worden 99-0. In 1913, Whitman gave up 100 points and scored none. After the Fort Worden game, Dobie is reported to have said to his team, "You were terrible, terrible, terrible. If you had been any good at all, you'd have beaten them one hundred to zero."

In 1910, rules of football changed to ameliorate the number of injuries incurred as a result of emphasis on

Guy Flaherty entered Washington having never played football. He was slender and weighed about 165 pounds. He played in every minute of every game during the 1906 and 1907 seasons. A severe case of boils on his arm prevented him from playing all but the first and last games of the 1908 season. Even when he was unable to play, Flaherty came to every practice and performed manager and assistant manager duties. His willing service to Washington football was recognized, and a medal was named in his honor. The Guy Flaherty Medal is awarded annually to the player voted "most inspirational" by his teammates and is considered the top award given at the end of each football season. It is believed to be the first such inspirational award in intercollegiate athletics in this country. Not surprisingly, its namesake was the first recipient of the award, in 1908.

If Dobie was the architect of Washington's success, **William "Wee" Coyle** was the field general. Coyle earned letters in three sports—football, baseball, and track—over the years 1908 to 1911, but he is best remembered as the quarterback of Washington's four undefeated teams from 1908 to 1911. His teams won 26 games and tied one.

He was the first-team quarterback on the All-Time Washington Team selected by fans in 1950. One of the voters said, "Coyle was the man who never made a mistake in his four straight years quarterbacking a major college team.... Had Coyle's light not been hidden under the bushel of limited competition, much too far out in the Indian country to jolt Walter Camp from the Big Three (Harvard, Princeton, and Yale) and Michigan, there is no doubt he would have been acclaimed one of the great quarterbacks of all time." Coyle was inducted into the Husky Hall of Fame in 1980.

Coyle takes it on the chin during Washington's shutout of the Beavers in 1910.

brute force in the old game. The new rules promoted more creative plays, liberalized passing rules, allowed more substitution of players, and changed the length of the game.

- The game was divided into four quarters of 15 minutes instead of 35 minutes per half.
- Players taken out of the game, except for disqualification, could return at the beginning of the next quarter. Previously, players removed from the game could not return to play. As a result, some players were exhausted in the later stages of the game and were prone to more injuries.
- Running backs could run the ball across the line of scrimmage at any point. The prior rule required the quarterback to run out five yards before heading up the field.
- The flying tackle was abolished.
- On a running play, the offensive team members were prohibited from pushing or pulling the runner. This rule change opened up the game and emphasized athleticism over physical force.
- The punter had to be at least five yards behind the line of scrimmage and the ball had to punted at least 20 yards downfield to be a free ball, available to each team—even before the receiving player had touched it.
- One forward pass per scrimmage of three downs was allowed. No pass could be more than 20 yards downfield.

More rule changes were added in 1912 to bring college football at that time closer to the type of games we see now.

- The football field was reduced from 110 yards to 100 yards and a 10-yard-deep end zone was added to each end of the field of play.
- The number of plays allowed to reach a first down was increased from three to four.
- Touchdowns counted for six points, up from five.
- No longer was the punted ball free for a member of each team to gain possession. The new rule required the receiving team to first touch the ball before it became "live."
- Passes could be thrown any distance downfield (instead of only 20 yards). With the addition of "end zones" beyond the goal line, a forward pass could be thrown into

the end zone for a touchdown. Catching a pass beyond the end zone was ruled an incompletion. However, the goal posts still remained on the goal line.

- If the opposing team intercepted a pass in the end zone, it was ruled a touchback and the ball was placed on the 20-yard line.
- A kickoff was made from the 40-yard line instead of the 50.
- The football's size, weight, and shape were standardized. When fully inflated, its elongated shape made it easier to grip and throw the ball. Such a change greatly enhanced the passing game and helped the thrower gain length and accuracy.

The "Bunk" Play

One of the trickiest plays in the Dobie era was designed for the Oregon game in Portland on November 18, 1911. Preparation for the game started about three weeks beforehand. Dobie did not even let the second team know about the new play he was going to use. Indeed, he asked the first team to take a pledge to keep everything they would learn about the new play in strictest confidence. At the end of each practice, the second team was directed to the locker room, after which the starters began another phase of practice, going through their secret play over and over.

On the Tuesday before the game, the second team lined up on defense and the secret play was given its first real test. The offense executed it to perfection. Dobie, along with quarterback Wee Coyle, met with referee George Varnell in his room at the Multnomah Hotel previous to the game. The coach proceeded to explain the play, step by step. Varnell and Dobie shook hands, and the referee said he would be on the lookout for the play. After the first quarter, with Washington up 5–0, Melville Mucklestone ran a punt back to Oregon's 40-yard line. Coyle quickly lined up his teammates and called for the secret play. The play was sort of a reverse to the end, except the center handed off the ball instead of snapping it to the quarterback, who was lined up as a setback.

The most accurate explanation of the play came from Coyle many years later. "The play had no signal of its own, but followed a given signal when a point midway between the goal posts and the sidelines had been reached. The backfield was in its regular position, the quarterback directly behind the center. On the word 'hike,' [Bevan] Presley, the center, passed the ball back into his stomach and started to count silently, '1, 2, 3.' [Wayne] Sutton, the right end, also started counting silently, '1, 2, 3.' The two guards fell in front of the center to protect him from attack.

"As quarterback, I made an obvious show of taking the ball from the center, at the same time pulling my headgear from my head and tucking it under my right arm so as to make it look like a football—the color of our headgear was the same as that of a football. The three backs made a pocket for me and we all beat it for the [right] sideline, not trying to make the distance. The whole Oregon team

Another outstanding athlete in the Dobie era was **Huber "Polly" Grimm**. A multisport athlete, he was a weight man in track-and-field events and a pitcher on the 1908 Washington team that made the first baseball trip to Japan. He was also the national Amateur Athletic Union (AAU) heavyweight wrestling champion in 1911. Only a lack of travel money kept him from representing the United States in wrestling in the 1912 Olympics. He later wrestled professionally after being shunned by the U.S. Olympic Committee.

In football, he starred on the 1905, 1907, 1909, and 1910 football teams as a tackle, place kicker, punter, and runner in a tackle-around play. On occasion, he was also a passer and a pass receiver. He was captain of the 1910 team and was picked third-team All-America by Walter Camp, becoming the first Washington player to receive national honors. Grimm was the only Washington and western college player picked by Gil Dobie in 1925, on his all-time national football team.

Polly had two brothers who also played for Washington. Warren was an outstanding end and a terrific pass receiver from 1908 to 1911 and Bill was a star tackle in 1915, 1916, 1919, and 1922.

A three-sport star, Huber "Polly" Grimm was selected third-team All-America by Walter Camp.

lit out in our direction, yelling, 'Get Coyle!' Six of them hit me as I ran out of bounds, throwing my headgear in the air as they ganged [up] on me. Meanwhile Presley and Sutton had finished their counts; Presley turned on his right knee, keeping very low. Sutton came out of the line. Sweeping close to the forwards, and under the cover of Presley, [Sutton] took the ball and ran in the opposite direction from me for a touchdown without being touched or even seen by an opposing player," wrote Lynn Borland, author of *Gilmour Dobie: Pursuit of Perfection*.

Coeds and the Hook

Washington yell leader Bill Horsley became a legend in 1911. Wearing a cap with a long peak and clad in peg-top trousers, he taught the student body at Washington how to cheer as a unit. He brandished a giant 10-foot hook carved out of solid oak that symbolized the supremacy of Dobie's football teams. Apparently, the idea came from the practice at the time of getting the "hook" out to unceremoniously pull actors off the stage. The hook was loathed by rivals, particularly when it was paraded around Denny Field in huge serpentine lines at halftime.

The Knights of the Hook were established to organize cheering at some of Washington's intercollegiate athletic contests. They were also involved in organizing entertainment for visiting teams and rooters, the comfort of old *W* men, support of the yell staff in all games played, ushering at games, and assisting the athletic manager in the advertisement of games, concerts, and debates.

Washington played Oregon on November 15, 1913, in Multnomah Stadium in Portland. There was great excitement leading up to the game. For the first time in the history of the University of Washington, a party of coeds and sorority girls made a trip away from campus to witness a football game. Washington men marched in a game-day parade from the new Multnomah Hotel to the stadium. Of course, the parade featured "the Hook."

There were 8,000 spectators, including 500 Washington rooters, on hand for the game. Washington quieted Oregon fans with a score in the first quarter after a drive that featured two pass plays capped off by a seven-yard plunge by Hap Miller. Wayne Sutton kicked the point after. In the

second quarter, Oregon scored on a 60-yard run after a fumble recovery by John Parsons. The point after tied the score 7–7. In the fourth quarter, Washington quarterback Charlie Smith called for a drop kick from a running formation. He backed up from his backfield position and calmly booted the ball through the uprights to win the game 10–7 and give Oregon the hook for good.

The 1914 season brought an end to the 40-game winning streak when Washington traveled to Albany, Oregon, to face Oregon State on a muddy, sloppy field. The game ended in a 0–0 tie. The Oregon State fans were quite jubilant, and rightly so. Their team had accomplished what no other team had done in the six years of Dobie's domination of Pacific Northwest football: holding Washington scoreless.

Dobie Resigns and the Pacific Coast Conference Is Born

Because of Dobie's success, he virtually ruled the PNWIC and dictated what teams would play Washington and on which dates. This behavior hurt him in 1915 when the other PNWIC graduate managers teamed up to force Washington to accept a schedule that included only one Northwest Conference opponent, Whitman. As a result, Dobie had to schedule two games with California, which had just begun playing football after dropping the sport for rugby between 1906 and 1914.

The first game with California was at Berkeley on November 6, 1915. California went into the game with a 4–1–1 record, and Washington had won its first four games. The Golden Bears took the position that if they won both games against Washington, they would be the West Coast champions. Washington fan support was tremendous. On November 1, more than 300 rooters and 20 band members had boarded the S.S. *Congress* with a special round-trip fare of $16. The following morning, the 20-member team along with university president Henry Suzzallo and his wife, boarded the Shasta Limited for the three-day train ride to Oakland. No one in the Bay area expected California to win but hoped they would put up a good fight against Washington. The final score was 72–0 in favor of the Huskies.

One week later, the two teams met again, this time on Denny Field. The outcome was much closer. California's defense was so strong that Washington gained yardage only eight times in the entire game. Washington scored with eight minutes to go to break a scoreless tie. The drive featured a long pass from Hap Miller to George Smith and several up-the-middle runs, including Walt Shiel's off-tackle dive for the score. Miller kicked the extra point. Moments later, California evened the score on a 55-yard pass play, and with the conversion, the score was tied. In the last minute of the game, Miller raced 50 yards to the Bears 5-yard line. Elmer Noble plunged in for the score and a 13–7 Washington victory.

During the week leading up to the California game, shocking news was reported from both the *Seattle Post-Intelligencer* and the *Seattle Times* that Dobie planned to resign after the season was over. Apparently, the University of Wisconsin had strong interest in hiring Dobie, and he did not deny the possibility of going. He said that after the Cal game he would be in a position to discuss matters more fully.

Shortly after the game, student body president Rusty Callow received a written resignation from Dobie. In the letter, Dobie indicated that he was a mental wreck and tired of coaching and of football. In December a student assembly and a special luncheon of the alumni association were held to honor the coach. Headlining the luncheon was university president Suzzallo, who in his speech heaped praises on Dobie. A national search for a new football coach was soon begun. Meanwhile, Dobie went to Berkeley to visit his sisters and relax. In mid-January, graduate manager Arthur Younger made a trip "someplace south" to talk with some coaching candidates and also meet with Dobie.

After Younger returned, he revealed that Dobie would stay. An offer was presented to the coach by Callow and Younger on February 5, 1916, but Dobie wanted to meet with Suzzallo before making a decision. They met and smoothed out any differences they had, and Dobie remained the coach.

The 1916 season was the hardest of Dobie's coaching career at Washington. The *Tyee* wrote: "In no other season were so many factors working against success. Seven men were gone from the previous season's team and three others were National Guardsmen stationed at American

UW yell leader Bill Horsley introduced the "Hook" to the Washington faithful in 1911.

The 1916 game against Cal was Dobie's last; the Huskies beat the Bears 14–7.

Lake near Tacoma. They could only come to practice on an irregular schedule." Practice games revealed weak spots in the backfield. The early season contest with Whitman took out two more backs to injuries. In spite of these issues, Dobie's team still went 6–0–1, the away game against Oregon on November 4 ending in a scoreless tie.

First Pacific Coast Conference Championship

Washington played the last two games of the 1916 season against California, winning 13–3 in Berkeley on November 18 and 14–7 at home on November 30. The home game was played before 9,000 fans, UW's largest crowd up to that point. Fighting through four periods of heartbreaking football, Washington completed its ninth-successive unbeaten season and won the first ever Pacific Coast Conference Championship.

Dobie had worked under a yearly contract, presumably because he wanted to keep his options open. In 1915, he had officially tendered his resignation and the board of regents had accepted it. In 1916, the situation was much different. When star tackle Bill Grimm was suspended for uncharacteristic behavior in cheating on a final examination, the students' Board of Control Committee recommended that Grimm's suspension begin on December 1, after the Cal game on Thanksgiving Day. The faculty-run Athletic Committee instead set the date at November 20, thus keeping Grimm out of the game. This date was officially announced as a joint unanimous vote of the Board of Control and the Athletic Committee. When the faculty moved the suspension to November 20, they decided that Grimm would be allowed to play in 1917. Supposedly, the faculty concession to let Grimm play was to get the student committee to accept the November 20 date.

Grimm's teammates resented the faculty decision. For two days, the players went on strike, refusing to practice and threatening to end the season prematurely. Suzzallo stood firmly behind the faculty; Dobie backed the players. The strike ended after some prominent alumni met with the players, urging them to abandon their protest. The Cal game was played without Grimm. In early December, four of the five members of the Athletic Committee opposed the renewal of Dobie's contract. On December 8, Suzzallo issued this statement: "Mr. Dobie will not be with us next year. That is now final. The chief function of the University is to train character. Mr. Dobie failed to perform his full share of this service on the football field. Therefore, we do not wish him to return next year."

Gil Dobie's teams never were invited to a postseason bowl game—partly because there were not many bowls in those days and partly for other reasons. In 1915, the Tournament of Roses' officials reinstituted football as the major sporting event in order to defray the expenses of the annual New Year's Day floral festival. The first Tournament of Roses bowl game was played in 1902, when Michigan thrashed Stanford 49–0. The next year, no West Coast team wanted to take on powerful Michigan, and so the festival reverted to holding other sporting events. Between 1903 and 1915, the Tournament of Roses contests included polo, chariot racing, tent pegging, and even a race between an elephant and a camel.

Football returned in 1916, and Washington State restored the honor of the West by defeating Brown 14–0. Lynn Borland asserts in his book, *Gilmour Dobie: Pursuit of Perfection*, that based on verified evidence, the Rose Bowl selection committee first invited Washington to the 1916 Rose Bowl ahead of Washington State. However, the students' board of control voted not to send the team because it was not in favor of postseason play, allowing WSU to get the bid.

Oregon got the Rose Bowl bid in 1917, though both Oregon and Washington were unbeaten. Borland asserts that Oregon had an ineligible player on its team, thus violating conference rules. Oregon's president Prince Campbell was informed of the violation and decided not to deal with it and thus did not forfeit the November 4 game against Washington, which ended in a scoreless tie. The Rose Bowl selection committee chose Oregon over Washington because the railroad fare for the entire team from Eugene to Pasadena was $250 cheaper than from Seattle. Oregon beat Pennsylvania 14–0 in the game.

After Washington, Dobie went on to coach Navy, Cornell, and Boston College. His 1921 Cornell team laid claim to a national championship along with California, Iowa, and

Washington captain in 1916, Louis Seagrave was selected as a first-team All-American by Paul Purman and as a third-team All-American by Walter Camp.

Lafayette. The Helms Athletic Foundation voted his 1922 team national champion. After the 1935 season, Dobie departed Cornell with an overall record of 82–36–7 (.684). His teams won more games than any in the school's history, and he served as a head coach for a longer period than any other Cornell football coach.

He finished the last three years of his coaching career at Boston College, resigning after the 1938 season. Dobie was replaced by Frank Leahy, who would record a 20–2 record before starting an 11-year career at Notre Dame that ended with 87 wins, 11 losses, nine ties, and four national championships. Dobie finished his coaching career in 1938 with a record of 183–45–15 for a winning percentage of .784.

Dobie was inducted as a charter member into the College Football Hall of Fame in 1951. He was also inducted as a charter member of the Husky Hall of Fame in 1979. He became the third president of the American Football Coaches Association in 1926.

1912*

Lynn Borland, in his book *Gilmour Dobie: Pursuit of Perfection*, determined that Washington won one more game in 1912. He reported that the September 28 preseason game with Everett High School was not included in the official records of Dobie's tenure at Washington. The *University of Washington 2012 Media Guide* similarly does not show the game. Searching the *Seattle Post-Intelligencer* for sports articles in late September 1912, I verified that the game was played on September 28, 1912, and Washington beat Everett 55–0.

With that additional game, Dobie's record becomes 59–0–3 instead of 58–0–3, Washington's unbeaten streak goes from 59–0–4 to 60–0–4, and the winning streak increases from 39 to 40. His overall coaching record went from 182–45–15 to 183–45–15. The University of Washington's Athletics Communications Department has contacted the NCAA to update Dobie's record and the Washington unbeaten streak.

CHAPTER 3

The Mountains, the Lake, and a Stadium

Gil Dobie left behind a lasting coaching legacy at Washington. Coaches who took over the football program after Dobie had a difficult time. In 1917, Claude Hunt was hired away from Carleton College, where he had coached for three seasons.

Washington opened the 1917 season with a victory over Whitman, 14–6, to keep the unbeaten streak alive. The following week, Washington suffered its first loss since 1907, when California shut out Washington 27–0. A scoreless tie with Oregon State and a 14–0 loss to Washington State ended the campaign.

In 1918, the war wiped out any semblance of college football. Until the World War I Armistice was signed on November 11, 1918, the Washington campus was studded with military barracks, and many student-athletes were in service. A Student Army Training Corps football team was formed and included a number of veteran players from other colleges. The team was coached by Tony Savage, a former star athlete at Washington and Lincoln High School (Seattle). He took over for Coach Hunt, who went off to service. The team played two games—one a 6–0 victory at home against Oregon State, the other a 7–0 loss at Oregon.

Coach Hunt returned from service in 1919, along with many Washington student-athletes. His teams won five games and lost one—a 24–13 loss to Oregon at University Field. One game was a resounding victory: a 120–0 shutout of Whitman College, the biggest margin in Washington history. Enjoying a 30-pound-per-man advantage, Washington sprinted to a school-record 19 touchdowns. Halfback Ervin Dailey scored seven touchdowns and amassed 350 rushing yards that included touchdowns of 70, 80, and 85 yards.

The game also included an amusing situation. In the second half, Washington's guard, Gus Pope, tore a big hole in his pants. Play was suspended while trainer Clarence "Hec" Edmundson hurried on the field to stitch the pants back together. Despite his pants-splitting antics, Pope was a world-class athlete. The first Washington athlete to win an Olympic medal, he received the bronze medal in the discus throw in the 1920 Antwerp Olympics.

The final game of the 1919 season, a 7–0 victory over California, was the last Thanksgiving Day game played on University Field. Nineteen thousand attended the game, the largest crowd up to that time. The 1919 team tied for first with Oregon in the Pacific Coast Conference. (Oregon

In 1919, **Hec Edmundson** became Washington's head track-and-field coach and athletic trainer. A native of Moscow, Idaho, he attended the University of Idaho. He was an outstanding runner for the Vandals and participated on the U.S. Olympic Team in the 1912 Stockholm Olympic Games, where he placed sixth in the 800 meters. He also competed in the 400 meters.

He became Idaho's head basketball and track-and-field coach in 1914. Five years later, he came to Washington and started an outstanding career that ended in 1954. His basketball teams won 488 games and lost 195 (.715%), including three Pacific Coast championships. He directed Washington to third place in the U.S. Olympic Trials Tournament in 1936 and the school's first NCAA tournament appearance in 1943. His wins and winning percentage are the best in Washington history. He was selected to the Helms Foundation Hall of Fame in both basketball and track-and-field.

His 1927 basketball team helped dedicate the Washington Pavilion on December 27, 1927, and beat Illinois 34–23. The building was renamed the Clarence S. "Hec" Edmundson Pavilion on January 16, 1948.

And where does the nickname "Hec" come from? While a young boy in the Idaho Palouse, he dashed down the road in his first makeshift track shoes—a castoff pair of his mother's rubbers. At frequent intervals, he criticized his own efforts with "Aw, heck."

played Harvard in the 1920 Rose Bowl and lost 7–6.) Despite the successful season, Coach Claude Hunt resigned on January 20, 1920. Ray Eckmann, a halfback on the team, recalled that the situation was practically impossible for a coach. "The reason was because Washington alumni and citizens were used to Washington winning nine years in a row. If a ballgame was lost, it was 'Well, what's wrong?'"

Edmundson coached basketball and track starting in 1914. In 1948, the Pavilion was named in his honor.

Leonard "Stub" Allison coached the football team during the 1920 season. He posted a 1–5–0 record, including the last game played on University Field. On November 5, Stanford beat Washington 3–0. Stanford's "Dink" Templeton made a successful drop kick from the 23-yard line in the second quarter. The ball "sped toward the Washington goal like a shot out of cannon." The *Seattle Times* reported that "the uncanny leg work of this phenomenal kicker from Palo Alto was the factor that decided a battle between the evenly matched elevens and swayed victory to the scarlet-jerseyed men from the South." The Denny/University Field era was officially over.

Stadium Construction

On the southeast corner of the Interlaken site to which the University of Washington moved in 1895, there was a large open area where the water of Union Bay lapped at its shore. The Laurelhurst Peninsula was nearby and Kirkland was in the distance to the east across Lake Washington. Not much happened on this somewhat swampy area until two major events occurred.

The first was the Alaska-Yukon-Pacific Exposition (AYPE), which was held from June 1 to October 16, 1909. On the slopes south of Denny Hall, exposition buildings were placed around a beautiful mall with a pool and a fountain at its center. The spectacular corridor of buildings was oriented around the Mount Rainier axis. The arrangement created an expansive outlook for the campus and an environmental partnership with the mountain. Eventually, the fountain and the mountain would become the primary features of the Rainier Vista. One of the other developments of the AYPE was the creation of an athletic field on the southeast corner of the campus, where some athletic contests were held during the exposition.

The second major event was the completion of the Lake Washington Ship Canal on July 4, 1917. The canal opened up passage from Shilshole Bay in Puget Sound, through the government locks, up to Salmon Bay, the Fremont Cut, Lake Union, the Montlake Cut, and Lake Washington. It was a very important project for Seattle and helped open up maritime transportation from Puget Sound and other large bodies of saltwater to the inland freshwater lakes and waterways. Lake Washington was lowered almost nine feet, and dirt and silt obtained from the digging of the Montlake Cut was deposited along the shores of Lake Washington for use in building Washington's athletic complex. The university began reclaiming Union Bay's wetlands in the 1920s, first using them for a landfill. Eventually, the area became the site for intercollegiate baseball and soccer fields, a track complex, university parking lots, and venues for intramural athletics.

During the 1919 football season, University Field was deemed inadequate for spectators. Thousands were turned away from the 1919 Thanksgiving Day game with California. Darwin Meisnest, the University's first athletic director, suggested a new stadium. What resulted was unequaled cooperation between university officials, students, and Seattle citizens. The whole project took a little more than 13 months, considered a record time to plan and build a large stadium. The construction of the stadium itself took only six months!

The editorial on the front page of the *Seattle Times* on November 26, 1920, the eve of the stadium's opening, cited the effort: "Man-made hills rising where hollows existed previously—towering earth banks swept away, seemingly in the twinkling of an eye—a monster ramp backing up far-reaching tiers of seats—concrete work everywhere—comfortable benches provided—the field completed and ready for use—what a magical creation it seems now that it is ready."

Meisnest's leadership was a crucial factor in the project's completion. Upon enrolling in the University of Washington, he had quickly become very involved in academic and extracurricular activities, including work with the Associated Students of the University of Washington (ASUW), the *University Daily*, and as student manager of the football, basketball, and track teams. He was the first man accepted into the Officer's Material Program of the Navy Training School, which had occupied part of the new stadium's site during World War I. He later received an ensign's commission. While still in the navy, he was elected in December 1918, as the graduate manager of the ASUW. He took office in March 1919, after his military discharge. One year later, the ASUW contributed $100,000 toward

PACIFIC COAST CHAMPIONSHIP
UNIVERSITY OF WASHINGTON
OF SEATTLE WASH.

The last Thanksgiving game on Denny Field, on November 28, 1919. Washington beat Cal 7–0.

the stadium construction, out of the $170,000 of annual revenue it was generating. Meisnest not only applied his industriousness and sagacity to the stadium project, but also displayed his uncanny ability to skillfully direct the work of others. One of his initial tasks was to convince the students that a stadium, not a student union, should be built first because it would receive the financial support of the business community, where the student union would not.

University president Henry Suzzallo and the board of regents moved quickly to approve the ASUW's recommendation to establish a broad-based Stadium Committee. The committee members actively engaged university architects C.H. Bebe and Carl F. Gould. The two men were appointed in early March and immediately proclaimed "that the stadium can be built by November 27, 1920 if the work is unhampered by industrial difficulties." Gould and university engineering professor and former Husky player Charles May investigated existing stadia, including the Yale Bowl, Princeton Stadium, Schoellkopf Field at Cornell, Michigan Stadium, and the Stadium Bowl in Tacoma. Plans were prepared to orient the stadium toward Lake Washington, the forested hills, and the Cascade Mountains. The University's astronomy department established the longitudinal axis of the stadium. The goal was to "avoid as far as possible the glare of the sun in the stadium for the benefit of the players." Based on the astronomers' measurements, the axis of the stadium was set approximately at right angles to the sun's rays—at 71 degrees 50 minutes west of north.

The stadium committee recommended a seating capacity of 60,000, to be constructed in two units, each with 30,000 seats. The structure would be an open-ended bowl that would preserve the site's scenic eastern views of the water and mountains. The height of the stadium when its second unit was completed would be 72 feet, with two great collegiate gothic towers surmounting the main entrance on the west. Four smaller towers were planned— two each on the north and south sides of the stadium. An encircling colonnade would provide a place for memorials, the inscribing of records, and a covered track. The field would be encircled by a quarter-mile track and a 220-yard straightaway on the north side.

A fund-raising campaign was launched in the spring of 1920 and was carried on throughout the state with the support of the Washington State Chamber of Commerce, its affiliated commercial bodies, and the alumni and students of the university. Every firm in Seattle was visited by loyal Washingtonians. Approximately 500 student salespeople sold small bronze plaques to those supporters who bought season tickets. The price was $50 for two years and $100 for five years; $25 and $50 for purchasers living more than 50 miles from Seattle. More than $260,000 of the funds raised prior to the completion of the stadium resulted from these efforts. Plaque holders received favorable seating in the new stadium and admission to all events in the stadium for the period related to the price of their contribution.

Ultimately, the stadium was built because of the commitment of the students of the University of Washington.

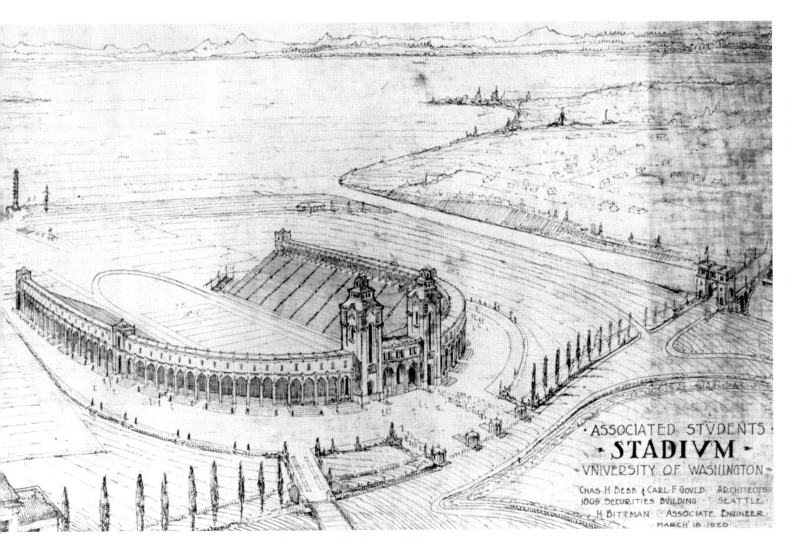

ASSOCIATED STVDENTS
· STADIVM ·
VNIVERSITY OF WASHINGTON
CHAS · H · BEBB & CARL · F · GOVLD   ARCHITECTS
1005 SECVRITIES BVILDING · SEATTLE
H · BITTMAN · ASSOCIATE ENGINEER
· MARCH · 18 · 1920 ·

Construction of Washington's football stadium, architects' rendition.

They approved an ASUW recommendation to raise student fees from $5 to $10 and to allocate $4 of the total fee to a building fund to help pay some of the initial stadium costs and to retire bonds that were issued to pay the contractor's fee. The fees provided almost $124,000 for construction of the stadium.

Sluicing

The contractor, Puget Sound Bridge and Dredging Company, used a unique method of construction that enabled the company to build the stadium quickly. On April 16, 1920, President Suzzallo and Seattle mayor Hugh Caldwell broke ground for the stadium with the assistance of students, faculty, and prominent stadium supporters. The contractor signed a construction contract with the ASUW on May 7, 1920. To clear the area, to build a burm around the stadium to be able to enter it from the Montlake

Boulevard level, and to reach a height of 18 inches for the crown on the field, the contractor used a unique method of excavation known as sluicing.

The entire excavation of the field and filling of the side embankments was done by hydraulic sluices and pumps. Great pressurized streams of water—687,000,000 gallons taken from the nearby lakes—cut into the earth and washed it into directed channels. There was 230,000 cubic yards of dirt and silt moved, leaving a drainable base of sand and gravel, onto which 4,000 barrels of concrete were poured. Reinforced by 106 tons of steel, the concrete formed the foundation for the stadium seats.

As the bowl took shape, 100,000 feet of Douglas fir were used to build 30 rows of benches in 32 sections. The aisles and seating pattern enabled the original capacity crowd of 30,000 to exit the stadium in seven minutes. To handle wet weather conditions that were sure to plague the field,

Looking east on October 30, 1920: 27 days to the Dartmouth game.

Looking west on November 13, 1920: 14 days to go.

8,000 cubic yards of drainage gravel were laid over and around 6,500 feet of four-inch drainage tiles.

Finally, 3,500 cubic yards of topsoil were hauled in to make the gridiron, and 2,000 cubic yards of cinder were used to make the running track. A sunken passage was built to separate the fans from the field, while also providing drainage. It was calculated that one inch of rainfall on the structural portion of the stadium would accumulate 36,000 gallons of water.

The entire field was 532 feet by 450 feet, built on two feet of ground. It was not a pleasant playing surface. Herman Brix, who starred as a tackle from 1925 to 1927 and was the world-record holder and 1928 Olympic silver medalist in the shot put, remembered: "To make the water drain quickly from the field, sand and sawdust was used.

As a result the field became very rough and abrasive when it became wet. It was like sandpaper." Chuck Carroll, a consensus All-American running back in 1928, agreed. "You had to run between the rocks. You could practically hide behind them. You would get stone bruises, and they would stay with you all season. You always looked forward to playing at Stanford because the Palo Alto stadium had a grass field."

A contest to name the field had been conducted before the stadium was completed. The service group of the University of Washington asked that the stadium be made a state memorial for those who gave their lives in World War I. To support this idea, the Student Building Committee recommended the stadium be named Memorial Olympian-U. More than 2,500 other names were entered, of which all but about 400 were duplications. The final three names considered were Crater, Cascadium, and Washington Field. The last one was declared the winner. It was suggested by Harold M. Sheerer, the plant engineer of the Seattle Shipping Board. He received $100 and immediately bought a seat plaque with his winnings. There were other names of a more humorous nature, such as Washington Dimple, Wash Bowl, Tub, and Basin.

The January 27, 1926, minutes of the ASUW's Board of Control included the final financial report of the stadium construction. It reported that the total cost was $565,034.98 and the payment sources were:

Plaque sales	$241, 102.00
ASUW Building Fund	123,519.48
Stadium non-football events, including pageants, concerts, and Fourth of July celebrations	107,100.00
Small donations	1,400.00
Rose Bowl Game, 1924	38,000.00
Rose Bowl Game, 1926	20,000.00
Excess funds from 1925 football budget	30,000.00
Refund from contractor	3,913.50
Total payments	$565,034.98

Washington Field was the first of its size built on the West Coast. Stanford's stadium was completed in 1921, and California's stadium in Berkeley and the Los Angeles Coliseum followed in 1923.

The stadium was completed 12 hours before kickoff on November 27, despite 46 days of rain during the construction period. To help celebrate the opening of the new stadium, many events were held to galvanize students, alumni, politicians, the business community, and fans. On Wednesday, November 24, the third homecoming in the history of the university was held. The university glee club and jazz band performed that evening in Meany Hall. On Friday, there was an automobile parade in downtown Seattle, with city officials and business leaders riding in cars decorated by fraternities and sororities.

That evening there was a big pep rally. More than 900 Washington rooters met on University Field and proceeded on a march north of campus, returning for festivities conducted around a big bonfire in a driving rain. The *Daily* reported: "The spirit shown by the turnout, in the face of the weather conditions, and the volume which the gathering was able to put into its cheers, convinced even the most pessimistic of supporters that Dartmouth will have to fight not only the Washington team, but the Washington student body, when it takes the field against the Purple and Gold football eleven."

Later that evening, about 1,200 men living in the Northwest—alumni of more than 70 schools—gathered in the gymnasium on upper campus for "College Night." The crowd joined in lusty singing of college songs and parading around the gym with standards bearing the name and colors of their schools. They closed the evening with each school group singing its alma mater. Alumni from more than 20 women's schools taxed the capacity of the basement of the home economics hall during the raucous occasion. The feature of the evening was a burlesque act performed by graduates of Smith College.

The "Big Green" Prevail

On game day, the University District displayed a brilliant lane of colors—purple and gold, green and white, and red, white, and blue—that stretched up 14th Avenue (today University Avenue). At noon, every store in the district closed in honor of the stadium opening; a city holiday was declared for the afternoon.

Fans arrived from all directions. They came on foot and by automobile, by bus and by trolley. Those coming by car from the south drove over the University Bridge and the Fremont Bridge, both recently completed as part of the Lake Washington Ship Canal project. The Montlake Bridge would not be completed until 1925, but a pontoon bridge was built across the Montlake Canal for pedestrians from the neighborhoods south of the canal. The arriving fans represented all walks of life—from the enthusiastic small child to the staid businessman, the high school student to the university professor, the flannel-shirted university student to the fur-coated society woman.

Of course, the Knights of the Hook were there. They roused the students and other Washington fans to cheer

Ready for the game. The seats are in, but the field looks pretty rough. Lander and Terry Halls, on the southwest side of the stadium, were built as barracks during World War I. Players dressed there before the Pavilion was completed in 1927.

U. of W. STADIUM

The first game in the new stadium. During halftime, many former players came out to greet Washington fans and formed the Hook.

wildly and enthusiastically. In the women's rooting section, a big purple and gold *W* was formed.

At 1:30 PM, a ceremonial procession of dignitaries in 16 automobiles started from Lander Hall. Led by the university band, decked out in blue coats and white trousers, the procession circled the running track and proceeded to the east end of the stadium and the speakers' platform. After short speeches by W.C. Lewis (representing the contractor), Meisnest, and Suzzallo, Governor Louis Hart was presented the gift of the stadium from Suzzallo to the service of the State of Washington. After the governor's acceptance, a detachment of soldiers from Camp Lewis fired a 17-gun salute. A detachment of U.S. Marines raised the American flag to the accompaniment of "To the Colors."

Then the mighty cheers of the fans came forth to welcome the teams as they emerged from a tunnel on the southwest side of the stadium—first the Dartmouth squad

and then Washington. This was the first intersectional game for Washington. In the 1920 season, football games between cross-country teams in many areas started to increase.

More than 24,000 spectators turned out to watch the Big Green (6–2) square off against 1–4 Washington. Bob Abel, Washington's quarterback and ASUW president, scored the first touchdown. After receiving the opening kickoff, Dartmouth began a six-minute drive that stalled at the Washington 15-yard line. Dartmouth attempted a field goal. Abel tore through the line and blocked the kick. The ball bounced into Abel's hands and he rambled 63 yards for the historic touchdown. Dartmouth scored in the second quarter to tie the score. In the third quarter, Dartmouth opened up its passing game and scored two more touchdowns. The visitors added one more score in the fourth quarter on a 50-yard pass play to win 28–7.

The Huskies Are Born

Up until 1922, Washington's football mascot was a three-and-a-half-foot wooden statute named Sunny Boy that was meant to symbolize "Joe College"—books under one arm and a football under the other. UW *Daily* editor Max Miller, who was on the committee that selected the school's new nickname, and his fraternity brothers at Sigma Alpha Epsilon provided the university its first live mascot. They acquired an Alaskan malamute, named him Frosty, and took him to games and other campus events. He served as school mascot until 1929. Other malamutes have followed Frosty as the school mascot.

Stadium Additions

In 1937, the first expansion of the stadium took place; 10,000 seats were added above the original seating, increasing the capacity to 40,000. A ticket office, concession stands, broadcast and public-address systems, and spotlights were also added.

The stadium took on a very different look when roof-covered stands were added to the south side. Harvey Cassill was Washington's athletic director (1946–56), and he wanted a 15,000-seat addition. Some called the new upper deck "Cassill's Castle." A cantilevered steel roof covered all seats in the upper deck as well as approximately 6,000 in the lower sections. To the rear of the structure, two silo-shaped ramps provided access to the upper-deck concourses. The additions cost $1.7 million and were financed by ASUW funds. A two-level press box and camera deck was also part of the project. Seating for about 75 members of the press provided a view 165 feet above the stadium floor.

In the 1950 season opener on September 23 against Kansas State, only 30,245 fans attended the game, but many of them ventured to the upper deck. Against Minnesota the next week, the upper deck was completely filled. The crowd of 49,704 set a stadium record.

Stadium capacity jumped from 55,000 to more than 59,000 in 1968 when 3,000 seats were added to the north side and portable bleachers were installed beyond the east end zone. Also, in that year, AstroTurf replaced the grass field, and an all-weather track was installed around the

The University officially accepted the nickname **Huskies** for its athletic teams on February 3, 1922. The announcement was made at halftime of the basketball game with Washington State. The nickname was selected by a joint committee of students, coaches, faculty, alumni, and business leaders. Students and fans did not like the old name of "Sun Dodgers." During the winter break in 1921, a group of athletic department administrators decided to use the nickname "Vikings," But when the students got back they rejected the name. Football captain-elect, Robert Ingram, presented the "Huskies" nickname. As he made his speech, large white placards were hoisted in the section occupied by varsity letter winners. The cards read THE HUSKY STANDS FOR FIGHT AND TENACITY, CHARACTER AND COURAGE, ENDURANCE AND WILLINGNESS. And with that, the name was adopted.

playing field. Washington was the first major college to install the synthetic surface. Because of the lack of similar surfaces in other stadia, Washington stocked more than 200 pairs of shoes for opponents to use during games.

The north-side upper deck, adding 13,000 new seats, was completed in 1987, bringing the stadium capacity to 72,500. The $17.7 million project was largely financed by donors. The hallmark feature of the project was a glass-enclosed reception area with a field view from goal line to goal line. Serving as an entertainment center for major donors and their guests on game days, the Don James Center has also been the site for banquets, social events, and many press conferences and athletic department meetings.

The last major construction in Husky Stadium before the 2011–13 renovation was completed in 1989, with the replacement of the west stands. The $3.7 million project gave Husky fans better seating, more concession stands and restrooms, a new first-aid room, a police security area, and a photo deck on top of the west scoreboard. During the summer of 1990, new aluminum seating replaced

Cassill's Castle.

the wooden bleachers in the north upper deck. The same process took place on the south upper deck in the summer of 1992.

In preparation for the 1990 Goodwill Games, the Seattle Organizing Committee provided $1.5 million to lay a new eight-lane synthetic surface and to convert the track to 400 meters. In preparation for the Seattle Seahawks' two-year stay at Husky Stadium, FieldTurf was installed in the summer of 2000. The cost of the new surface was underwritten by a gift from Paul Allen, one of the University of Washington's greatest benefactors.

Other Events in the Stadium

The availability and capacity of the University of Washington Stadium quickly attracted events other than Husky football. During the week of July 23, 1923, there were several major events in Seattle. Many ships of the U.S. fleet arrived in Seattle; their crews performed many activities for the public, including rowing navy cutters over a two-mile course on Lake Washington. A major merchant's exposition was held all week. The clear highlight of the festivities was on Friday, July 27, when U.S. President Warren Harding arrived as a part of his 22-day trip that covered more than 5,200 miles. He ended his Seattle tour with a speech at the stadium before 40,000 people. Having just returned from Alaska, he told the crowd about his observations of the territory and his interest in its becoming a state. It was one of Harding's last speeches. He died in San Francisco on August 2, 1923.

Track-and-Field Meets

Many track-and-field meets and running events have been conducted in and around the stadium. University of Washington teams have hosted hundreds of dual meets against opponents across the nation. Many conference championship meets have been held in the stadium, starting with the Pacific Coast Conference championship in 1922, which was won by Washington. Some of the more entertaining track-and-field events have been the Pacific Coast Relays, National Collegiate Athletic Association (NCAA) and the Amateur Athletic Union (AAU) championships, and the Goodwill Games.

In 1972, the AAU track-and-field championships were held in Husky Stadium. The outstanding performers were Dave Roberts, who cleared 18 feet in the pole vault and became only the fourth man in the world to clear that height or higher at that time, and Lee Evans, the 400-meter world-record holder and the 1968 Mexico City Olympic Games gold medalist in the 400 meters and the 1,600-meter relay, who won the 400-meter dash. Rod Milburn swept over the high hurdles to win his event. Dave Wottle, his signature cap on his head, raced to victory in the 800 meters. Milburn and Wottle won gold medals later that year in the Munich Olympic Games.

The biggest track-and-field event ever held in Husky Stadium was in the summer of 1990, when the Goodwill Games were held in Seattle. The Games spanned 17 days, from July 20 to August 5. More than 2,500 athletes from 33 countries participated in 21 sports. The ceremonies stressed the theme of friendship and peace and featured a parade of athletes. In addition to the athletic events, many artistic events were performed as part of the Goodwill Arts Festival. The Games were the largest multisport event in the U.S. since the 1984 Los Angeles Olympics.

Charity Football Games

Spurred by the efforts of the *Seattle Post-Intelligencer*'s sportswriter Royal Brougham, a series of football games were started to benefit the *P-I*'s Christmas fund for needy children. The first charity game was played on December 1, 1930, in Civic Stadium between the Olympic Club of San Francisco and the West Seattle Athletic Club. Both teams featured ex-collegians. West Seattle was led by 1928 Husky All-American running back Chuck Carroll. West Seattle prevailed 13–6. In 1931, the venue was Husky Stadium, and 15,000 people attended the Thanksgiving Day game between Gonzaga University and West Seattle. The Yellowjackets won 13–12. One of the game's biggest attractions was Jim Thorpe. During halftime, he and other contemporaries demonstrated the formations of the early 1900s and wore the uniforms of yesteryear.

On December 10, 1932, Washington hosted the Yellowjackets for the city championship. The day before the game, the temperatures dipped below freezing, and the

President Warren G. Harding gave a speech in the stadium on July 27, 1923, after a tour of the western states and the territory of Alaska. It would be one of his last speeches; he died less than a week later.

stadium field turned into an ice rink. Washington coach Jim Phelan bought tennis shoes for all of his players, thinking they would provide better traction than football cleats. Phelan had his troops warm up in cleats, then just before the kickoff, they made the switch. The Huskies rolled to a 66–0 halftime lead as the Yellowjackets went slip-sliding all around the field. During the intermission, the West Seattle outfit rounded up some tennis flats of their own. In a shortened second half, both teams went scoreless.

Starting in 1933 and ending in 1942, the Seattle Parent-Teachers Association paired up with the *P-I* to continue charity games in the stadium. Typically played on Thanksgiving Day, Seattle's best high school teams played for the city championship.

Professional Football

As business leaders and others in the Seattle community started to push for a professional football franchise in Seattle, Husky Stadium hosted NFL exhibition games. Under the sponsorship of Greater Seattle, Inc., the first game was played on August 20, 1955, between the New York Giants and San Francisco 49ers. More than 49,000 watched former Husky quarterback Don Heinrich lead the Giants to a 28–17 victory. His former Husky teammate, 49er running back Hugh McElhenny, did not play because of an injury. However, on the sideline, in street clothes, McElhenny received a thunderous ovation from the crowd during the pregame introductions.

The last exhibition game, other than Seahawks games, was played on September 7, 1975, the New York Giants beating the Cleveland Browns 24–20. Only 20,000 people attended. Presumably, the small crowd was a result of an NFL franchise having been awarded to the Seattle Seahawks earlier that year. Already, 59,000 season tickets had been sold. Presumably professional football fans in Seattle felt that they didn't have to go see a couple of barnstorming teams in preseason when they would have their own team for the entire 1976 season.

The Seattle Seahawks used Husky Stadium in 1994 when their home stadium, the Kingdome, had problems with falling ceiling tiles. That season, they played two preseason games and three regular-season games in Husky Stadium. In 1996, Paul Allen entered into an option to buy the Seahawks. Ultimately, Allen purchased the Seahawks, and a new stadium was built. During its construction period after the Kingdome was imploded in March 2000, the university agreed to rent the stadium for the 2000 and 2001 seasons.

The Montlake Dump and the University of Washington Golf Club

There are two parking lots adjacent to Husky Stadium, on the north and south sides. There, tailgaters spend several pregame and postgame hours—some in rather elaborate fashion. The north lots were once part of 200 acres that comprised Seattle's largest landfill—the Montlake Dump. The university claimed the area, then wetlands, in the mid-1920s. It operated as a landfill from 1926 to the early 1960s. In its later years of operation, it received between 40 and 66 percent of Seattle's annual garbage. Once the landfill was covered, the area was converted to parking lots, in addition to intramural playfields, the Husky baseball and soccer fields, a golf driving range, and a wildlife refuge. In 2013, a new track-and-field facility was opened just north of the soccer field.

The parking lots to the south of the stadium were built on what was once a golf course. In 1912, golfing enthusiasts among the university faculty members received permission from the board of regents to establish a golf course along the shores of Lake Union and what would become the Montlake Cut. It was a very short nine-hole course requiring only iron and mashie shots. In 1913, several putting greens were also constructed. In March 1914, the University of Washington Golf Club was organized. A clubhouse was built and opened on New Year's Day, 1915. Eventually, nine holes totaling 3,150 yards were developed, with seven holes on the west side of Montlake Boulevard and two holes east of Montlake and south of the Husky Stadium site. In the early 1950s, the area on which the holes west of Montlake were located became the new Health Sciences Building. In the early 1970s, the last two holes finally met their demise.

CHAPTER 4

The Welshman and the Irishman

After completion of Husky Stadium, there were two very successful eras in Husky football before World War II. One period—from 1921 to 1929—was presided over by a Welshman named Enoch Bagshaw. He compiled a record of 63–22–6 (a .725 winning percentage) over nine seasons, a mark that still stands as the fourth-best in Husky history. Then from 1930 to 1941, Jimmy Phelan notched a record of 65–37–8 (.616). His 1937 team recorded the first bowl game victory in Husky history.

Enoch Bagshaw

Languishing in the years after Gil Dobie's dismissal, Washington's football program was in need of sweeping change. It needed a better coach and better players. The coach they settled on was familiar, a former Washington standout. Born in Wales, Enoch Bagshaw arrived in Seattle as an infant with his parents. He attended the old Central School and then Broadway High School. When he entered the University of Washington, he had plans to become a mining engineer. He was fascinated by tales of ore in the Cascade Mountains.

He also joined the football team. Between 1903 and 1907, Bagshaw played end, halfback, and quarterback.

When he graduated in 1907, the Cascade ore had already been depleted, so Bagshaw instead turned to teaching and coaching at Everett High School. Against high school opponents, Everett lost only one game in 12 years. In his last year of high school coaching, Bagshaw's team beat Sedro-Woolley 68–0, Navy Base Hospital 84–0, and Salt Lake's East High 67–0. The team capped the season with a 16–7 victory over East Tech of Cleveland, Ohio, in the National High School Championship Game.

In 1921, Washington, for the first time in the century, had a coach who was a Washington graduate. In his first year, Bagshaw inherited a pitiful group of players from Stub Allison's 1920 team and had to beg players to come out to fill the roster and practice squad. The team went 3–4–1 and suffered its worst slaughter to date. California, coached by Andy Smith, was determined to avenge the lopsided shellacking the Bears had received in 1915—72–0, the worst in their history. Before the game, Smith told his players that he wanted them to score as many points as UW had scored against them. After scoring nine points in the first quarter, Cal racked up three touchdowns in the second period. In the final five minutes of the fourth quarter, with the game clearly out of hand for Washington, Smith sent

First Game with the Trojans

Washington opened the 1923 season with four-straight wins. Then the Huskies played the University of Southern California for the first time, before a home crowd of 21,500 on October 20. Washington stopped the first Trojans possession after three downs. USC punter Otto Anderson dropped back to kick, but the snap sailed over his head. He scrambled and recovered it on the Trojans 4-yard line. Washington's George Wilson scored four plays later, putting Washington ahead 7–0. The Huskies cruised to a 22–0 shutout. "The Huskies swarmed over the touted Trojans like ants on picnic pie," wrote well-known Seattle sportswriter Royal Brougham. The game was considered the turning point in rebuilding the Husky program.

In their last six games, Washington lost only to California 9–0 in Berkeley, where the Bears played for the last time on their historic California Field built in 1904. For the fourth-straight year, California won the Pacific Coast Conference title—but they turned down the Rose Bowl bid. Cal players had been to the Rose Bowl in 1921 and 1922 and did not want to spend another Christmas away from their families. Based on its 10–1 record and second-place mark in the conference, the game was offered to Washington, who would play Navy in their first-ever Rose Bowl.

The Huskies' First Rose Bowl

Navy came into the game with a 5–1–2 record, having lost to eastern powerhouse Penn State 21–3 and tied Princeton and Army. Some say the Naval Academy had been picked for the game even before the season started. It was reported that Rose Bowl officials had hoped to stage an Army-Navy game, but West Point officials declined.

The Midshipmen dominated the first quarter with a spectacular passing game. They completed their first six passes and scored on a 22-yard throw. On their next possession, the Huskies tied the score. George Wilson burst through the line on an off-tackle slant and drove 23 yards for the score, slamming and bouncing off most of the Navy secondary en route to the end zone. Les Sherman, a reserve quarterback, came into the game to kick the extra point.

Enoch Bagshaw, Husky football coach from 1921 to 1929.

in an entirely new team of scrubs, and in the final five minutes, they romped for five more touchdowns. The final score was 72–3.

Despite such grim beginnings, it did not take long for Bagshaw to catapult the Huskies into national prominence. Bagshaw's 1922 team started the season with five-straight victories and ended the season with six wins, one loss, and one tie. The season's total attendance was 95,900—up almost 42 percent from the year before. Over the next three seasons, 1923 to 1925, Bagshaw's teams won 28 games, tied three and lost three and appeared in two Rose Bowls. In that period, the Huskies outscored their opponents 1,135-to-141.

He wore a size 12 shoe instead of his normal 8, protecting a broken toe. His toe held up, and the kick was perfect. Navy scored again on a 78-yard drive, taking a 14–7 lead into halftime.

There was no scoring in the third quarter. With about six minutes to play in the game, Navy had the ball on its own 30-yard line. A bad center snap sailed over the punter, and Roy Petrie, the Huskies' right tackle, recovered the ball on the Navy 10. In two plays, Washington lost two yards. Coach Bagshaw called a timeout to call a special play. The Huskies lined up in an unbalanced line, with the fullback on the line and the end in the backfield. This formation made weakside guard, James Bryan, an eligible receiver. The Middies stacked the defensive line with eight men, and nobody covered Bryan, who delayed his move momentarily and then dashed to the end zone to grab a pass from Fred Abel. Sherman again hobbled onto the field and split the uprights to tie the score at 14.

With about three minutes to play, Husky Chalmers Walters intercepted a Navy pass and returned it to the Navy 44. Wilson received a short pass from Abel and raced to the 21. On fourth down, Leonard Ziel tried a field goal from the 32. It was high enough and long enough, but it sailed just wide right. Two minutes later, the game ended in a tie.

Goal Posts Get in the Way

Before the 1924 season started, Husky fans and the media alike had great expectations for a conference championship and a Rose Bowl victory. The Huskies started the season with six-straight victories, scoring 235 points and holding opponents to just 10. They traveled to Eugene to face the Oregon Ducks on November 1. For the first time ever, the game was telegraphed to Seattle. The Huskies were held to just three points, while Oregon scored a touchdown on a very unusual play. In those days, the goal posts were situated on the goal line instead of behind the end zone. George Wilson set up to punt behind the goal line, and as the snap came, Oregon's right end darted in, requiring Wilson to turn to avoid the charging end. Wilson booted the ball squarely, but it hit the crossbar. A wild dash for the bouncing ball ended when the Ducks' Otto Vitus—or "Saint" Vitus, as they called him after the game—cradled the ball to his chest behind the Washington goal line, scoring a touchdown. Oregon won the game 7–3.

In 1925, the Huskies were 4–0 when they traveled to Lincoln, Nebraska, to play the Cornhuskers for the first time in school history. Nebraska scored first, but the Huskies tied the score in the fourth quarter; the game ended in a 6–6 tie. Washington's next two games were runaways—beating Whitman 64–2 at home and Washington State 23–0 on the road. Stanford, who won the conference title in 1924 and advanced to the Rose Bowl, was next in their path.

Huskies Knock Nevers Dizzy

Coached by the legendary Glen "Pop" Warner, Stanford came north to play Washington. Both teams were unbeaten in conference play. Both featured All-American running backs. Stanford had captain and fullback Ernie Nevers; Washington countered with George Wilson, a triple-threat star. The winner of the contest would have the inside track to the Rose Bowl.

In the first quarter, Washington dominated, keeping the ball in Stanford's territory for most of the period—partly the result of Nevers' poor punting. Washington opened the second quarter on Stanford's 43-yard line at third-and-5, setting up this time in a different formation. Wilson was in punt formation, the ends were in the backfield, and Herman Brix lined up as a tackle and eligible receiver. The diversion worked; Wilson passed to Brix for a 20-yard gain. Captain Elmer Tesreau then rolled through left tackle to the Stanford 14. After a five-yard loss on an end sweep, Wilson passed to quarterback George Guttormsen, who fell into the end zone. Guttormsen's kick was no good, so the Washington lead was just six. The Huskies threatened one more time before the half ended, but Guttormsen's drop kick from the Stanford 25-yard line went wide.

Husky defense in the third quarter was the key to Washington's victory. After several exchanges of punts, Stanford started a drive on its 34-yard line. With Nevers running and passing, the Cardinal had a first down on the Husky 20. On fourth-and-2, Nevers attempted to leap over the center of the Husky line. Tesreau and Wilson suddenly hit him, lifting the Stanford star off the ground and knocking him out. Guttormsen punted out of danger to the Husky 41-yard line.

The momentum then shifted to Stanford. With a relentless combination of passing and running, the visitors soon had a first down on the Husky 8. Mike Murphy gained two on a crisscross play; Nevers picked up three over tackle. Again, Nevers got the call over the center of the line. Tesreau unleashed all his force into Nevers, and the big back bounced backward as if he had hit a stone wall. Nevers dumped a pass into the end zone, with no receiver in the area. Coach Warner said they had called a running play, but Nevers' dazed condition caused him to miss the signal.

In the fourth quarter, Washington regained the momentum, and they never gave Stanford another scoring opportunity. About midway in the quarter, Stanford's Don Hill threw a short pass that was picked off by another Tesreau, Elmer's brother Louis. He stiff-armed Hill as he picked up several blockers and raced 60 yards for the touchdown. Les Sherman converted the extra point to give the Huskies a 13–0 lead and the victory.

The season ended with a 15–14 win over Oregon at home. With a 10–0–1 overall record and a 5–0 conference record, Washington won the Pacific Coast Conference and, for the second consecutive season, led the nation in scoring, racking up 461 points. (Only one team in Husky history—the 1991 national championship team—has since bested that mark.) Washington had the opportunity to go to their second Rose Bowl, but most of the Huskies did not want to go. When the matter was put to the players for a vote, they voted it down twice. Guttormsen said, "We'd been there two years before and I think some of the older men were not too excited about going back… about missing Christmas at home. But, there were two other reasons. First Dartmouth, champion of the East, had turned down the invitation. Second, Alabama was selected and we didn't know anything about them. So we voted against going a second time." Darwin Meisnest, then

George Wilson, one of the greatest running backs in Husky history and the school's first consensus football All-American.

the athletic director, stepped in and pressured the players to vote for a third time. The vote passed by a narrow margin.

One of the Greatest Rose Bowl Games Ever

Alabama came into the 1926 Rose Bowl with a 9–0–0 record, having outscored its opponents 277–7. They were crowned national champions, along with undefeated Dartmouth, after the 1925 regular season ended. The

Crimson Tide played in the Southern Conference, coached by Wallace Wade and led by halfback Johnny Mack Brown.

George Wilson was sensational in leading Washington to two touchdowns in the first half and a 12–0 lead (both conversion kicks failed). Then midway through the second quarter, he was knocked unconscious and was carried off the field on a stretcher. The Crimson Tide went on to score three touchdowns in the third quarter with Wilson on the bench. With two successful conversions, Alabama led 20–12 at the end of the third stanza. Amazingly, Wilson reentered the game in the fourth quarter and engineered an 88-yard scoring drive, capped off by a 27-yard touchdown pass from Wilson to Guttormsen. This time George Cook was brought in to kick the extra point to bring Washington within one point of Alabama with eight minutes to play. The kick succeeded, but it was the last score of the game, which ended 20–19 in Alabama's favor.

With Wilson in the lineup, Washington had gained more than 300 yards and scored 19 points. Wilson rushed for 139 yards and completed 5-of-11 passes for 77 yards and two touchdowns. During his 22 minutes out of game action, the Huskies gained only 17 yards, were held scoreless, and gave up 20 points. Wilson was voted the game's Most Valuable Player, along with Alabama's Brown. The game was regarded as one of the greatest Rose Bowl games ever. It was also the first time that the Rose Bowl game was broadcast by radio.

The 1926 Rose Bowl also closed out the collegiate careers of many fine Husky players, including Wilson. Two weeks later, he became a professional. He led a team—the Wilson Bearcats—against a traveling group of all-stars headed by Red Grange. Wilson kicked off to Grange, and after running downfield, he hit the "Galloping Ghost" so hard that Grange became a groggy ghost. Wilson gained 128 yards to Grange's 30. A week later, he again outplayed

During 1924 and 1925, **George Wilson** was one of the best all-around players in the United States and is certainly considered one of the finest backs in Husky history. Grantland Rice, who made All-American selections for *Collier's Magazine* during Wilson's era, named him to his first-team All-America backfield along with Illinois' Red Grange and Stanford's Ernie Nevers.

Wilson was the first consensus All-American in Husky history. His selection was even more noteworthy when taking into account the geographical bias of the Eastern sportswriters on football coverage at the time. Damon Runyon, a New York sportswriter, actually saw Wilson play in the 1926 Rose Bowl against Alabama. The reporter described Wilson as "one of the finest players of this or any other time."

In 1923, his sophomore season, Wilson was a key figure in the Huskies' first trip to the Rose Bowl. As an offensive back and a punishing defensive player, he could dictate games from either side of the line. In 1924, Wilson led Washington to an 8–1–1 record and was a second-team All-American selection. He ran, he threw, he caught passes, and he boomed long punts. He blocked and tackled. He was fast and quick and utterly fearless. He had a terrific stiff-arm, and he used it on many of his runs. In one game, he knocked five defenders off their feet, stiff-arming his way to a touchdown. In his senior season, Wilson scored 14 touchdowns and 85 points and capped off his brilliant career in the 1926 Rose Bowl. His jersey No. 33 was retired after his last season.

In 1969, the centennial of college football, Wilson was named to the All-Time Western All-Star football team. In the backfield were Nevers, Morley Drury of USC, and the Trojans' O.J. Simpson. As Steve Rudman points out in the book *100 Years of Husky Football*, "This was a backfield…that did not include Norm Van Brocklin, Kenny Washington, (Heisman Trophy winner) Terry Baker, Herm Wedemeyer, Frankie Albert, or Mike Garrett. Or even Hugh McElhenny." Wilson was elected to the College Football Hall of Fame (1951), the Husky Hall of Fame (1980), and the Rose Bowl Hall of Fame (1991).

Herman Brix was the Huskies' star tackle from 1925 to 1927. However, he was better known for his world-class abilities in the shot put. He won the NCAA title in the shot put in 1927. The next year, at the 1928 Amsterdam Olympic Games, he set a world record in the event—51'8". Moments later, his teammate John Kuck bested Brix's mark by about five inches to win the gold medal. Brix won silver. After graduation, he competed for the Los Angeles Track Club. He won four consecutive American Amateur Union (AAU) shot put titles (1928–31). Brix set his second world record in the shot put in 1932 with a heave of 52'8½".

After retiring his spikes, Douglas Fairbanks helped Brix begin a career in motion pictures that spanned more than 150 films. He appeared in many classics, including *The Treasure of the Sierra Madre* with Humphrey Bogart. In Hollywood, Brix is best known as the pre–Johnny Weissmuller Tarzan.

At the age of 94, Brix returned to the Husky football scene when he visited one of Washington's practices in preparation for the 2001 Rose Bowl. Brix was overcome by emotion, telling the players that even 75 years afterward, he still vividly recalled playing in the 1926 Rose Bowl. Later in the week, Neuheisel used Brix's comments to motivate his players: "Seventy-five years later, he still gets choked up talking about playing in the Rose Bowl. If that does not get you fired up to play in this game, nothing will."

Husky tackle and 1928 Olympic silver medalist Herman Brix.

Grange. A San Francisco newspaper report read, "Wilson plainly showed that he is a great football player, as great if not greater than Harold 'Red' Grange." Wilson subsequently played for Akron's professional team before drifting into professional wrestling.

Washington continued to produce winning seasons in 1926 through 1928 but would finish no higher than fourth in the conference. For the Huskies, 1926 was a rebuilding year, with nine of the 11 starters from the 1925 squad having graduated. Washington registered four shutouts in its first five games and wound up winning eight contests. Unfortunately, both losses were to conference opponents, and the Huskies finished fifth in the conference. That season also brought the debut of Charles "Chuck" Carroll. He and Herman Brix became the stalwarts of the team.

In 1927, the Huskies won nine games and lost two—again both to conference opponents Stanford (13–7) and USC (33–3). The 1928 season started well, with five-straight wins including a double-header with Willamette

Chuck Carroll (No. 2), the second consensus All-American in Husky history.

(26–0) and the USS *Tennessee* (41–0) on September 29. Carroll scored 37 points—three touchdowns against each team and a point-after. But after back-to-back shutouts by Oregon (27–0) and Oregon State (29–0) in midseason and two more shutouts near season's end, the fans and administration began to think about a new coach.

When USC beat the Huskies 48–0 in the third game of the 1929 season, whispers to fire coach Bagshaw turned to cries. On October 23, 1929, in the middle of the 1929 season, Bagshaw resigned, offering to remain until the end of the season. The Huskies went on to notch a 2–6–1 season, and their dismal 0–5 conference record put them dead last in the conference standings. Washington's

Coach Jim Phelan.

Chuck Carroll was a consensus All-American selection in 1928. He is one of the most outstanding running backs in Husky history. He could run through and around his opponents with great speed and agility. He was an excellent passer and punter. He was also a punishing linebacker. During his three seasons (1926–28), he led the Huskies to a 24–8 record. He scored 104 points in 1928, which still ranks him sixth-best in Husky history. His 32 career touchdowns are fifth all-time. After Carroll's brilliant play in a Husky loss at Stanford, Cardinal coach Pop Warner said, "These old eyes have never seen a greater football player." President Herbert Hoover, a Stanford alumnus, called Carroll "the captain of my All-America team."

In 1927 and 1928, Carroll led the Pacific Coast Conference in scoring and was second in the nation in 1928. He won the Flaherty Award as the most inspirational team player in 1928. His jersey No. 2 was retired after his last game.

Carroll was inducted into the College Football Hall of Fame in 1964 and was inducted into the Husky Hall of Fame in 1979. He went on to practice law and served as King County prosecuting attorney from 1948 to 1970. He passed away in 2003 at the age of 96.

governor, Roland H. Hartley, appointed Bagshaw State Supervisor of Transportation on March 24, 1930. He died six months later of a heart attack. He was inducted in the Husky Hall of Fame in 1980.

James Merlin Phelan

Coach Phelan took over the football program in 1930. A graduate of Columbia Prep School in Portland, Oregon, he learned his collegiate football from Knute Rockne while playing quarterback at Notre Dame from 1915 to 1917. After that he went into the service, where he got his first taste of coaching. First Lieutenant Phelan advised

Paul Schwegler was a letterman in the 1929–31 seasons. From Raymond, Washington, he initially enrolled at Northwestern University but returned to Washington after a brief stay in the Midwest. The Huskies were glad to have him—he became one of the best tackles in Washington history. He was an All-American tackle in 1930 and 1931 as well as an All-Coast selection in those years. Stanford coach Pop Warner rated Schwegler as one of the four best tackles in the country. In 1931, he was the Husky captain and won the Flaherty Award. He played in the East-West Shrine Game and was picked as the contest's defensive star.

He was elected to the College Football Hall of Fame in 1967 and became a member of the Husky Hall of Fame in 1983.

Paul Schwegler was one of the best tackles of his era.

a military occupation team in Germany in 1919. His superior officer was a University of Missouri graduate, and Phelan received an army "assignment" to go to Columbia, Missouri, as associate coach in 1920. Phelan became the Tigers' head coach in 1921, then went to Purdue, where his Boilermakers won 35, lost 22, and tied five over eight seasons (1922–29).

He is considered the most colorful head coach in the history of Washington football. Then again, Dobie and Bagshaw were anything but colorful. One was called the "Dour Dane" and the other "aloof and all business." It was Emmett Watson who may have placed Phelan in the best perspective. In one of his *Post-Intelligencer* columns, Watson wrote, "He coached hard, drank hard, and was anything but circumspect; he was the antithesis of the Organization Man. He said almost anything that was on his mind. He was an individualist, a swift-moving catalyst, who saw all too clearly that the means of football coaching survival were not always on the field. 'I'd rather,' he once said, 'outsmart those bastards on the upper campus than knock off Oregon State.'"

Phelan coached the Huskies for 12 years (1930–41), compiling a 65–37–8 (.616) record. His winning percentage ranks fourth in Husky history among those who coached five or more seasons. His 1936 team reached the Rose Bowl and was ranked fifth in the nation; his 1937 team won the first bowl game ever won by a Husky team. He was also the first coach in school history to lead Washington to consecutive bowls. He also tutored nine All-Americans (more than any other coach except Don James).

A record crowd of almost 37,000 attended the season opener against Minnesota in 1936.

In 1930, a new attendance record of more than 42,000 was established when the Cougars came to Seattle to face the Huskies. The men from the Palouse won 3–0. It would be 11 years before the Huskies played a home game before a larger crowd.

In Phelan's first four seasons, his teams never reached higher than fourth in the conference. In 1934, the Huskies went 6–1–1 and finished third in the conference. USC and Stanford were the dominant teams in the early '30s.

During the seasons from 1932 to 1934, Washington had two All-American ends—Dave Nisbet in 1932 and Bill Smith in 1933. Nisbet was selected for his blocking, defensive skills, and punt blocking. He played in the summer East-West All-Star Game. He was elected to the Husky Hall of Fame in 1988. In 1933, Smith became the Husky captain. He was the second-best scorer in the conference, scoring 39 points as an end and place kicker. Smith was elected to the Husky Hall of Fame in 1991. Both

were selected to the All-Time Washington Football Team of the first 50 years of the 20th century.

In 1935, the Huskies dropped to sixth in the conference after losing three conference games. But they beat Washington State 21–0 and received the Governor's Trophy for the first time. The trophy had been established in 1934, but the previous year's contest ended in a scoreless tie. In 1962, the Governor's Trophy became the Apple Cup and was won by the Huskies in that year. Washington State would not win its first Apple Cup until 1967.

"You Scored Two for Them and Now Get Six for Us"

On December 7, 1935, Washington played USC in the Los Angeles Coliseum. Husky halfback Byron Haines scored every single point in the game. On the opening kickoff, the Trojans' Jim Sutherland booted the ball short, but it took some lucky bounces down to the Husky 1-yard line. Haines picked it up, fumbled it, then picked it up again. He then took off along the goal line to evade the horde of maroon-jerseyed giants sweeping in on him. Ultimately, he was tackled in the end zone and USC had two quick points.

In the second quarter, tackle Vic Markov said in the huddle to Haines, "You scored two for them and now get six for us." Washington took over on the Trojans 42-yard line after a USC punt. After getting a first down on the 25, Haines scampered through the left side for a Husky score. The extra point failed, and Haines had scored all eight points in the 6–2 Husky victory.

Phelan's squad had a breakout year in 1936. The Huskies had a 7–1–1 regular-season record, losing only to Minnesota in the season opener. Washington's only conference blemish was a 14–14 tie with Stanford. They rose to eighth in the national polls after beating Oregon State at home 19–7. The next week they climbed to fourth after shutting out California 13–0 . The Huskies closed out the regular season with victories over 15th-ranked USC at home and 20th-ranked Washington State on November 26.

The Perfect Game

The Cougars came into Husky Stadium on November 26, 1936, trailing the first-place Huskies by one game in the conference standings. It was the first time that the cross-state rivals would battle for the Pacific Coast Conference championship. But what was touted as the National Game of the Day quickly turned into a rout.

Husky fullback Al Cruver blasted over left guard for the game's first touchdown. Less than three minutes later, he broke through a huge hole for a 15-yard scoring run. The Huskies built their first-half lead to 20–0 when Husky quarterback Fritz Waskowitz found wide-open Byron Haines for a 37-yard touchdown pass. The Huskies scored twice more, in the fourth quarter, before Cruver finished his remarkable performance for the game by scoring a

Max Starcevich, unanimous All-American guard in 1936.

In 1936, **Max Starcevich** became Washington's third consensus football All-American. He was an All-Coast selection in 1935 and 1936, despite playing only one year of high school football. He worked in a steel mill in his hometown, Duluth, Minnesota, after high school until he encountered job difficulties brought on by the Depression. He decided to enter college and chose Washington with the help of Washington alumnus Dr. Alfred Strauss. In his first Husky season, he played fullback and then switched to guard for his last two seasons. He played in the fourth Chicago All-Star Game (1937) that pitted the defending NFL championship team against recently graduated college stars. The collegians were the first all-star team to beat the professionals, defeating the Green Bay Packers 6–0.

Starcevich was elected to the College Football Hall of Fame in 1990 and the Husky Hall of Fame in 1989.

third touchdown. He intercepted a pass at the Cougars 34-yard line and rumbled into the end zone for the final score of the game.

The victory was considered the most dominant in the series to that point. The Cougars did not even register a first down until the fourth quarter and recorded only two first downs in the game. They never once got into Washington territory; the closest they came was their own 44-yard line. Washington State gained only 61 total yards to the Huskies' 359 and had five interceptions.

As conference champions, the Huskies were invited to the 1937 Rose Bowl. As Rose Bowl hosts, Washington could choose its opponent. Most bowl officials and enthusiasts wanted Louisiana State, the top team in the South and No. 2 nationally. But Coach Phelan wanted Pittsburgh because he wanted to beat the great Pitt coach Jock Sutherland.

Panthers Claw Huskies

Pittsburgh entered the 1937 Rose Bowl game ranked third in the nation. The Panthers lived up to their ranking by whitewashing the Huskies 21–0. Pitt gained 300 total yards and held Washington to just 153. In the first quarter, the Panthers scored on a 65-yard drive and in the third put together a 74-yard scoring drive, featuring a 44-yard run by halfback Bobby LaRue. The final score came in the fourth quarter, when All-American end Bill Daddio intercepted an attempted Husky lateral and ran 71 yards untouched into the end zone. Daddio also booted all three extra points.

At Last, a Bowl Victory

In the 1937 season, Washington finished third in the conference and recorded an overall record of 7-2-2, losing to Oregon State and Stanford and tying California and Washington State.

After the 1937 season ended, Hawaii beckoned with an invitation to play in the Pineapple Bowl—then called the Poi Bowl—on New Year's Day against the University of Hawaii in Honolulu Stadium. In front of 13,500 spectators, Washington rolled to a 53-0 lead before Husky reserves mercifully allowed the Islanders two touchdowns in the last stanza. The play of the game was halfback Joe Dubsky's

Vic Markov was named an All-American tackle in 1937.

39-yard punt return to the Hawaii 11, where he lateraled to tackle Rich Worthington, who rumbled into the end zone. The final score was 53–13, and Washington had its first bowl victory.

Then on January 6, the Huskies defeated the Honolulu Townies 35–6. Al Cruver scored three touchdowns and kicked two conversions.

In 1938 and 1939, the Huskies suffered losing seasons. In 1940, the Huskies' only conference loss was to Stanford, 20–10. The Indians, led by All-American quarterback Frankie Albert won another conference title and beat Nebraska in the 1941 Rose Bowl. In 1941,

Vic Markov played on Phelan's football teams from 1935 to 1937. He was considered the premier tackle on the West Coast during his career. Markov improved his strength by wrestling. He qualified for the NCAA heavyweight finals in 1936. He also competed in the shot put and discus throw for the Huskies' track-and-field team.

He made the All-Coast teams in 1936 and 1937 and was an All-America selection in 1937. A 1938 College All-Star, Markov received the second-highest number of votes and was selected captain of the team. The collegians faced the Washington Redskins, led by quarterback Sammy Baugh, on August 31. The All-Stars won 28–16.

In 1976, Markov was inducted into the College Football Hall of Fame and entered the Husky Hall of Fame in 1980.

1941 consensus All-American guard Ray Frankowski.

Washington went 5–4–0 and finished second in the conference. Soon after the season ended, Phelan's contract was not renewed.

Despite their records, there were plenty of standout players on those squads. Rudy Mucha was a consensus All-American in 1940. He was the first Husky center to be named an All-American. He played that position from 1938 to 1940 and also handled the kickoff duties. Mucha became a star guard for the 1946 Chicago Bears, who won the NFL championship. He was elected to the Husky Hall of Fame in 1990.

Ray Frankowski earned three letters in football (1939–41) and was also a two-time All-Coast selection (1940 and 1941). He was named to one All-America team in 1940 and earned consensus All-America honors in 1941. He was picked on the All-Opponent teams in 1940 and 1941. He was also a two-time letterman in wrestling in his junior and senior years and was the only Husky matman to capture a Pacific Coast Northern Division title in 1940, winning the heavyweight class. Frankowski earned a sixth letter as a member of the fencing team in 1941.

Professionally, he played with the Green Bay Packers (1945) and the Los Angeles Dons (1946–48). He was elected to the Husky Hall of Fame in 1986.

If ever anybody had a big disadvantage upon accepting a football head-coaching position, it was Ralph "Pest" Welch. World War II was in full tilt as Welch took over, and it significantly impacted the entire Husky athletic program. All Pacific Coast Conference football rosters were limited to 28 players. The Washington crew team had to row back at the old Leschi-Madison Park course because of military restrictions near Sand Point Naval Station. In fact, no Intercollegiate Rowing Association (IRA) regattas were held for five years (1942–46). Jack Torney, tennis and swim coach, entered the Navy at the close of the 1942 swim season. Other coaches followed. More than 100 faculty members and many more students served in the armed forces. A navy V-12 unit was established on campus and the Applied Physics Laboratory was created to do naval antisubmarine research. It was the first special contract research agency established on campus.

Welch had previously been an assistant for all but one of the 12 Phelan years. The two came to Seattle together in 1930 after each had played significant roles in Purdue's undefeated charge to the Big Ten championship in 1929. Welch was a running back on that team and became the first Boilermaker All-American. He brought his nickname from home. Growing up, he always played with older children. "At fourteen, I wanted to wrestle with some of them," he said. They would call him a "darn pest." The name stuck.

Welch's first season as the Huskies' head football coach ended with a 4–3–3 record. He coached for six seasons (1942–47) and had an overall career record of 27–20–3.

Husky Stadium was a venue for many military-related events during the war. In 1942 and 1943, Governor's Day was held there. Washington governor Arthur Langlie, a former Husky tennis and baseball player, reviewed the assembled student military units. Several war shows were held by military and civilian defense forces. The last was held on July 4, 1944. The highlight of the event was a flyover of a Boeing B-29 Superfortress flanked by two B-17s.

There were many recorded acts of heroism by Washington students and graduates serving in the armed services. On September 29, 1942, Lieutenant Fritz Waskowitz, Husky football captain in 1937, became the first Husky athlete to be killed in action. Major Robert Galer, Husky basketball captain and All-American in 1935, received the highest military award, the Congressional Medal of Honor, in 1943. Galer led his Marine Corps fighter squadron against Japanese forces in the Solomon Islands. His superb airmanship, outstanding flying skills, and personal valor helped him shoot down 11 enemy bombers and fighters in a 29-day period. Overall, he and his squadron shot down 27 Japanese planes.

The "West Coast" Rose Bowl

Because of wartime travel restrictions, the 1944 Rose Bowl invited the Pacific Coast Conference Northern and Southern Division champions to play each other. Washington won the Northern Division title by default when other conference schools in the Northwest failed to field teams. Washington's record was 4–0, with wins over Whitman and three military teams. Washington controlled the first period against USC, twice driving deep into Trojans territory but failing to score. Late in the second period, USC turned to the air, neutralizing Washington's size advantage with quick passes to their fleet ends. With 40 seconds in the half, the Trojans had fourth down on the Washington 11-yard line. Trojans quarterback Jim Hardy tossed to halfback George Callanan, who made a final move at the goal line for the touchdown. Dick Jamison kicked the point after and the Trojans had a 7–0 lead going into the half.

USC scored midway through the third quarter on another Hardy-to-Callanan hookup, and Jamison converted to put USC up 14–0. Late in the third period, Hardy tossed his third touchdown pass to George Gray. Gray scored again in the fourth quarter on a throw from left-handed

Arnie Weinmeister entered Washington in 1941 and became a starting end on the freshmen football team. He starred as an end on the 1942 varsity before entering military service. He returned to Washington in the fall of 1946 and became the Huskies' starting fullback. In 1947, he was shifted to tackle and earned his third varsity letter. He played in the 1948 East-West Shrine Game and on the College All-Star Team.

Weinmeister played professional football for the New York Yankees in the All-America Football Conference in 1948 and 1949 and was named Rookie of the Year in 1948. He starred on the National Football League's New York Giants for four seasons (1950–53). As All-NFL selection in each of those seasons, Weinmeister started in the first four Pro Bowl games (1951–54). He was admitted to the Pro Football Hall of Fame in 1984, one of only three Huskies to be selected (Hugh McElhenny and Warren Moon are the others). He entered the Husky Hall of Fame in 1982.

Husky Stadium was a venue for military events during World War II.

Campus life in the 1940s: the Husky athletic facilities, campus, and vistas of Green Lake and Puget Sound.

substitute quarterback Ainslie Bell. The Trojans added a safety by blocking an Everett Austin punt into the end zone that was recovered by the Huskies' fullback, Wally Kramer. The final score was 29–0.

One oddity in the game involved Bill McGovern, the only substitute tackle the Huskies had. On Thanksgiving Day 1943, McGovern was playing for Stadium High against Lincoln in Tacoma's annual crosstown turkey fest. On December 10, he enrolled in one of the service programs at Washington, making him eligible for UW football. So on January 1, 1944, he played his first college game—in the Rose Bowl! McGovern went on to earn four more letters in football and was the team captain in 1945.

"Couskies"

During the war years, there were eight known football players who suited up for both Washington and Washington State athletic teams. These "Couskies"—Al Akins, Tag Christensen, Wally Kramer, Vern Oliver, Jay Stoves, Bill Ward, Hjalmer "Jelly" Andersen, and Jim Thompson—all began their college careers at Washington State. During World War II, the navy and marines transferred new enlistees to Washington for the equivalent of officer-candidate training. WSC's football program, already depleted by military call-ups, was curtailed until 1945. The first six players listed above played for Washington in 1943 after wearing crimson and gray in the previous season. All but Akins had played Cougars football. Akins had lettered on WSC basketball teams in 1940 and 1941. In 1944, he started in the Husky backfield in the 1944 Rose Bowl. Anderson and Thompson lettered in 1942 for Washington State but played for the Huskies after the war ended.

The Huskies ended their 1946 season with a 5–4–0 record. Fred Provo received the Flaherty Award as the football team's most inspirational player. He was also their leading rusher. Husky fans knew him as a hard driver with the speed of a gazelle. Few knew that he sustained an injury in the Battle of the Bulge in late 1944 and was told he would never play football again.

After a tumultuous wartime tenure, capped off by a 3–6–0 season in 1947, Welch resigned as head football coach.

"Cassill's Castle"

Generally, college athletic directors keep a relatively low profile, except when major changes are required. Athletic director Harvey Cassill was a notable exception. For 11 years, from 1946 to 1956, Cassill had a high profile and was extremely controversial. Despite controversy, he developed Washington into a major athletic power. During his tenure:

- Washington football teams played games against major intersectional powers such as Baylor, Michigan, Minnesota, and Notre Dame.
- An upper deck to Husky Stadium was added in 1950, which provided 15,000 additional seats—a total of 55,000—to attract nationally ranked teams who were interested in a share of larger gate receipts to play in Seattle.
- The NCAA swimming championships were held at Washington in 1947.
- Washington hosted the NCAA Basketball Final Four in 1949 and 1952 in Edmundson Pavillion.
- The NCAA track and field championships were held in Husky Stadium in 1951.

Cassill was also in charge during the exciting tenures of Hugh McElhenny and Don Heinrich. He introduced airplane travel to Husky athletes when the football team flew to Pullman in 1946. He also hired Tippy Dye, who coached Husky basketball teams to national rankings. Dye's 1953 team reached the Final Four, taking third place in the consolation contest. His coaching accomplishments have never been equaled.

Cassill's greatest achievement, and maybe the most controversial, was the addition of the stadium's south-side upper deck. The new stands were called Cassill's Castle. Some criticized his boldness in building the upper deck at a time when the Huskies had trouble filling the seats already available. In 1949, the Huskies averaged slightly more than 30,000 fans for their six home games—in a stadium that seated 40,000. Cassill prevailed.

One of the most important tasks that Cassill faced was the hiring of a football coach for the 1948 season. He embarked on a coaching hunt that, in his opinion, was never quite satisfactory. Cassill settled on 37-year-old

Howie Odell, a University of Pittsburgh graduate who had established an impressive record in six years as head coach at Yale. Cassill would later say, "I hired the guy [Odell] with some misgivings." One was that Ivy League coaches did not feel that recruiting had to be very extensive because of the number of student-athletes who were already interested in attending Ivy League schools.

Cassill made Odell's job a little tougher and the Huskies' strength of schedule much greater when he scheduled a home-and-home series with Notre Dame. Minnesota, another powerhouse, was already on the schedule for the next five years. The Notre Dame games called for gate receipts to be split, and Cassill told the Irish coach, Frank Leahy, that he would raise ticket prices for the home game from $3 to $5.

Shortly after arriving at Washington in 1948, Odell was confined to bed with a kidney ailment. Reg Root, a Yale graduate and one of Odell's assistant coaches there, took over the head coaching responsibilities in Odell's absence.

Following an opening home-game loss to Minnesota, the Huskies won just two of eight Pacific Coast Conference games and tied another. They finished the season with a 46–0 loss to Notre Dame before 52,000 fans in South Bend, Indiana, to finish the season 2–7–1. The Irish, meanwhile, ended the season ranked second in the nation behind Michigan.

Although the 1948 Washington–Notre Dame game in South Bend was a disaster on the football field, the Washington Alumni Association was pleased to recover Sunny Boy, Washington's mascot before the 1920s. Sunny Boy's portrait appeared on the masthead of the *Sun Dodger*, the lusty campus humor magazine in 1919. In 1923, Sunny Boy was removed from the trophy room of a university fraternity house as a prank and shipped to South Bend to keep in hiding. Curly Harris, the alumni association director, mentioned the legend of the statue to Midwest sportswriters prior to the Notre Dame game. A farmer living outside of South Bend read the story and matched the description of the mascot with one gathering dust in his barn. Sunny Boy was presented to university officials at

Howard Odell coached the Huskies from 1948 to 1952.

the football game and has resided on the UW campus ever sense.

The Huskies had not speeded Odell's recovery as they went through that dismal 2–7–1 season. The season was also darkened by the death of two players—Henry "Mike" Scanlon and Al Kean. Scanlon received the Flaherty Award in 1948.

Odell went on to spend the next four seasons as head coach. In 1949 through 1951, some of the greatest players in Husky history would arrive on the gridiron.

CHAPTER 5

The King and His Cohorts

Hugh McElhenny was probably one of the most prized recruits in Husky history. He was certainly the most spectacular running back in the history of Washington football. He provided Husky fans with three seasons' worth of electrifying runs. Even before McElhenny arrived in Seattle, his abilities were well known. At George Washington High School in Los Angeles, he was an outstanding football player and hurdler. In 1947, he was unbeaten in the long jump and both the low and high hurdles, winning the California state championship. He ran the 120-yard high hurdles in 14 seconds flat and ran the 100 yards in 9.7 seconds. McElhenny graduated from high school in February 1948 and enrolled in a University of Southern California extension school program that would make him eligible to enter USC. For three months, USC had Hugh in tow. He was signed to a football and track scholarship. But he left after the school reneged on its offer to pay him $65 per month for the chore of watering the grass around the Tommy Trojan statue.

He enrolled at Compton Community College in the fall of 1948 and led the school's football program to the Junior Rose Bowl. Meanwhile, many colleges were pressuring him. The hassle over the job USC had promised led McElhenny to consider other avenues. Finally, on March 22, 1949, Hugh's father called the *Seattle Times* and announced that his son was coming to Washington.

Also enrolled at Washington when McElhenny arrived was Don Heinrich, who had played on the 1948 Husky freshmen team after graduating from Bremerton High School. Heinrich was well known to college recruiters for his outstanding passing ability, and because of Coach Odell's emphasis on a strong passing attack, Heinrich chose the Huskies.

With both Heinrich and McElhenny slated in the same backfield for three years, the Huskies' future looked very bright. Unfortunately, because of injuries, they played together for only one year.

1949 Season

On September 17, 1949, the Huskies won their opener against Utah 14–7. Next was an away game with Minnesota, who would finish the season ranked 16th in the nation. Before the fans had time to settle into their seats, they witnessed one of the fastest opening-play touchdowns in school history. McElhenny gathered in the kickoff with a graceful sweep of his arms, cut sharply to his right, and

The King.

The following week, the Huskies hosted Notre Dame before a record 41,948 spectators. The Irish, national champions in 1946 and 1947, came to the stadium with a string of 29 wins. They featured All-American running back Emil Sitko and tight end Leon Hart, a two-time consensus All-American and the first and only lineman to ever win the Heisman Trophy (1949). The Huskies struck first in the opening quarter when Don Heinrich found halfback Roland Kirkby open on the Notre Dame 20. He threw a 35-yard pass to his fleet teammate, who sped to the end zone. Unfortunately, the Irish held the Huskies scoreless for the rest of the game and scored four touchdowns of their own for a 27–7 victory. The Irish would go 10–0–0 and win another national championship.

1950 Season

The full potential of McElhenny and Heinrich blossomed in 1950, and Huskies enjoyed their most successful season since 1936. With the south-side upper deck in place, Washington opened the season with a 33–7 win over Kansas State on September 23, 1950. The *Seattle Post-Intelligencer* opened its account of the Kansas State game with this paragraph: "Hammer blows, precise as the swing of a section hand's sledge, and pin point aerial accuracy, brought victory to the Washington Huskies...Husky backs splattered all kinds of all-time records as they romped to the runaway win."

The game was a showcase for McElhenny, who ran for the third-best single-rush mark in Husky history and also set the team record for most rushing yards in a game (177). He would eclipse that record later in the season. He also ran for a 91-yard touchdown. That run still stands as the fourth-longest in Husky history. Not to be outdone, Heinrich put on a display of his own. He and halfback Roland Kirkby combined for three touchdown completions. The quarterback broke three Husky records: longest gain on a forward pass and run (65 yards), most touchdown passes (4), most yards passing in a game (292).

A week later, Washington vanquished Minnesota 28–13, ending the Gophers' seven-game winning streak over the Huskies.

faked giving the ball to another Husky running back, Roland Kirkby. He found a lane, and with his sprinter's speed and a couple timely blocks by alert teammates, he sped down the field completely untouched into the end zone. The 96-yard kickoff return established a Husky record and today stands as the sixth-longest return in Husky history. It also incensed the Gophers, who battered and shattered the Washington defense and sent the Huskies home with a 48–20 defeat. Worse still than the loss of the game was the loss of McElhenny, who was sidelined for most of the remainder of the season by a first-half foot injury.

The need for a bigger stadium became apparent when Notre Dame visited in 1949.

McElhenny picks up big yardage in the Huskies' 21–20 defeat of UCLA in 1950.

Battle with the Bruins

Ranked 10th in the country, Washington played its first conference game of the 1950 campaign against 13th-ranked UCLA. The Bruins, coached by Red Sanders, featured a high-scoring single-wing offense and one of the toughest defenses on the West Coast. UCLA took advantage of a first-quarter fumble by Washington to jump to a 7–0 lead. The Huskies tied the score in the second period when Heinrich capped an 82-yard drive with a two-yard quarterback sneak.

In the second half, Washington wasted little time moving in front. On the fourth play of the quarter, Heinrich connected with Fritz Apking for a 50-yard touchdown.

On the ensuing drive, UCLA quarterback Joe Marvin found Isaac Jones in the end zone for a 38-yard score. But Bob Watson missed the extra point, and Washington clung to a 14–13 lead.

A break that would have ruined the morale of many football teams came in the fourth quarter. Washington had stopped a Bruins attack on the Husky 25-yard line. On fourth down, Coach Sanders called for a short punt just over the heads of the two safeties. Dick Sprague sensed the purpose of the play and ran away from the ball to let it roll over the goal line. His teammate Anse McCullough tried to retrieve the bouncing ball and touched it, making it a live ball that was recovered by the Trojans at the Husky 3. UCLA's John Florence crossed the end zone one play later. With the successful extra point, the Bruins led 20–14.

With two minutes to play, the Huskies started a drive from their 15-yard line. McElhenny scored from the UCLA 1-yard line to even the game. In came straight-A student Jim Rosenzweig, who would later become an outstanding faculty member in the UW Business School. He set up for the winning extra point and then kicked the ball straight through the uprights to clinch the victory for Washington.

For the Conference Title

After defeating Oregon State, the Huskies traveled to Palo Alto, where they beat Stanford 21–7. On November 4, defending conference champion and sixth-ranked unbeaten California came to town. Cal was led by two-time consensus All-American lineman Les Richter and future All-American running back Johnny Olszewski. Everything was on the line in the game: a conference title and a trip to the Rose Bowl.

Washington got the first break. Husky safety Dick Sprague picked off a Cal pass near midfield. Eight plays later, halfback Bill Earley dove over the center pileup for a touchdown. Rosenzweig's kick made it 7–0. Just a few minutes later, Cal evened the score after a 63-yard drive and Richter's conversion.

In the third quarter, the Bears scored on a 26-yard pass play. The Huskies had two great chances to score near the end of the game. They got to the Bears 2-yard line on one drive. On fourth down, Heinrich tried to pass, but the ball was batted out of his hand and the Bears recovered. Then, with a little more than four minutes left in the game, Cal fumbled and left tackle Ernie Stein recovered on the Bears 9. But the enraged Cal defenders rose up one more time, smearing McElhenny for a six-yard loss. On second down, Heinrich lost another fumble.

The Bears took the game 14–7, won the conference, and advanced to the Rose Bowl. In the locker room after the game, several players said with tears in their eyes, "Twice on the 10-yard line. Twice! And we couldn't score. I don't know what to think... We should have won."

A Bizarre Finish and Two Husky Records

On November 25, 1950, in Spokane's Memorial Stadium, Heinrich and McElhenny were not only trying to help the Huskies beat the Cougars, but also trying to break national and conference records. Heinrich was trying to break the national passing record for completions in a season, which was set by Mississippi's Charley Conerly in 1947. Meanwhile, McElhenny was chasing the conference single-season rushing record, set in 1948 by Cal's Jackie Jensen.

Washington made no bones about trying to put Heinrich and McElhenny in position to eclipse the records. With less than two minutes left, Washington led 45–14. Earlier in the game it had been announced that Heinrich had set the national record, so the Huskies focused on helping McElhenny get his. It was later discovered by the official statistician that Heinrich had only tied the record. Husky coaches tried to relay the need for one more pass to the bench, but the lines went dead. So the public-address announcer was asked to bellow forth, "Heinrich needs one more." There was just one problem: the Cougars had the ball.

Clyde Seiler, a Husky defensive tackle, rushed on the field yelling, "Let them score! Let them score!" On the next play, John Rowley caught a Dick Gambold pass and ran into the end zone untouched. With 50 seconds to go, Kirkby took the kickoff and ran straight out of bounds to stop the clock. Heinrich's first pass attempt, to Joe Cloidt, was incomplete. The next one was complete—a short pass in the flat to Kirby. Heinrich then turned to McElhenny: "I've got mine, now let's get yours." Heinrich pitched the ball to his teammate, who raced for 84 yards and his fifth touchdown of the day. The late-game run gave McElhenny 296 yards for the game (still a Husky record) and 1,107 for the season—a new conference record.

"The Day That Hope Died"

As the 1951 season approached, the memory of the disappointing loss to California the year before began to ebb behind the prospect of what was ahead. Heinrich, who had been named to two All-America teams in 1950, was back with McElhenny. Coaches and fans had every reason to believe that 1951 would be the year that Washington would return to the Rose Bowl.

But on the afternoon of September 8, two weeks before the season opener, Heinrich suffered a shoulder separation while participating in a scrimmage. He was hit by a third-stringer, who was so mortified that he quit the team and left school. Heinrich was sidelined for the season. Jack Hewins, an Associated Press sportswriter, called it "the Day That Hope Died." Hewins described the atmosphere in the coaches' locker room after the fateful practice. "The coaches weren't weeping... A couple of them said, 'Well, what the heck? What can you say?'" Others were quiet, trying to recall something from their own experiences that would match the catastrophe. Odell said, "We'll still be tough... We'll surprise a few people."

The "surprises" came early in the season. The Huskies walloped Montana 58–7 and went to Minnesota the next week and beat the Gophers 25–20. Then began the team's downfall; they lost the third game when 12th-ranked Washington lost 20–13 to USC.

The Punt Return Everybody Remembers

Whenever you ask fans about Hugh McElhenny's most memorable moments, they often recount his 100-yard punt return on October 6, 1951, against the Trojans. After a grueling three-plus quarters, USC clung to a 13–6 lead. With fourth-and-9 on the Husky 48, USC's short-yardage punter Des Koch was sent in to kick instead of Frank Gifford, the regular long punter and one of the best running backs in the nation. Koch punted the ball toward the Washington goal line. All the coaches were yelling at McElhenny to let the ball roll into the end zone. McElhenny had other ideas.

"I thought I was between the 5- and 10-yard line. It was probably stupid, but it's sort of a runner's feeling that you go for it," he later recalled. Sidestepping the first tackler, the King shook off another and started to sprint up the

No football player in Husky history has made more people say "I don't believe that" or "Did you see that move?" than **Hugh McElhenny**. John Jarstad was the radio voice of the Huskies during the star's playing days. "I know everything that was written about him, and none of it was adequate. Hugh was always doing the impossible," Jarstad said. "He drove tacklers batty. The idea that Hugh was a great runner because of how he practiced was garbage. He was a free spirit, often goofed off during the week, and was called on the carpet. What he did on Saturdays wasn't taught. It came straight down from heaven."

The player set Husky records for longest kickoff return, longest punt return, and longest run from scrimmage. All of them were for more than 90 yards and all for touchdowns. He also established a school record for rushing yards in a single game—296 yards—which still stands, along with his punt-return mark. In his senior year, he finished the season with 125 points, a total that was just one point less than the nation's leader, City College of San Francisco's Ollie Matson. "He was the darndest animal," said UCLA coach Red Sanders. "He ran around you, through you, and if the situation demanded it, right over you."

An All-American selection in 1951, he played in the 1952 East-West Shrine Game, the Hula Bowl, and the College All-Star Game. He was a first-round draft pick of the San Francisco 49ers in the 1952 NFL Draft and won the Rookie of the Year Award. In his 13-year NFL career, he gained 11,375 all-purpose yards. He was a charter member of the Husky Hall of Fame (1979) and was inducted into the Pro Football Hall of Fame in 1970 and the College Football Hall of Fame in 1981.

north sideline in easy strides. Suddenly, with a burst of speed and Husky blockers upending Trojans defenders all over the field, a clear path opened down the length of the field. McElhenny turned on the speed. "It was like a

Don Heinrich finished his career regarded as one of the greatest quarterbacks in college history. After leading Bremerton High School to a state football championship in 1948, he entered UW in 1949. As a sophomore in his first varsity season in 1950, he was named to the Associated Press' All-American and All-Coast teams. In that year, he set an NCAA record for passes completed (134) and completion percentage (60.6). Out of action with a shoulder injury in 1951, he returned in 1952 and again led the nation in passing, throwing 137 completions and finishing his Husky career with a school-record 4,392 yards and 33 touchdowns. He still ranks 10th in Husky history in career passing yards, and his 80-yard touchdown pass to George Black in the 1952 UCLA game ranks ninth all-time. He was an All-Conference and All-America selection in 1952.

Heinrich went on to play seven seasons in the NFL, with the New York Giants and the Dallas Cowboys. He played in three NFL Championship Games with the Giants and won one, beating the Chicago Bears 47–7 in 1956. Heinrich capped off his career by being selected to the Husky Hall of Fame (1981) and the College Football Hall of Fame (1987).

All-American quarterback Don Heinrich.

touchdown out of a cornball movie...only it was real," Gifford said. McElhenny's return is still the longest in Husky history. Less memorable was the outcome of the game: the Huskies missed the extra point and then allowed the Trojans to score again, for a 20–13 final score.

The Huskies finished the season by beating Oregon 63–6 but then losing 27–20 at home to eighth-ranked Illinois. After the season ended, Odell's relationship with Cassill began to deteriorate. The coach was asked to resign but refused to do so. He stayed on to coach in 1952, Heinrich's last season in purple and gold.

About a week prior to the last game of the 1952 season—against the Cougars in Spokane—Don Heinrich was inducted into the army. It took a weekend pass issued by understanding officers at Fort Lewis to let him play. He played very well in the Huskies' 33–27 victory and once again set a national record in passes completed.

Another outstanding player in the 1950–52 seasons was Dick Sprague. An All-American defensive back in 1950, he and Heinrich were the first sophomores in Husky history to earn All-America honors. Sprague made seven interceptions in 1950, a record that is still fifth all-time in school history. His speed and athleticism enabled him to play several positions during his career. In addition to being a defensive back, he played offensive halfback, performed punting duties, and returned punts and kickoffs. He entered the Husky Hall of Fame in 1995.

The People's Choice

Less than a month after the last game of the 1952 season, Coach Odell was out of work. University president Dr. Henry Schmitz approved Cassill's recommendation that Odell be fired even though he had a year to go on his contract. Schmitz said, "There was no consideration of the won-lost record nor was there any criticism of Coach Odell as an individual. Rather, the problem concerns itself entirely with relationships in the general management of the athletic program." Unhappy marriages bring about unhappy endings.

Seattle fans had a lot to do with the selection of Johnny Cherberg as Odell's replacement. They had followed the "Cowboy's" football career from its beginning at Queen Anne High School in the mid-1920s. Harvey Cassill was not very interested in Cherberg but wanted Skip Stahley, who had served with Cherberg on Odell's staff. But Cassill and his superior, university vice president H.P. Everest, recognized the public's desire and on January 31, 1953, named Cherberg Washington's head coach.

Since his high school playing career, Cherberg had built up a faithful following. He was a running back on Coach Phelan's first three Washington teams, from 1930 to 1932. After his graduation, he became a successful coach at Cleveland High School, and then at his high school alma mater. In 1946, he joined Coach Welch's staff as the backfield coach. He was retained in 1948 by Odell, who appointed him freshman coach at Washington. During his five seasons with the freshmen, his teams won 22 of 23 games. He lost his first game to the Oregon Ducklings 25–24 and then won the next 22.

Unfortunately, Cherberg was not as successful with the varsity squad. He compiled a 3–6–1 record in 1953. The next year the Huskies went 2–8–0 and finished eighth in the conference. The next season became a pivotal year for not only Cherberg's coaching future, but for the entire Husky athletic program. In the season opener, Washington beat Idaho 14–7 but set a school record by fumbling 11

Harvey Cassill, UW's athletic director from 1946 to 1956.

times. On the road, they shut out Minnesota 30–0 and beat Oregon at home 19–7.

Facing 10th-ranked USC at home, they fashioned one of the most memorable plays in Husky football history to beat the Trojans 7–0. With 6:20 remaining, the Huskies had the ball on their own 20-yard line. Quarterback Steve Roake threw a 20-yard pass on a crossing pattern to right end Jim Houston. After running five yards, Houston was hit as left end Corky Lewis was coming up to block. As Houston was falling on the 45-yard line, he lateraled the ball to Lewis, who was in full stride. Lewis raced past a would-be tackler and headed straight downfield 55 yards for the game's only touchdown. It was the Huskies' first win over USC in Seattle since 1945.

After that triumph, the season began to unravel. At home, the Huskies lost to Baylor and Oregon State and tied Stanford. Away, they lost to Cal and fourth-ranked UCLA. Before the Bruins game, Cherberg asked Torchy Torrance, a Washington alumnus and one of the Huskies' most ardent football boosters, to talk to the players. It was a "pep" talk, and it almost worked; the Huskies went out and nearly upset UCLA, who went on to win the 1955 Pacific Coast Conference title.

A few days after the loss to UCLA, Lewis and a few other players visited Torrance to discuss a coaching change. Torrance advised them to talk to athletic director Harvey Cassill and encouraged them to go out and play a great game against Washington State in the season finale. The Huskies did just that. Credell Green ran for 258 yards to lead Washington to a 27–7 victory. Washington finished 5–4–1 and fifth in the conference.

Soon after, the players turned in their equipment and about 30 of them went to see Cassill. Lewis said, "We told Harvey we could not play for Cherberg anymore." After the meeting, Cassill immediately went to Cherberg and said, "I think you should meet with the players." Cassill and Cherberg met with the players together. "The players would not repeat what they told me. They were afraid of John. And I had to agree with John, at the end of the session, that there was no reason for him to do anything. As far as the player revolt was concerned, there wasn't any," said Cassill.

Several players who were on Cherberg's squad when he was freshman coach said he became a different man when he stepped up to the varsity. Some felt "he couldn't take the pressure," particularly as the losses mounted in the latter part of the 1955 season. Cherberg started to lash out at the coaches, players, and others in a manner that startled those who were his targets.

Lewis recounts an incident when Cherberg charged into the locker room while the players were dressing for a game. Lewis was standing nude just inside the door to the room, when Cherberg screamed at him, "Are you ready? Are you mad?" Lewis replied, "Coach, I am ready. I'm always ready." Cherberg bellowed, "Are you really ready? I want you mad, really mad." He then stomped his cleated foot right on the top of Lewis' bare one. Was Cherberg's action intentional? Probably not. Was it called for? Definitely not. Did it hurt Lewis? During the game, Lewis had to loosen his shoe because his foot was swollen and bruised.

Players remember Cherberg blowing up on a charter plane ride home in 1955. On team trips during the Cherberg era, the stewardesses, after takeoff, would serve trays of fruit. On this trip, when Cherberg saw the stewardesses start down the aisle, he charged out of his seat and hit the trays from below with his fist, sending fruit flying everywhere. Then he shouted, "Don't you ever feed fruit to my players without asking me first!"

Reports of the players' unrest ultimately got out, but public opinion rested mostly with the coach. Many of the fans' reactions were published in the *Seattle Times*, a sampling of which indicated just how many felt about the players:

"Those kids are squawking like a bunch of babies."

Roscoe "Torchy" Torrance was known as Mr. Everything in Seattle. The University of Washington never had a more loyal, devoted alumnus than Torchy. His love affair with Washington began in 1918, when he enrolled as a freshman. He played baseball for four years. After graduation, he became the university's property manager and assistant trainer, and in 1922, he was appointed freshmen baseball coach and ASUW assistant graduate manager. After leaving the university in 1924 to pursue business interests, he continued his active support of the Husky program. He was an avid recruiter, raised funds, and found jobs to help athletes through school. His fund-raising efforts led to the formation of the Greater Washington Advertising Fund, which is used to help players with expenses.

"We've been too considerate of the younger generation. We've been babying them, and when they get into something highly competitive like college football they can't take it."

"The ball players should not run the team. Johnny is running his own show and he is capable of doing it. He's a fine gentleman and a good coach."

"In my estimation, there are not enough boys with the extreme desire to play football today. Too many are just going along for the ride."

As the controversy mounted, the university administration and student governing body weighed in. They agreed that the administration should start a complete investigation of the situation. Ultimately, the Board of Control of the Associated Students of the University of Washington (ASUW) voted 12–2 to fire Cherberg.

On December 10, a semblance of quiet was restored when the university's board of regents voted unanimously to rehire Cherberg on the condition that he mend the situation and develop harmonious relations with the team. In an executive session prior to the public portion of the December 10 meeting, the regents gave Cassill the sole responsibility to decide whether or not Cherberg had accomplished that objective. Unfortunately, the coach made little change. In mid-January, Cassill met with the players, after which many came to the conclusion that the situation would not improve with Cherberg at the helm.

It was a touchy situation. Players received bribes and threats from Cherberg boosters. Lewis, a premedical student with outstanding grades and an impressive roster of campus activities, remembers getting a phone call from an unidentified booster who threatened that he would never get into Washington's medical school if Lewis did not stop the players' revolt. When Lewis reported the threat to Everest, he responded, "Corky, with your grades and activities you should have no worries about getting into medical school. There are not enough strings for anybody to have to prevent your being accepted."

The players had a meeting early in 1956. Lewis indicated that some players had received $50 bills before the meeting. One of the team members stood up during the meeting and said, "God came to me and told me to vote for Cherberg." Another player asked, "Did God leave $50 under your pillow?" The whole meeting room rocked with laughter, and then the players agreed to meet with Cassill to discuss their decision to ask for Cherberg's dismissal.

An editorial in the January 26, 1956, *University Daily* called for Cherberg's resignation. On January 27, Cassill fired him. Cherberg immediately went public, firing several volleys at the university administration, Cassill, the ASUW, and prominent boosters who paid players. As reported in the article "Boosters Mess It Up in Washington" in the February 20, 1956, issue of *Sports Illustrated*, Cherberg said, "The filthiest thing in the world is to corrupt young Americans with dough. I may never coach again, but, God willing, I'm not going to let them corrupt any more kids." Later in the article, he added, "I went along all right—with the full knowledge of my superiors. No coach has any other choice under the unrealistic rules which prevail in the Coast Conference and others like it." In another publication, he said, "For the good of the University and for the benefit of my successor and other coaches out there, right-minded citizens should take affirmative action to fire Cassill, establish an athletic administration that will operate for the benefit of the students, and create a program without any connection with any downtown interests."

Lewis and other teammates felt Cherberg's words took a holier-than-thou stance because they knew he had directly sent players to boosters for financial assistance. Lewis, for example, got into financial trouble at the end of his sophomore year. "I had no money to pay my Sigma Nu house bill. I could not work the required hours for grant-in-aid payments because of my considerable lab studies in the spring quarter. So I went to Cherberg and told him I needed a loan. He sent me downtown to meet with a booster and the booster starts paying me $50 a month to be his 'campus representative.'"

University of Washington administrators denied the allegations. Pacific Coast Conference (PCC) commissioner Victor O. Schmidt suggested an investigation of Washington's athletic program. In the PCC in those days, up to 60 student-athletes participating in the men's intercollegiate athletic program—which consisted of nine major sports and a few minor ones—could be provided tuition from university funds in any one year, and all student-athletes could be given a campus job and/or summer jobs. Other athletes could receive tuition funds from money contributed by boosters. The rate of pay for campus jobs was $1.50 per hour, with a maximum of 50 hours ($75 per month). Any payments in excess of $75 per month were in violation of PCC rules. Some players who had a high grade point average in high school could also receive academic scholarships.

"I Took a Pay Cut After Leaving the UW for the Pros"

One of the most widely circulated stories related to the payments made to Husky All-American running back Hugh McElhenny. After McElhenny left Washington to join the San Francisco 49ers, his former teammates jokingly said that the star running back was the only college football player to take a cut in salary when he turned professional. During the PCC investigation of Washington in 1956, McElhenny said he and his wife had a combined income of $800 per month while in Seattle. He said he received $75 a month from an on-campus job. His wife earned $300 per month working for King County Medical. The balance of $425 was earned, he reported, for doing "public relations" work for Seattle's Rainier Brewing Company. While he signed with the 49ers for $7,000 a year and a $500 bonus, he admitted, "The remark about me taking a cut in pay wasn't entirely off base."

Before and during the Cherberg years, funds were paid directly to Husky football players by businessmen boosters. The largest source was the Washington Advertising Fund, which was established to receive money earned from a professional football exhibition game in Husky Stadium in August 1955. Torrance was instrumental in creating the fund through his association with Greater Seattle, Inc., the game's sponsor. Torrance talked the teams into coming to Seattle. He convinced the directors of Greater Seattle to sponsor the game. He persuaded the university's board of regents to allow professional teams to play in Husky Stadium for the first time—for a percentage of the gate receipts.

More than 49,000 watched former Husky quarterback Don Heinrich lead the New York Giants to a 28–17 victory over the San Francisco 49ers at Husky Stadium. The game was a whopping success. Each team made $36,586; the ASUW received $28,361 for stadium rental and management fees; and Greater Seattle turned a profit of $7,021. After taxes, there was $28,000 left. In accordance with a previous agreement with Greater Seattle, Torrance tucked it into the Washington Advertising Fund to pay Husky athletes.

Many groups weighed in after the Cherberg firing, and the issues became polarized. The Organization Assembly, representing more than 200 of the university's student organizations, voted 44–9 in favor of Cassill's action. A group of Washington alumni and athletic boosters announced it would circulate a statewide petition urging Cassill be fired. Cassill didn't need to be fired; he resigned on February 9. As a result of the most tumultuous period in Husky athletics, the University of Washington was without leadership in two important positions: athletic director and head football coach. Athletic probation was a very real possibility, the community was still divided over the Cherberg-Torrance-Cassill hassle, and spring football practice was due to begin in a few months.

Probation

To fill one of the two positions, Washington hired 31-year-old George Briggs as AD. He had previously been the assistant athletic director at the University of California. Everest recommended him because he was young and a capable athletic administrator and because "he had no connection with any factions or any group associated with this university. I feel the best interests of the university will be served by a man from outside the university circles.... Mr. Briggs has accepted his post with the definite understanding that the development of all university athletics must be conducted entirely within Pacific Coast Conference rules and policies." Briggs was given complete control of the Department of Athletics.

A former Seattle resident, Briggs graduated from Seattle's Roosevelt High School in 1943. He entered the marines' V-12 program at Washington and graduated in engineering from the University of California. He was a member of Washington and Cal's swim teams and also played on the junior varsity basketball team at UW. A veteran of World War II and the Korean War, he completed his military duty as a marine captain and battery commander of an artillery unit.

Around the time of Briggs' hiring, a Washington State Legislature review of the athletic situation began, as did investigations by the Pacific Coast Conference and the National Collegiate Athletic Association. As a result of the investigations, all Washington teams, except crew, were placed on a two-year probation starting July 1, 1956. The investigations disclosed that 27 football players had received an average of $60 per month more than the allowed $75. The PCC ruling prevented any Washington team from winning any conference championships, the football team from appearing in the Rose Bowl, and the basketball team from competing in postseason games. The school could not participate in the distribution of receipts from the Rose Bowl game, including receipts for radio and television rights, and could not nationally televise any home games or events. It was estimated the loss of receipts from the Rose Bowl would amount to $53,000 over the two probationary years. All other sports, excepting crew, could not compete for championships.

Later, the NCAA declared all Washington teams ineligible to participate in postseason and national championship events. But because sports other than football had not violated the PCC rules, there was a significant outcry. When the NCAA put the crew team on probation, the Washington State Senate sent a letter to the NCAA and the Intercollegiate Rowing Association urging them to stop "the unreasonable, uncalled-for, and unwarranted indictment" of the Washington crew program. The IRA did not agree.

Later in 1956, three other schools in the conference were placed on probation—California for one year, USC for two, and UCLA for three years. In January 1959, the NCAA again placed USC on probation until January 1961 for recruiting violations. *San Francisco Chronicle* columnist Art Rosenbaum wrote about the future of the conference, wondering if all the other conference schools were innocent as uncharged. It was inconceivable that the recruitment programs at the other schools were completely unsullied, after all. "To get hot college athletes, a recruiter must outbid the other school... The whole thing has become an 'arms race,'" he wrote.

Briggs' first order of business was to clean house financially. He got all the contributors to the Washington Advertising Fund, the Quarterbacks Club, and other booster groups together and declared he was going to form the Tyee Club. He explained the Tyee was a Pacific Coast Native American word meaning "the chief." It was also used to describe Chinook salmon of 30 pounds or more. Briggs wanted the "big fish" boosters to contribute to the Tyee organization. All contributions to the athletic program would be funneled through this new group but under the control of the university and the administration of the athletic department. The funds would be used for grant-in-aid to athletes under the PCC rules. In exchange for their contributions, Tyee members could purchase football and basketball season tickets in favorable viewing locations.

Next, Briggs focused on hiring a new football coach. He wanted someone who was tough on conditioning and discipline and who could win games in the fourth quarter. "We were getting a reputation in the Pacific Coast Conference as a party, playtime, and country club in football. The conference champion would advance to the Rose Bowl and summarily get its butt kicked by the Big Ten victor. They would eat our lunch in the third and fourth quarters." He was right. Since the Rose Bowl Committee formed the pact between the Big Ten Conference and the Pacific Coast Conference champions in 1946, the Big Ten representative had won nine of the 10 meetings.

Briggs continued, "I called the three best coaches in the country—Michigan State's Duffy Daugherty, Texas A&M's Bear Bryant, and Bud Wilkinson of Oklahoma. I didn't expect any of them to accept my offer to be Washington's head coach. Each of them felt he was running a better program and did not want to start all over again."

Briggs asked each of them who they would hire, were they in his position. On everybody's list was Darrell Royal, the head coach at Mississippi State. Briggs flew to Mississippi to meet Royal and his wife, Edith. "I spent the day with them, offered him the job, and Royal accepted it," he said.

Royal's $17,000 salary created a lot of controversy on campus. The *University Daily* polled the school's faculty on the matter and reported that 79 percent of the faculty felt football should be deemphasized and 81 percent thought that the new coach's salary was too high. *Time* magazine declared that the faculty had reason for outrage, considering the average annual pay was $8,469 for a full professor (not teaching in the professional schools such as law, business, and medicine). A few days later, local sports columnist Emmett Watson noted in the *Seattle Post-Intelligencer* that football coaches were typically paid more than professors because they got fired more frequently than professors. Any job with a high turnover, Watson explained, usually commands good money. He then went on to quote an unidentified coach: "A biology professor can flunk twenty-five percent of his class and nobody pays any attention. But let Royal send a football team out next fall that flunks one test in front of fifty thousand people and he's in thick soup." Watson added, "The conclusion is clear: big-time football is a thing apart from education, and a professor might as well fret over the salary paid Groucho Marx as worry how much the football coach makes. Both are in the entertainment business, and both had better produce—or else."

When Royal arrived in Seattle, he said he would like to put his suitcases in the attic and stay a while. After graduating from Oklahoma in 1950, where he played under Coach Bud Wilkinson and was an All-American quarterback in 1949, Briggs began his coaching career. His first stop was as the backfield coach at North Carolina State in 1950. He went to Tulsa in 1951 and Mississippi State in 1952. He received his first head-coaching assignment in the Canadian Football League in 1953, as the leader of the Edmonton Eskimos. Edmonton won the Western Division Championship that year with 12 wins and four losses. Royal returned to Mississippi State as head coach in 1954.

Royal began to build a good football program in Washington. In the spring of 1956, he introduced the Split-T offense he learned under Coach Wilkinson at Oklahoma. By the time practice started in late August, Husky fans

Darrell Royal went on to a stellar coaching career at Texas A&M.

were more interested in the team's upcoming season than in rehashing its painful past. In the season opener, the Huskies rolled up a school-record single-game 430 yards and 33 first downs (still the second-best in Husky history), defeating Idaho 53–21. It was an impressive debut for Royal. The next week, Minnesota gave Royal his first Husky loss, 34–14. Then 13th-ranked Illinois came to town. Washington beat the Illini 28–13, a contest that featured Dean Derby's 92-yard touchdown run on the Huskies' second play from scrimmage.

In their fourth-straight home game, the Huskies beat Oregon 20–7. The fans were flying high and thinking about a conference title. They were quickly brought to earth when the Huskies lost their next four games, all to conference foes. The Huskies closed out the season with wins over Stanford and Washington State.

With a 5–5 record, Royal had laid a solid foundation. He stressed that team members be great representatives for the university. He said, "If a player behaved in such a manner as to embarrass the university and the rest of the team, we are better off without him." He also emphasized academics: "Players must give the same kind of attention to their studies as we expect them to give to football." He wanted his relationships with faculty to be positive, so he began inviting three professors each week to join the team from the Thursday before the game to the end of the game. Royal wanted them to see what the coaches did and what the team did. Many believed Royal was a better teacher than most faculty members.

Everybody looked forward to a Royal future, but after the 1956 season, Texas came calling. At a Husky home basketball game in early December, George Briggs was in the athletic director's aisle seat near the court. Royal came down and sat next to Briggs and said that he had just gotten a call from Texas asking if he was interested in their head-coaching job. Royal didn't want to respond to Texas before talking with Briggs because he knew what Washington was trying to do, the kind of commitment he had made, the four to five years it would take to turn the program around. Briggs asked Royal, "What do you think of the Texas job?" Royal replied, "I think it's the best football coaching job in college today." Briggs said, "Let's go right now and call Dana Bible [the Texas athletic director]."

"I called Dana and told him he would be crazy if he didn't hire Royal. My theory was, even though I might have been able to convince Darrell to stay, he would be looking over his shoulder all the time wondering why he stayed. He would be thinking, 'Should I have gone, what would I have accomplished?' That's not the kind of situation you want in football coaching or in any other business," Briggs later said.

Soon after, Briggs was visited by a prominent group of alumni who said they had already selected a new coach—

Joe Kuharich, coach of the Washington Redskins. Briggs firmly told them that he would not pick anyone they had chosen, saying, "If the new coach is not selected by the athletic director and the university administration, then the coach isn't working for us." Otherwise, Briggs reasoned, the university would be in the same position as in the recent past, when outsiders were actively involved in activities impacting the athletic program.

Briggs went back to the list of head-coaching candidates he had compiled just 10 months ago. One of the names on his list was Jim Owens. "The reason why he wasn't a candidate for me the first time was that he was not a head coach," Briggs explained. "I didn't believe I could come to Washington with all the turmoil we had and bring in an assistant coach, however good he was, and get away with it. I had to have a head coach then."

Briggs thought the situation in 1957 was much different than it had been in 1956. He had been the athletic director for almost a year and had cleaned up the boosters' mess. He had achieved some stabilization and confidence in the program by interacting with fans, faculty, students, alumni, and other supporters. He also felt he had a broader array of candidates. Still, the program had its outside influences.

Owens' skills had been highly developed by several great coaches. He played at Oklahoma University for two outstanding coaches—Jim Tatum and Bud Wilkinson. He was an assistant for six years under the legendary Bear Bryant at the University of Kentucky and Texas A&M.

On January 21, Owens became the Huskies' head coach. He signed a three-year contract for $15,000 a year. An editorial in the *University Daily*, while bemoaning the size of Owens' salary, cited that football was now big business and said a good football coach was a priceless commodity.

In his introduction to the media, Owens was announced to be 30 years old. In fact, he was about a month and a half shy of his 30th birthday. He silenced any critics who still had thoughts of Royal's quick departure after one year. In his first public appearance in Bremerton a few weeks later, he said, "When I first saw Mount Rainier, I felt like a displaced person seeing the Statute of Liberty for the first time. I'm here to stay."

CHAPTER 6

From Ashes to Roses

Growing up in Oklahoma City, Jim Owens knew he wanted to be a football player—not just that, he wanted to play for the Oklahoma Sooners. Owens' quest for Oklahoma began as a teenager at Classen High School in Oklahoma City. "In my junior year, I played a lot," said Owens. "We had a good team that year. In my senior year, we had the best team that had been around in a long time. We won the 1943 state championship and I made the All-State team."

After high school, he joined the navy and was discharged in time to begin his freshman year at Oklahoma three years later, in the fall of 1946. Oklahoma had a big-time football program. Beginning in 1946, the Sooners were ranked in the top 20 for 14 consecutive years, winning national championships in 1950, 1955, and 1956.

Owens was ready for such a program. He had grown to 6'4" and weighed about 220 pounds. Following World War II, there were no restrictions on freshmen's eligibility to play varsity, so Owens started for the Sooners right away. Owens was a standout at Oklahoma, named cocaptain of the team in his senior year and selected as an All-American. He graduated in three years and entered Oklahoma Law School in the fall of 1949.

He joined the professional football ranks, signing a contract with the Baltimore Colts in 1950 for $4,500 plus a $500 cash bonus. He played both ways for the Colts, as an offensive and defensive player. Near the end of the 1950 season, the Colts faced the Steelers in Pittsburgh. Owens, then on defense, was hit in the kidney. Though injured, he finished the game. Afterward, he complained to the team physician about feeling sick, and the doctor found a blood clot in his kidney. His professional football career was over.

Owens then returned to Oklahoma Law School and worked as a student assistant during the 1951 football spring practice. Owens had several interests at that point, including law, politics, and coaching. A coaching opportunity soon came. In the spring of 1951, Oklahoma coach Wilkinson conducted a football clinic for high school coaches. Wilkinson invited Bear Bryant to speak at the clinic. Bryant needed several men to demonstrate a point he was making and chose several of the Oklahoma student assistants, including Owens and Darrell Royal. A few weeks later, Owens received a call from Bryant asking him to meet in Dallas. Over that lunch meeting, Bryant asked Owens to sign on as his end coach at Kentucky. "By the time that Bryant finished talking to me, I was ready to go. He was very persuasive," Owens said.

Owens coached the next three years at Kentucky and joined the Bear at Texas A&M in 1954. Bryant and his staff faced a monumental rebuilding challenge with the Aggies, who had not won a conference championship since 1941 and had lost five games in 1953 by a combined score of 133–46. Bryant approached the rebuilding of the A&M football program with three major tenets: sacrifice, hard work, and self-discipline. "My approach to the game has been the same at all the places I've been. That means, first of all, to win physically. If you get eleven on a field and they beat the other eleven physically, they'll win. They will start forcing mistakes. They'll win in the fourth quarter," Bryant said.

It was these tenets that Owens took with him to Washington in 1957. In his first meeting with the team, on January 30, 1957, he impressed his young players. Physically, he was an imposing figure, but he also possessed those characteristics everybody pictured in a football coach: energy, a straightforward style, leadership, a bounce in his step.

Twenty-four hours after Owens was hired, he had already chosen three assistant coaches—Bert Clark, Tom Tipps, and Chesty Walker. Clark had been a teammate of Owens' at Oklahoma. Tipps had served on the coaching staff with Owens at Texas A&M. Walker, 52 when he joined the Washington staff, was the "old man" of the group. "The winningest high school coach in Texas," he took on the role as "Father Confessor" for the team, providing a lot of counsel to Husky players over the years.

Owens installed a system similar to what he knew under Bryant. None of the coaches had any specific designation, such as end coach, backfield coach, or line coach. Instead, they each worked with all the players, while highlighting their specific areas of expertise. Most important, they all worked with the freshman team during the 1957 season. They recognized that the future of the program rested with the incoming class, many of whom they had recruited and all of whom possessed the characteristics the coaches wanted.

The Coaches Were "Working Sons of Bitches"

The coaches started shaping their approach to spring practices. The first goal was team unity. Owens was not interested in players who focused on personal statistics and making All-Star teams. His teams had no names on their jerseys. He recruited players who were smart and who would sacrifice their own recognition for that of the team. He would have shirked the Husky Sports Information Department's press releases and the hype that surrounds the college football scene today. He did not even care about the Heisman Trophy, All-America selections, and All-Coast recognition. If it came to some players that was fine, but team success and recognition were paramount.

His second point of emphasis was defense. His players might have been small, but they were quick and tenacious on defense. Owens would get the Huskies to commit to football "from the defense out." In his mind, playing defense was the real test of a player's love for the game. The best defenders ultimately would be the best football players. If a player couldn't or wouldn't play defense, he didn't get much playing time under Owens' system.

A third fundamental was conditioning. Owens and his staff believed that being physically and mentally tough was the key to winning football games. They wanted the Huskies to be in better shape than any opponent and thereby wear the opposition down. The coaches pushed their players to the limit. "You run drills to get a player to a physical and mental point where he believes he can't give anymore and then you continue to push him so he has to fight through the 'breaking point' and so he understands that he can handle more pain and sacrifice," Owens said. "Football is a game of power and you beat opponents by beating them physically."

Finally, Owens expected his players to "pay the price." He firmly believed that the best football teams were those that did whatever it took on the practice field to prepare for each Saturday afternoon. "To do that demands sacrifice and the desire to succeed. I want the kind of player who is willing to pay the price," Owens stated. One drill they would implement exemplified this. At the end of a grueling practice, when all the players were exhausted, Owens would have the offense attempt to run 10 plays perfectly—not only that, but mess just one up, and they had to start again from zero. Once the players accomplished 10 in a row, everybody could go to the locker room.

There were 58 players at the start of that spring practice. Twenty were letter winners, 17 were freshmen, and two were junior college transfers. Only one returning letter winner, fullback Jim Jones, had been an All-Coast player. Additionally, the team was without Al Ferguson, the starting quarterback in 1956, who was recovering from an off-season shoulder operation.

Owens ran the team like a drill sergeant. Everything was done quickly, with military precision. All players wore their helmets at all times. Emmett Watson reported in a story about a day in spring practice in early May when the coach exhibited his own physical toughness: "Owens moved from group to group, working with quarterbacks and centers, then the backs, then the tackles and finally the guards. Wearing only practice pants and a light T-shirt, he crouched down in front of a bucking sled to demonstrate. Abruptly, he raised up, slammed his elbows and head into the sled, driving it back a few feet. At one point as the players hit the sled, Owens' voice suddenly rose and he said, 'I don't see anybody trying to break the sled. Go ahead, break it—we'll buy a new one. Deliver the blow! Deliver the blow!'"

Keith Jackson, the renowned college football broadcaster, was then sports director for KOMO, the ABC affiliate in Seattle. He said, "The coaches worked like no coaching staff I can ever remember. They were working sons of bitches. The coaching staff was just like a bunch of Marines trapped in a lonely place. They backed each other up and committed themselves to each other and to their philosophy."

"The Death March"

As the 1957 preseason got under way in September, Owens and his coaches continued to see two problems: the lack of depth on the roster and inexperience at quarterback. To compensate for the lack of experience, Owens continued to stress fundamentals and conditioning. "When you have less depth than others, you have to look for any edge you can

Coach Jim Owens.

find. We decided to excel in the conditioning area because we hadn't had much time with the players and hadn't had the time to get our philosophy installed in the program," he said. After the first week of practice, many players had already shed several pounds. Even so, the coach was still concerned about their physical and mental fitness. On September 10, he decided to find out.

In the second of two practices that day and with the temperature eclipsing 90 degrees, Owens held a four-quarter scrimmage. Unsatisfied, he ordered two more quarters. Fuming, he ordered his players down to the practice fields east of Hec Edmundson Pavilion. He lined the players up in teams and had each squad cover punts. "Nobody fielded the punts," Carver Gayton recalled. "We just went full bore down the field and stayed in our lanes. After covering eight or ten punts, we figured that was going to be it."

The drills continued. Owens ordered all the players to line up on one goal line. Each player started in a three-point stance, and on Owens' whistle, they ran up the field about 15 yards. Another whistle, another three-point stance, another whistle. They continued the wind sprints over the entire length of two football fields and then turned around and came back. After several round trips—some say up to 15 of them—the group ended up in a kind of V-shape, with the more conditioned and committed players leading the pack. Some staggered and fell. Then they crawled. "They babbled and cried like babies as the assistant coaches ran down the field and urged them on," reported sportswriter Mike Donohoe.

During all of the practice sessions, nobody was allowed to drink water, which was the accepted treatment of the day for athletes, military personnel, and others in tough conditioning situations. Conventional wisdom said you would get cramps if you drank water.

Once the team was finally dismissed, everyone was exhausted. Many had severe cramps; seven of them were hospitalized. John Owen, a noted sports columnist for the *Seattle Post-Intelligencer*, remembers when Donohoe, who was covering the Huskies for the *P-I* in 1957, came into the sports department after the practice and told his fellow reporters about the "death march." He exclaimed, "They ran the kids up and down the field. If they fell down, they called them 'gutless bastards.'"

John Thompson, the director of public relations for the athletic department, can still remember the death march. "When it was all over, I had to take the reporters to visit with Jim. He was almost crying. He said, 'I hope I never have to do that again.' The death march—physical and mental toughness—made Husky football and ultimately revived the Pacific Coast Conference." Coach Tipps agreed. "The Death March was a big deal. West Coast football had a reputation of being a soft touch. We went in the opposite direction. People made a big deal of what we were putting

the players through at Washington. I think we brought back a hard-nosed approach to football in the Pacific Coast Conference."

It was the defining moment for the 1957 team, etched in the minds of all who endured it. The stories about that day would become the stuff of legend, recounted to incoming players for years to come. There is no doubt that Washington's reputation for toughness, tenacity, and endurance was cemented in 1957.

Owens implemented other innovations, too. At the time, the conventional football-coaching technique was to have a player use his shoulders to hit his opponent. If a player missed with his shoulder, even just a little bit, he would have a difficult time executing the block or tackle. But if he used his helmet and face mask, his odds improved dramatically. Tipps explained, "In football, you can't put your one shoulder against your opponent's one shoulder without giving up some advantage. So we taught the players when making a block or a tackle to focus their target on the very center of things. The center of things is the opponent's helmet."

The helmet was not only used for blocking and tackling but also for punishing an opponent. Dick Dunn said, "If you get a clear shot at a running back or a quarterback hung up in a pile, you were instructed to spear him helmet on helmet. You put a stop to whatever he was trying to do and he might not get up. We were also encouraged to block anybody still standing. You could be ten yards from the end of the play that was nearly over. If the whistle had not blown and an opposing player was nearby, you just flattened him."

"Fire out and hit them with the helmet" was a rallying cry of the Husky linemen. "We all still have noses and foreheads with big scars on them," Tim Bullard proudly proclaimed. "When an opponent got hit with the helmet enough times, he was pretty well beat up by the fourth quarter. We went right for the ear hole of the helmet on some plays and tried to knock him out."

Another hallmark of the new and improved Huskies was their punt game, something Coach Owens drilled into them over and over. Bob Schloredt, one of the nation's best punters from 1958 to 1960, summed up their objective.

"We gave up about two yards a punt. We averaged about 10 yards on punt returns. So figure the math. If we played great defense, punted the ball, played great defense, punted the ball—after about four series without giving up a first down, we would be in the opponent's end of the field, many times in four-down territory. That was as simple as you could make it."

His math was pretty good. In 1960, the Huskies had an average punt return of 14.2 yards compared to their opponents' average of 3.8. The margin still stands as the high mark in Washington history.

A Tie Is Like Kissing Your Sister

In the season opener, before a crowd of almost 35,000, the Huskies greeted the University of Colorado Buffaloes. The game satisfied no one except those who delighted in Indian summer sunshine; it ended in a 6–6 tie. In his postgame interview, Owens sat all alone in the Washington equipment property room, legs stretched straight out, leaning against the wall, and chin in hand. He looked for all the world like a western marshal after some cowboys had shot up his town and ruined his first day in office. "I feel sick because we didn't win," Owens began. A few minutes later, after summarizing his misery in technical football terms, he mustered a grin and said, "A tie game is like kissing your sister." He had a point: there was no exhilaration in either act.

The next week, in Minneapolis, the Gophers thoroughly trounced the Huskies 46–7 before a sellout crowd of 63,500. Washington played a little better at home on October 5. They almost held Ohio State even in the first half, 7–7. However, a Husky fumble allowed the Buckeyes to score about five minutes before halftime. Three more fumbles in the second half enabled the Big Ten powerhouse to breeze to a 35–7 victory.

The next week, the Huskies opened their conference schedule with UCLA in Los Angeles. They suffered their only shutout of the season, losing to the Bruins 19–0. The following week, the Huskies put together the best showing yet but still lost to Stanford 21–14.

Oregon State was next. It was Owens' first meeting with Tommy Prothro, the Beavers' head coach. Not only

were the Huskies mad as they ran out of the tunnel into Husky Stadium, but they were ready to show something new to the visiting Beavers. They did, and beat the Beavers 19–6. For his excellent offensive and defensive play, the Associated Press selected Jones as the national "Back of the Week." (By season's end, Jones was named to the All-Conference and All-Coast teams, to the Hearst Publications All-America second team, and received honorable mention on the UPI and Football Coaches All-America team.)

Game number eight was in Portland's Multnomah Stadium against Oregon, the conference leader. Playing with fervor, intelligent defense, and a solid running attack, the Huskies defeated the Ducks 13–6. After the game, players presented the game ball to Owens. Even though their season record was not very good, positive things were brewing on the Washington football scene. Owens was getting recognized as a fine young coach. United Press International named Owens the national "Coach of the Week" for the upset of Rose Bowl–bound Oregon.

On November 16, the Huskies journeyed to Berkeley to face quarterback Joe Kapp and his bunch of Bears. Washington completely dominated the first half and held a 21–7 halftime lead. California stormed back in the second half, but the Huskies hung on to record a 35–27 victory. The season ended with a 27–7 loss to Washington State. The Huskies finished sixth in the nine-team conference, besting Cal, USC, and Idaho.

The Demise of the Pacific Coast Conference

In December 1957, actions were taken that would lead to the breakup of the Pacific Coast Conference. In May 1956, Washington had been placed on athletic probation for two years beginning July 1, 1956. California, UCLA, and USC were also put on probation. In December 1957, the three announced that they would quit the Pacific Coast Conference—USC after July 1, 1958; Cal and UCLA on June 30, 1959; and Stanford on July 16, 1959. In May 1958, Washington's board of regents voted to have the Huskies join the new athletic conference. In a meeting on August 8, 1958, faculty representatives and athletic directors of each of the nine PCC member schools voted to dissolve the conference and distribute its assets. They also voted to participate in the 1960 Rose Bowl; thus in 1959, all schools would participate for the right to be the conference representative for the last time.

Meanwhile, another team—the Husky Pups—was forged in 1957. On October 2, the Class of 1961 attended their first day of classes at Washington. Five days later, 83 reported for the first turnout of the freshman football team. When practice started on October 7, the freshman squad had already heard about the Death March and the physical punishment the varsity was enduring in practices. "It was scary for us to hear about," recalls Dick Dunn, '61. "The doctor who gave us a physical and shots at the beginning of our season would ask us, 'Do you really want to be here? Do you know what this place is like? Guys are getting hurt here.'"

Owens' goal was clearly stated: "We may not win a freshman game. Our job is to get them ready for next year's varsity. We want to get them indoctrinated in our system. We want to get the boys ready to move right into the varsity next spring and fall. All of the coaches are going to spend a lot of time with the youngsters."

The Youngest Team in America

In the 1958 season, most of the Huskies' starting players were sophomores. They got off to a quick start, beating San Jose State and Minnesota. Hopes were high as Ohio State hosted Washington. The Buckeyes were ranked third in the country and coming off a national-championship season. Washington gave the Buckeyes all they could handle. After scoring on their second possession, the Huskies led 7–0, but Ohio State snuck away with a 12–7 victory. Owens and OSU head coach Woody Hayes met at midfield after the game. Hayes skipped the platitudes and instead said, "Coach, I think you're going to have to work real hard on your offense." (In 1966, Washington again faced the Buckeyes in Columbus. Donnie Moore rushed for 221 yards as the Huskies pasted Hayes' charges 38–22. Owens later said it took all his discipline and biting of his tongue to not say, "Coach, you have to work on your offense.")

The Stanford game in Palo Alto indicated Washington was not yet a good team. The Indians had the Huskies

groveling on the ground and recorded their first win of the season, 22–12. Stanford, who had lost their first three games by the combined score of 98–13, outgained Washington 378 yards to 207. Husky mediocrity continued the next week when the UCLA Bruins came to Seattle and left with a 20–0 victory. Fortunes didn't improve on October 25 in Portland's Multnomah Stadium as the Oregon State Beavers downed Washington 14–12. Even so, one thing had become very clear: Owens' tough punting drills were paying off. Opponents were being held to very little return yardage and sometimes were fumbling deep in their own territory, giving Washington great field position. With Schloredt, the Huskies had a punter who could kick the ball high and deep. The coaches were also developing punt-return schemes featuring the smooth gliding and shifty running style of George Fleming and the vicious comeback blocks of the linemen.

Frustrated by four-straight losses, Owens announced at the Monday practice, normally a comparatively light one, that he was sending the team back to first grade. "All eleven positions are wide open." He then proceeded to send his charges through the roughest, toughest drills they had experienced. Owens told the squad that during the week there would be a decided emphasis on the fundamentals of blocking and tackling and the basics that win football games. On the next day, the practice ended with a scrimmage that became all-out donnybrook, with everybody socking everybody else. After the practice, Owens vowed "there would be more earthy-type football in preparation for Oregon." In addition to weekly challenge drills, his first and second units would fight it out—head to head—for starting positions. He and the other coaches were mad, and the players were motivated.

Against Oregon, the fans witnessed a tough defensive struggle. The Ducks seemingly had all the offense in the world at their command as they marched up and down the field. However, when they got into scoring territory, the Huskies shut them down. The game ended in a 6–0 victory for the Huskies. It was Owens' first shutout at Washington and the first Husky shutout in 33 games.

Sadly, the Oregon win would be the Huskies' last for the season. On November 16, Quarterback Joe Kapp led his

Rose Bowl–bound California Bears into Husky Stadium. The Huskies led 7–6 at halftime. The Bears drove 65 yards to go ahead 12–7 late in the third quarter after being denied several times deep in Washington's end of the field.

After the game, Owens said, "We're the youngest team in the United States. Nobody comes close to us. Today we had eight sophomores, one junior, and two seniors in our first unit. We had seven sophomores and four juniors on our second unit. I was real proud of the way those kids hung in there and hit back. That was a top team effort, and I'm not down a bit over the way they played." Kapp agreed, "Washington has a real tough team. They hit as hard as any team we've played. I can't understand how Washington ever loses, the way they hit. And they're all young guys. In another year, that bunch is going to be hard to beat."

On November 18, the NCAA approved 11 postseason bowl games. The four traditional games—the Rose, Cotton, Orange, and Sugar Bowls—were to be played on January 1. Some of the others were the Mineral Water Bowl, the Bluegrass Bowl, the Gator Bowl, the Tangerine Bowl, and the Sun Bowl—all of which would be played before New Year's Day.

The Huskies closed out the season in Spokane with its traditional Governor's Cup game (the Apple Cup did not come into existence until 1962) against the Cougars. The Washington State fans cheered on their team but listened for the final results from Berkeley. The Bears edged Stanford 16–15 to finish one-half game ahead of the Cougars in the conference standings. Washington State hung on to defeat the Huskies 18–14, delivering the final mark in Washington's 3–7–0 season and 1–6–0 conference record.

First Conference Title Since 1936

The 1959 Husky football team was loaded with juniors who had acquired significant experience in 1958. They had gained confidence from close games with Ohio State, Oregon State, and California and wins over Minnesota and Oregon. And with the preparation that Coach Owens had instilled in them, few teams could match the

Don McKeta won the Flaherty Award in both 1959 and 1960 and was only the second player in Husky history to that point to receive the honor twice. Time after time, he rallied his teammates to make big plays on offense and defense. And in many very close games, he was the one who broke tackles and rushed for needed yardage or the one who made a defensive stop or an interception to turn the tide for a Husky victory.

He is the only player in Husky football history to twice lead Washington teams in the Rose Bowl and served as cocaptain for both teams. He was named All-Conference in 1960. In 1998, McKeta received the All-American Football Foundation's "Unsung Hero" Award. He was selected to the Husky Hall of Fame—first as an individual in 1984 and again as a member of the 1959 football team in 1994.

Huskies in fundamentals. Although most of their 1958 opponents beat them in the scoring column, they never beat them physically. Washington had won the respect of their opponents for its hard hitting, crisp tackling, and aggressive play.

The Owens-Tipps doctrine of rough, physical, hard-nosed football was paying off. By the start of Owens' third season, Washington football was on solid ground. Players who were not willing to pay a sometimes-painful price had been drummed out or quit. The survivors were close-knit as a team. There were still no names on the jerseys, no big stars. They were simply a bunch of guys who liked to play football, who liked to knock their opponents down, and who supported one other.

What had emerged at the beginning of the 1959 season was a team with unshakable self-confidence and absolute unselfishness. "There wasn't any Rose Bowl talk before the season opened. I told them they had the ability to become a fine team. They had learned to pay the price for greatness, in work and practice," Owens said.

Don McKeta (No. 36), the most inspirational player of the Owens era.

Bear Bryant once said, "Football games are won in the trenches." Washington had some great players up front. In 1959, the linemen were tabbed the "Sturdy Seven." They held opponents to 65 points in the 10 regular-season games during 1959 and recorded four shutouts. They held their opponents to 216.5 yards per game. They were disciples of Owens' philosophy that the game of football started with defense.

In 1959, Owens' first unit was an all-junior squad, excepting sophomore John Meyers. The second team would usually consist of four seniors, five juniors, and two sophomores. Owens had established a weight-training program in 1958. He enlisted the aid of Harry Swetnam, a noted Seattle physical culturist, to design a set of bodybuilding exercises that echoed the movements of the players on the field. The program wasn't compulsory, but the team's leaders got together to promote it. Soon many of the players were weight lifting. In many instances, they increased their body weight by 10 to 15 pounds without adding any fat.

The Huskies opened the 1959 season on Folsom Field in Boulder, Colorado. Before the game, Don McKeta rallied his band of brothers around and said, "The only way for us to win is to reach down and play it from the heart." The slogan "Play It from the Heart" became the season's rallying cry.

The Huskies' first four games ended in victories, with Washington outscoring its opponents 105–18. Seventh-ranked USC was next. The Trojans had opened the season with a 27–6 win over Oregon State and shutout victories over Pitt and Ohio State. The Huskies were convinced that if they played their best game, they would produce one of the major upsets of the week, maybe the season. "The club has jelled," Owens said during the week. "Nearly all of these boys were recruited by my staff and are playing their third season together. They've matured."

A Classic Matchup

The Trojans featured the McKeever twins—Marlin, an end, and Mike, a guard—tackle Ron Mix, and halfback Jerry Traynham. Willie Wood, USC's cocaptain and one of the few African American quarterbacks in college football, had been sidelined with a shoulder separation and was only available for limited action.

A homecoming crowd of 54,500 filled Husky Stadium. Some had pregame jitters, but none more than Jack Ehrig, the homecoming chairman. His wife said that he was so nervous when he awoke on game day that he shaved with Pepsodent and brushed his teeth with Burma Shave.

The contest had all the makings of a classic—power plays, stirring defense, momentum shifts, great strategy, artfully executed plays, a minimum of errors, and victory in the balance until the final seconds. For many a long turn of the clock, it appeared that the Huskies would be overrun by the invaders from Troy. Pulling their fast guards and ends ahead of the ball carriers, USC swung the Husky flanks and powered up through the tackles. The Trojans scored the second time they had the ball and again in the second stanza to lead 14–0.

After Bill Kinnune recovered a USC fumble on the Trojans 47, the Huskies unveiled a new offensive formation: the bug eye. They set the line strong to the left with the swing end split left and the left wingback set in the slot between the end and the rest of the line. It was essentially a flood-pass formation. Immediately, Schloredt hit Lee Folkins, the swing end, who got down to the 35. After several runs got the ball to the Trojans 12, George Fleming ran wide around the left end and fumbled. Lineman Chuck Allen saved the drive by recovering on the enemy's 14. Schloredt hit McKeta on a short pass to the 9-yard line. On the next play, Schloredt faked a pass, tucked the ball firmly away, and charged between two defenders into the end zone. The Trojans were penalized 15 yards on the successful extra-point play. Fleming tried an onside kick from the USC 45, but Roy McKasson dove on the ball just inches short of the required 10 yards, giving possession to the Trojans.

Early in the fourth quarter, Schloredt punted the ball high and long—47 yards—and as it came down, it drifted away from Traynham, the Trojans' returner. Unable to get his hands squarely on the ball, he fumbled and Don Millich smothered the pigskin on the USC 20. Then a little razzle-dazzle unleashed a crowd roar that was heard across the lake and into the eastern foothills. Schloredt pitched to

Coach Owens is carried off the field after the Huskies win the 1959 conference title and a bid to the 1960 Rose Bowl.

Millich, who handed it back to Schloredt going back to the right. The Husky quarterback hit John Meyers, his tight end, for a first down on the 6. On second down, Schloredt went to the spread offense again. After rolling to his left, he slanted back and into the end zone to pull within one point. Owens detested ties, so there was no question he would go for two. Schloredt just ran the same play, and the Huskies were on top 15–14 with 10 and a half minutes to go.

Wood and his teammates then drove 80 yards for a touchdown. On the second-and-goal on the Husky 6, Wood ran a bootleg to the left and danced into the west end zone. Then he passed for the two extra points and the Trojans regained the lead, 22–15.

The Huskies fought back and nearly pulled the game out in the final eight minutes. On their first series, Schloredt's long pass to McKeta in the clear was just beyond his fingertips. After Schloredt's 52-yard punt rolled dead on the Trojans 18, the Huskies forced a quick kick and took over on their own 49. Washington drove to the USC 17. Schloredt lost four, and then his pass to Dick Aguirre fell incomplete. Jim Everett came in during the series to replace Schloredt, but his pass was intercepted by Don Morgan. And with that, the Huskies lost a heartbreaker.

For Washington to stay in the race for the Rose Bowl, the players had to cast aside the what-ifs from the USC game and look squarely ahead to the next five games. The next one was in Portland's Multnomah Stadium against undefeated Oregon. Before a turn-away crowd of about 37,000 in Portland on October 24, the Huskies staged a great come-from-behind triumph to shoot the Ducks 13–12. They followed that up with four wins, including a shutout against Washington State. The Huskies finished the season 10–1–0 and 3–1–0 in the conference. With the Beavers beating the Ducks and UCLA upsetting USC in the final week of the regular season, Washington tied with the Trojans for the Big Five title. The Huskies finished ahead of all the old Pacific Coast Conference teams eligible to be selected for the 1960 Rose Bowl. (USC was still on probation and thus could not go to the Rose Bowl.)

There was only one sign that had stayed in place in the locker room since Owens brought it to Washington three years earlier: TOUGHNESS IS A QUALITY OF MIND.

WITHOUT IT, PHYSICAL CONDITION IS A MOCKERY. His team was mentally and physically tough. They were good players who had bonded together to become a great team. "We might not have any All-Americans, publicity-wise," said Schloredt, "but this team is great, simply great." McKasson, the Huskies' center and linebacker, chimed in, "It's what the coaches taught us, that's what made this team good. All season, we've had a chance to apply what they taught us. We saw other teams make mistakes that shouldn't be made, and we had the chance to see the value of our coaching."

Eventually, after the Oregon game, the locker room thinned out and became quieter. McKeta, the toughest of the tough, sat on a bench, still wearing some of his battle gear. He was tired and beat up. His elbows rested on his knees and his head was down. In one hand was a red rose.

With the dissolution of the Pacific Coast Conference, the Big Ten Conference faculty representatives failed to renew the 1946 agreement between the Big Ten and PCC for Rose Bowl participation. Even so, they did not exempt any Big Ten team receiving a bid to play in Pasadena from accepting. Shortly after the regular season ended, athletic directors from Washington and Wisconsin accepted the bid for the 1960 Rose Bowl, the 46th in its glorious history. The Badgers were ranked sixth in the nation, the Huskies eighth, in the final regular-season Associated Press poll.

Washington's First Rose Bowl Victory

Both teams were looking to reverse their fortunes from previous Rose Bowl games. The Huskies had not won in four previous appearances. The 7–2 Badgers had appeared in the 1953 affair but lost to USC. Worse, it was the only loss by a Big Ten representative in the 13 years of Rose Bowl games played between Big Ten and PCC teams after World War II.

The Badgers fielded a mostly senior team in the Rose Bowl. Their offense was built around Dale Hackbart, 6'3" and 200 pounds, who also lettered in baseball and basketball. The defense was led by All-American tackle Dan Lanphear and cocaptain and All–Big Ten guard Jerry Stalcup. The men from Madison fielded a typical Big Ten team—huge on the line and heavy in the backfield. Their line averaged 15 pounds more than the Husky front wall. Oddsmakers quickly established the Huskies as a 6½-point underdog.

Owens and his staff, focused on beating Wisconsin, chose Long Beach as their base of operations, to avoid the distractions of Los Angeles. Owens would let the players go to the functions required by tournament hosts—Disneyland and Lawry's Prime Rib House, and a few others—but quickly reminded them that they were in Long Beach to work. "We were really concentrating," Joe Jones said.

On the evening of December 30, the Badgers and the Huskies attended dinner together. Some of the Wisconsin players were already seated before the Huskies arrived. The Huskies had been taught that nobody sits down until the whole team was together. Some of the first Huskies to arrive stood waiting for their teammates. The Badgers players kept saying, "Boys, you can sit down. Wisconsin has arrived," emphasizing "boys" as they teased them. Some other Badgers called the Huskies "Loggers." McKeta remembered that moment. "It is so important for teams to realize how words can change the complexion of the game before it starts. Their words certainly fueled our fire," he said.

When the teams had been together a few days before, one of the crooners entertaining the teams sang "Danny Boy" to acknowledge the presence of Wisconsin's Dan Lanphear that evening. About two-thirds of the way through the song, Husky assistant coach Norm Pollom's voice could be heard loud enough so every Husky around him could hear: "That son-of-a-bitch better screw on his helmet tight. We're coming right after him."

Early New Year's Day morning, the Huskies awoke to do battle. They ate mostly in silence, their minds weighed heavily on the task before them.

When the Huskies entered the field for their pregame warm-up, the frost on the grass glistened as it slowly disappeared under the rays of California sunshine. The contest would be played under bright sunshine, but cold winds from the north would blow bitterly. Assessing their opponent, already on the field, Kermit Jorgensen observed, "They may outweigh us. But we are trim, lightweight guys

in much better shape than they are. We are going to kick the shit out of them."

George Fleming remembered, "Playing in the Rose Bowl was a childhood dream of mine. I had watched Rose Bowl games growing up in Dallas. I wanted to go to UCLA or USC to play in the game." A few days earlier, Fleming had suffered a knee injury when he banged into McKeta in practice. The decision to play him was going to be made right before the game. He was heavily taped. When the Huskies trotted off the field back to the locker room, Owens asked, "Can you go?" Fleming replied, "Try and keep me off the field!"

Owens spoke briefly to the players before they returned to the battleground. He told them they were faster and quicker than Wisconsin. He told them that they had paid the price all season, that this game was the payoff. Joe Jones thought, *We are in better shape than they are. I believe the price is right.*

The Badgers won the toss and elected to kick off and defend the north side. When asked why, Coach Milt Bruhn replied, "We've got a good kicker and there was a strong wind blowing [from the Wisconsin players' backs]." For the next few minutes, Bruhn's decision seemed sound. Fleming stood near the 10-yard line waiting for the ball. He was hit at the 27, fumbled, and recovered his own miscue. After getting a first down, the Huskies were stopped. Schloredt arced a 42-yard punt down to the Badgers 12, where sophomore quarterback Jim Bakken fielded the bouncing ball and was immediately knocked out of bounds.

Their defense had stopped the Huskies, and the Wisconsin offense thought they would push their lighter foe down the field. Instead, Washington stuffed them on three plays. Fleming returned Hackbart's punt 14 yards to the Wisconsin 49. On fourth-and-1, Schloredt ran a keeper to the right for six yards and a first down on the Badgers 34. On third-and-9, Schloredt lobbed a short pass to Ray Jackson sliding out of the backfield for seven. Schloredt rolled left for a first down on the 23. All-Conference lineman Kurt Gegner already was seeing the chinks in Lanphear's armor. He said, "He tries to run around my blocks instead of hitting me head on. Our line is getting off the ball very quickly and opening some huge holes. We are sticking our helmets on their chests and driving through."

On the next play, Schloredt faked to McKeta, rolled right, and ran 17 yards to the Badgers 6. On the 10th play of the drive, the entire right side of the Husky line sealed off Wisconsin's left side by driving their opponents back and inside. Left guard Chuck Allen pulled to the right and hit the cornerback on a perfect block. Jim Skaggs fired out from the left-tackle spot and drove the left outside linebacker almost into the end zone. McKeta cut up inside Allen and raced untouched into the end zone. McKeta thought, *This is too easy.* Fleming's kick put the Huskies up 7–0.

The Badgers were back on their heels. On their first play from scrimmage after returning the kickoff to their 23, they met the Huskies' alternate unit. They got a rude welcoming. Halfback Billy Hobbs fumbled after colliding with end Stan Chapple, and Brent Wooten recovered for the Huskies on the 29. A double reverse, Bob Hivner to Don Millich to Wooten, gave the Huskies a first down on the 19. On fourth down at the 18, Fleming kicked a 36-yard field goal into the wind that put Washington ahead 10–0.

Four plays later, the Huskies were on the scoreboard again. With a vicious charge, Kinnune knocked his opponent into the backfield and stretched out and blocked the ball. Bakken recovered and was hit by Meyers on the 4-yard line. On fourth-and-17, Bakken punted again, this time booming it 49 yards. Fleming took it on the second bounce on his 47, raced laterally to the far side, and cut inside the first would-be tackler. He then picked up some initial blocks to clear a lane. He sped through the next wave of defenders, keeping his eye on Gegner. The German immigrant was blocking Bakken inside; Fleming darted outside and cruised the last 15 yards into the end zone.

There was no celebration. He had been in the promised land before and didn't need any high fives or hugs or to spike the pigskin. He calmly tossed the ball to the official and trotted back to get the kicking tee. After the 53-yard play, the Huskies had really popped the Badgers' balloon. The score was 17–0, and Wisconsin still didn't have a first down.

With two minutes left in the half, Schloredt teamed up with split end Lee Folkins on the most spectacular play of the game. Schloredt rolled right. "What I was taught

George Fleming was named co-MVP in the 1960 Rose Bowl.

was that when I came to the corner, I am coming to run, and unless the defensive back leaves somebody open, I'm running the football. I would run with the ball high most of the time and throw the baby right at the last moment," Schloredt later recalled. "I ran on two-thirds of the pass plays I called. So the coaches designed a play where the right halfback would roll left and I would drop back and semi-roll to about the tight end spot on the right side of the line. We would have several pass routes. One was a post—

usually the split left end. The right halfback would swerve the other direction and go down the far sideline. The tight end would look like he was going the other direction from the rollout." It was called the Utah Special.

Schloredt continued, "As I rolled right, I was looking to see where the safety was and the safety gave me room down the middle. I saw Lee and he was pretty even with the safety and I just led him into the post." Folkins raced left to right between two defenders. The Husky quarterback threw it up high and Folkins launched his 6'5" frame and long arms as far as he could and caught the ball on his fingertips. "I threw the ball where he had a chance of getting it and the defensive backs didn't. Lee goes up and makes one of those damn finger tip catches," Schloredt said. Folkins deftly brought the ball into his chest as his outstretched body landed in the end zone to complete one of the most amazing touchdown catches in Rose Bowl history.

Wisconsin threatened on their next series. A 43-yard field-goal attempt by Karl Holzwarth, the Badgers' 245-pound tackle and Dale Hackbart's brother-in-law, was straight, but it sailed under the crossbar. The Huskies went into the dressing room ahead 24–8. The Badgers had outgained the Huskies 145-to-124 but had lost three fumbles and had given up almost 121 yards on punt returns to Washington's zero. The press corps was buzzing during the intermission, wondering, "Who are these jackrabbits? Who is this guy Fleming?"

As the players returned to the field for the second half, Owens took Schloredt aside and stressed the importance of the Huskies' first possession; they were about to receive the kickoff. Owens said, "This is a very important time. We have to go down and drive and let them know they are not going to get back in this ballgame." He told Schloredt if the Huskies scored, it would break the Badgers' hearts and souls.

Fleming got the Huskies in good field position by returning the kickoff 29 yards to the Washington 34. The Huskies executed Owens' directions perfectly. In just more than four minutes, Washington ran 11 plays, most of which were just smash-mouth football. Barry Bullard and Meyers cleared the way over the right side, and Jackson followed. He ran the football five times through that side for 47 yards. After Jackson's first carry over the right

George Fleming was one the best all-purpose players in Husky history. He was a running back and an excellent punt returner, kickoff returner, and defensive back on the 1960 and 1961 Rose Bowl teams. In 1960, he earned All-Conference honors when he converted 25 of 26 points after touchdowns and led the team in scoring with 70 points. In 1959, he returned 26 punt returns and averaged a record 13.6 yards per return—still 10th in team history. In the 1960 Rose Bowl, Fleming sparked the Huskies to a 44–8 win over Wisconsin with a 53-yard punt return for a score and a 65-yard pass reception to set up another touchdown. For his exploits, he was voted Co–Most Valuable Player in that game. In the 1961 Rose Bowl, he kicked the longest field goal in Rose Bowl history up to that time—44 yards. He was inducted into the Rose Bowl Hall of Fame in 2011.

He ended his career with 49 punt returns for an average of 12.6 yards per return—still the fourth-best in Husky history. Fleming went on to serve in the Washington State Legislature, where he spent two years in the House and 20 years in the Senate, 18 of them in leadership positions. He was the first African American member of the Senate. In recognition of his distinguished career, his name, along with former Washington State lieutenant governor Joel Pritchard, are on the state's Pritchard Fleming Building in Bellevue.

guard, where Lanphear was defending, Bullard and Meyers came back to the huddle and told Schloredt, "We think we hurt Lanphear on that last play." Schloredt decided to take advantage. He said, "I was calling the plays and we ran the next three over Lanphear's side." Lanphear eventually went out of the game.

On his third-straight carry, Jackson's 25-yard rumble put the ball on the Wisconsin 16. Schloredt then threw the only pass of the drive to Lee Folkins in the end zone, but it fell incomplete. So he went back to Jackson for six

George Fleming and Bob Schloredt receive a key to the city of Seattle from Mayor Gordon Clinton.

yards to the 10. Then the drive appeared to have stalled out. Schloredt rolled right down to the 4, where he was hit; the ball popped loose back to the 11. But there was Fleming. Trailing the option play, he recovered the football. Again, Schloredt faked the pitch, kept the ball, and muscled his way around end down to the 6. After the play was dead, Hackbart came up out of his defensive back position and tried to level Fleming, who was standing out of bounds. The referee threw his flag, and the Badgers were penalized for a personal foul down to the 2—half the distance to the goal from the spot of the transgression. On the ensuing play, Jackson shook off Stalcup, Wisconsin's

All-Conference guard, with ridiculous ease to score standing up. Fleming again scored the conversion. Speaking later, the modest Jackson commented on the drive, saying, "When they called my number, I just ran. I never remember individual plays." At the end of the game, Tipps went over to Jackson and gave him a little kiss on the forehead.

The Huskies led 31–8 with less than 26 minutes to play, but the game was over for the Badgers at that point. They were being annihilated, and they knew it. The Huskies scored two more times in the fourth quarter and won 44–8.

In the postgame analysis, Wisconsin's coach, Milt Bruhn, paid tribute to Washington's overall speed. "This team had more speed than any we met all year... Their line speed was most impressive and was about the only thing—except for the final score—that surprised us," he said. He praised many Huskies.

People in the press box were very impressed with Washington's tremendous pursuit. They observed that a Husky player might have been knocked to the ground, but he never stayed there. Wisconsin's Hackbart sighed and said, "It was discouraging to see our guys put some good blocks on the Washington players and then have them get up and run back to the play. We've never seen tigers like that in the Big Ten—*never!*"

Newspaper reports lauded the Huskies—none more so than Lloyd Larson's column in the Milwaukee *Sentinel*: "What an unhappy New Year's afternoon. Really unhappy and just as shocking. Yup. It's true what they say about Bob Schloredt. And George Fleming. The same can be said about all those Huskies from Washington. As a group, they were quick, alert, poised, aggressive, and razor sharp. Man, O Man, were they ever ready."

Keith Jackson had this perspective: "The score shocked the country, particularly the middle of the country. The 'big dogs' back East thought they ruled the world back in those days, and they did. Remember, in those days, you were talking about Seattle, which was geographically isolated. The whole Northwest was isolated from the rest of the country because of the mountains and the population. Not a hell of a lot of people on the East Coast paid any attention to what was going on in Seattle."

Fleming and Schloredt were named Co–Most Valuable Players for their outstanding performances. The Husky halfback gained only five yards on three carries, but he racked up 122 yards on punt returns, including one for a touchdown, and 80 yards on kickoff returns. He also caught one pass for 65 yards. His place-kicking was perfect—one field goal for 36 yards and five conversions. All told, he had 272 all-purpose yards. His teammate Schloredt passed and rushed for 183 yards, completing four of seven passes. He scored one touchdown and averaged almost 40 yards on four punts.

A distant observer of the game who had watched it on national television called Owens after it was over. It was Owens' former coach, Bud Wilkinson. After congratulating his pupil on the stunning victory, he said, "It would be hard to find a club anywhere, anytime, that played a sixty-minute period any better than that team that day."

The Huskies spent three days celebrating in the Los Angeles area before arriving home on the evening of January 4. A large crowd greeted them at the airport, and Seattle mayor Gordon Clinton gave a symbolic key to the city to Fleming and Schloredt. Giant searchlights pierced the sky and illuminated the airport arrival area. A presidential-style motorcade, led by the police motorcycles from the city and county police departments, gave escort to buses filled with Husky players and their wives as they wound their way from the airstrip and north onto Highway 99. They proceeded through the city and the university district and down to the University of Washington crew house. All along the route, people lined both sides of the road, waving and cheering the victorious band of brothers.

Keith Jackson remembers, the reception was "like we won the war. It was the first time in my life that I fully realized how a college football team could pick up an entire state and region and revitalize it."

CHAPTER 7

National Champions

In 1960, the entire starting lineup from the Rose Bowl victory, plus 10 other lettermen who saw considerable game action, returned to the Husky squad. Because of their success in 1959, they would have a bull's-eye on their backs. Owens warned them about this but also reminded them about the upside—what they had been through, what they had accomplished, and what they could achieve in the upcoming season.

The team would be buoyed by several sophomores, up from the 1959 freshman squad, including linemen Duane Locknane, Ray Mansfield, Dave Phillips, and Rod Scheyer, and running backs Charlie Mitchell and Bob Monroe.

Several linemen who had played backup roles in 1959 had to step up in 1960 because of injuries to the Rose Bowl starters—among them, senior ends Stan Chapple and Pat Claridge; senior interior linemen Ben Davidson, Dick Dunn, Dave Enslow, and Sam Hurworth; and juniors Tim Bullard and Jim Skaggs.

Despite the players' experience, Owens felt the 1960 team wasn't as strong as the 1959 squad because their roster was not as deep. The Huskies also would not surprise any of the powerful teams they would face in 1960 the way they had the previous year. All of their opponents

would have ample incentive to knock off the Rose Bowl champion. The Northwest schools particularly pointed for Washington, given that they had not been invited to join the Big Five conference. As if that wasn't enough, the new conference was strong. Washington had their work cut out for them.

Don McKeta thought the coaches did a great job deflating the Rose Bowl balloon. He said, "They said the starting eleven has been told that they are the greatest team ever to hit Washington. They said you guys hardly even have to practice. So we will work with these other guys to get them up to your caliber."

It bred healthy competition at all positions. In the intrasquad game at the end of spring practice, the second-team Gold unit whipped the starting Purple unit 33–0. The Rose Bowl starters were so embarrassed by their lethargic and haphazard play that they challenged the second team to an extra quarter. The Purple unit capitalized on two Gold fumbles and won the additional stanza 13–0 to gain some solace.

Owens announced at the end of spring practice that the days of the 1960 Rose Bowl starting unit were history. "We won't have the Rose Bowl team next season. Next fall, you'll find several—or even many—new faces on our first unit," he said. He also told the Purple players and others that they had better get in shape during the summer because they "will have a hell of a lot of competition coming in this fall."

Several off-field changes took place during the spring. Owens took on the additional job of athletic director after George Briggs resigned in early 1960. Assistant coach Norm Pollom left for a similar role at USC; he was replaced by Don White.

KOMO-TV won the bid for the television rights to replay Husky games on the Monday evening following each game. The program went head-to-head with *The Huntley-Brinkley Report*. The ratings on the Husky show, anchored by Keith Jackson, beat out the renowned newscasters.

The Big Five conference continued its policy of picking the best team in the country, not just from one league, as its opponent in the Rose Bowl. Meanwhile, the Big Ten voted to reverse its previous decision of barring member schools from competing in postseason play.

When fall practice commenced on September 1, the coaches were very focused on achieving as much, if not more, success in 1960 than in 1959. They wanted nothing less than another conference championship and a repeat as Rose Bowl champions.

Bill Kinnune said, "The coaches worked us very hard. Many of us had come back out of shape. They put us on two meals a day during the two-a-days." Challenge drills were intense. At the end of the first week, very few of the Rose Bowl starters were on the Purple unit.

Slowly, as the Rose Bowl heroes got the message, the more familiar names from the 1959 team emerged on the first unit. By the end of the preseason, nine Rose Bowl starters were on the Purple unit for the season opener. Lee Folkins and John Meyers, the two other starters, had been edged out by Pat Claridge and Jim Skaggs, Meyers in part because of an ankle injury.

Ranked third in the preseason polls, Washington rolled over its first two opponents with ease. The Huskies crushed the College of Pacific 55–6. The following week, the Huskies stomped Idaho 41–12. Sophomore Charlie Mitchell showed early promise. He led the Husky ground game in the College of Pacific game with 100 yards in eight carries and had another dazzling performance against the Vandals, gaining 71 yards on eight runs in the first half and scoring Washington's first touchdown by racing nine yards around left end. After he returned the second-half kickoff 85 yards for another touchdown, Owens put the beaming sophomore on the sideline.

In the high perches of the stadium, scouting the game, was Navy's assistant coach, Steve Belichick, whose son Bill had been cavorting as a youngster at Navy practices and who was just beginning to accumulate football knowledge. The senior Belichick felt the Huskies had played the game "under wraps." He added, "Last year we played [national champion] Syracuse and this year we got Washington. I'd rather play Syracuse. You know what they're going to do. You don't know what this team is going to do." His Navy team would soon find out.

By the Length of a Salmon

The easy games were over. The 17th-ranked Midshipmen from Annapolis were next. The Huskies would not see a finer running back all season than Navy's Joe Bellino. Although it was a nonconference contest, the buildup was enormous.

Navy and Army were the perennial top-ranked teams in the 1950s and 1960s. The service academies—Army, Navy, and later the Air Force Academy, which opened in 1955—were respected and admired for their mission as well as the commitment and discipline of their students. The teams and their supporters always seemed to do things with a measure of class and élan. The service academies teams had to get a lot out of its student-athletes to be competitive because they were not typically as big or fast as their opponents.

Early in the week, it was announced that the game would be piped in to most of the corps of 3,100 midshipmen back in Annapolis, who had taken a collection to pay for the lease of a direct phone line from Seattle to a field house on the Navy campus. There, a battery of microphones was set up. And with special loudspeakers set up behind the Middies' bench in Seattle, the players would hear the cheering and singing of their fellow students.

The only time the two teams had faced off previously was in the 1924 Rose Bowl, when they played to a 14–14 tie. At Sand Point Naval Air Station on Lake Washington, north of the Washington campus, all hands and cooks were preparing for the arrival of the Midshipmen. The naval station had been King County's gift to the navy in 1922. Expanding to 460 acres, Sand Point hosted more than 5,600 naval personnel, more than 2,400 civilian workers, and hundreds of aircraft at its peak during World War II. Units who trained there fought in some of the most critical battles in the war's Pacific campaign.

Excitement for the game was so high that two tickets were being scalped for up to $100, about 10 times the face value of a pair of ducats. Bill Stern, one of the country's most famous sportscasters, came to town to broadcast the game nationally over the Mutual network. "Washington is one of the most-talked-[about] teams in the country," he said. "If the Huskies can beat Navy and their great halfback Joe Bellino, it will add a lot to the prestige of Jim Owens' team."

Sports Illustrated, then a fledgling sports weekly, whetted the appetites of gridiron followers with a cover photo of Bob Schloredt and a feature story about the All-American quarterback and the success of the Husky program. Schloredt was the first Husky player on an *SI* cover.

At a Navy League luncheon the day before the game, Schloredt received a Presidential Unit Citation from undersecretary of the navy Fred Bantz, in recognition of the quarterback's efforts to further the employment of physically handicapped people. With only 10 percent vision in his left eye, Schloredt had written many letters over the previous year to boys and girls who had lost an eye, and their families.

Washington was favored by 13 points—largely on the strength of the Huskies' alternate unit, which was deemed to be far stronger than Navy's second unit. The then-largest crowd ever to see a Husky home game—57,379—got their five dollars' worth. Washington's famed first team won the game statistically. They held Navy to 69 yards on the ground—Bellino got 53 of them—and 138 in the air. Washington rushed for 193 and passed for 82 yards.

Bellino was all he was touted to be. He accounted for 145 all-purpose yards and was a threat every time he touched the ball. Kermit Jorgensen remembers his legs: "He

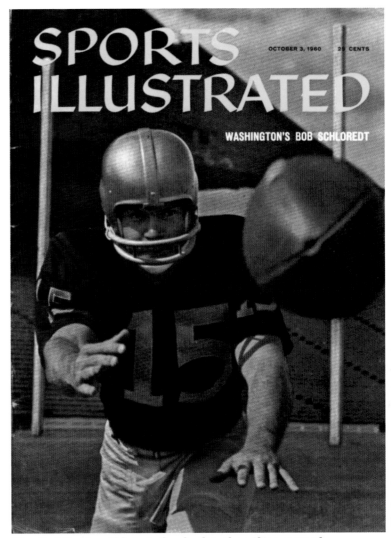

The first Husky athlete to be depicted on the cover of Sports Illustrated.

had calves you wouldn't believe. He could change directions and he could rip out of a tackle so quickly." His calves were indeed huge—they measured 18 inches in circumference. He could run as well laterally as forward. He also seemed to be bottom-heavy. When he got knocked in the air, he invariably landed on his feet.

Navy received the opening kickoff but went three-and-out, giving Washington excellent field position after the punt on the Navy 48. The Huskies immediately went into the Bug Eye formation to throw off Navy's stunting defenders. Both the halfbacks set up behind the strong side of the unbalanced line. From the 31, Schloredt threw to McKeta. Still favoring his foot, injured in the Idaho game, he ran for the score. Fleming's kick was good, and the Huskies were up 7–0 with just about four and a half minutes gone in the quarter.

Navy battled right back. Bellino fielded Fleming's kick at the goal line and weaved and darted upfield for 30 yards. The all-purpose back was starting to make the Huskies miss. Bellino then passed 20 yards to running back Ron McKeown to midfield. Eleven plays later, they were in scoring position. On third-and-goal, Bellino launched himself high over the left guard to reach the end zone. Greg Mather's kick was no good, so Navy trailed by one.

Early in the second quarter, Washington seemed almost a lead-pipe cinch to score again. The Huskies drove from their own 30 to the Navy 5 on the combined efforts of Jackson, Fleming, Schloredt, and a personal foul assessed to Navy. The Huskies went for it on fourth down, and Schloredt hit Claridge for a touchdown. Unfortunately, offsetting penalties nullified the play. Still fourth-and-5, Schloredt then ran a keeper around the right end but came up a yard short.

The Huskies threatened again near the close of the half. McKeta intercepted Bellino's pass on the Washington 20 and returned it 18 yards. On second-and-16 on the Navy 36, Schloredt hit McKeta for 14. Navy's Frank Dattilo was ejected from the game after taking a wild swing at Husky lineman Jim Skaggs after the play. The ball was moved to the Navy 9. The coaches had sent in Fleming to try for a field goal but reversed their decision after the penalty and elected to go for six instead. Schloredt rolled left to the 4, and time elapsed. Fleming remembered the play saying, "McKeta was open in the end zone but Schloredt didn't see him." At halftime, the second-guessers had lots to discuss about the play calling.

After an exchange of punts to open the second half, the Huskies took possession on the Navy 43 and struck pay dirt after eight plays. Jackson, Mitchell, and Schloredt did most of the damage to the Midshipmen, and Jackson scored on a three-yard rush up the middle. Fleming's kick made it 14–6.

Bellino again gained big yardage on the kickoff, returning it 23 yards to the Navy 30. Eschewing the ground game, the Middies went airborne with quarterback Hal Spooner, who was supposed to be in sick bay, directing the aerial assault. He hit Lawrence Graham for 15, then McKeown for 12, and the team was then aided by another Husky personal foul. Spooner's last bomb was to W. Allen Hughes (a great name for a future navy officer) who beat Bob Monroe into the end zone, capping a 26-yard play. Navy attempted to rush for the equalizing points but was stopped by the Washington front wall.

The drama reached its climax late in the fourth quarter. On third-and-4 on the Husky 33, Schloredt rolled around the left end with a clear field ahead, but he stumbled and gained only one yard. He then set up to send a booming punt deep into Navy's territory to put the Middies in poor field position to mount a scoring strike. Dunn's snap was low, and Schloredt, who had injured his thumb earlier in the game, couldn't control the shoe-top pitch. It rolled to his left—the side of his bad eye—and he momentarily lost sight of it. Those few seconds allowed the Navy defenders to swarm in and tackle Schloredt on his own 24, where the Midshipmen took over on downs.

Spooner, on a passing attempt, was chased back to the Husky 35 and thrown for an 11-yard loss. Bellino made up for it on the next down, weaving his way down to the Husky 16. Captain Joe Matalavage hit over left guard for six and a first down on the Husky 10. Bellino again, for one. Spooner then found floater back Hughes in the end zone. Inside the Navy field house in Annapolis, the Middies were listening to Bill Stern's play-by-play broadcast. When Hughes caught the pass for what seemed to be the winning score, they broke from the stands, wildly cheering and shouting odes of joy. The Huskies regained hope when the play was called back for an illegal shift. Everybody—in the stadium and in the Navy field house—was on their feet. Just 14 seconds remained on the scoreboard.

Navy place-kicker Greg Mathers trotted onto the field and set up his field-goal attempt at the 31. The kick away, it seemed to hang in the air forever before barely dropping down over the crossbar. An ear-splitting naval salvo exploded after each Navy score, and this time the exuberant gun crew couldn't resist. It fired two double-strength shots.

In Owens' postgame interview, he simply said, "Our ball handling was too sloppy to win. Mistakes always beat you and we made more than Navy did." The Huskies had fumbled four times in the game and lost three of them.

Navy's center Frank Visted added, "We're supposed to cover after the field goal kick. But I just stopped and prayed. It was all or nothing. The ball cleared the bar by about this much," holding his hands out as if measuring a fair-sized salmon.

Washington players felt that they should have won the game. To this day, they still have vivid memories. "Navy was the only team that I ever played that was actually afraid of us at the start of the game. And then we turn around and lose to them. Too many mistakes," remembered McKeta.

In 1959, Washington's seven starting linemen had been nicknamed the Sturdy Seven. None of them played less than 333 minutes out of a total of 600 in the regular season, Folkins played a staggering 436 minutes. But in 1960, injuries severely impacted the line. Meyers suffered an ankle injury early in the season, Allen had a groin injury, and Bullard got hit with a comeback block on his knee in the Navy game. "From then on, I was not able to play much," Bullard later said. "They would tape my body from my hip to my ankle. They would spray on a substance so the tape would stick to my legs. When the tape stretched, it would pull the skin off, and I was bloody from the hip down," he added.

Other teammates would have to step up and get ready for the Huskies' first conference game, in Palo Alto against Stanford. They were led by Dick Norman, one of the top quarterbacks in the nation. The game was nationally televised—in those days a much bigger event than it is today. Washington received $85,000 from the network to cover the game.

Like all great teams and athletes, the Huskies didn't dwell on the Navy loss but focused on the next game and defending their conference title. They jumped out to a 10–0 lead in the first six minutes and won 29–10.

"The Cardiac Kids"

Several of the last six games of the season put Husky fans with heart problems at serious risk. "The Cardiac Kids" won four of the six games by a margin of five points—three of them involving come-from-behind game-winning drives late in the fourth quarter.

The first heart-stopper was against UCLA in Seattle on October 15. The Bruins were playing their first conference game. They had not played in two weeks and were well rested and well prepared to battle the Huskies. UCLA featured Bill Kilmer, the triple-threat tailback, in the Bruins' single-wing offense. He had excellent receivers, including Jim Johnson, the brother of Bruins alumnus Rafer Johnson, the 1960 Olympic gold medalist in the decathlon.

A midweek newspaper column compared Kilmer and another triple-threat star, the Huskies' Schloredt, and felt Schloredt had the edge over Kilmer on defense. The article described the Husky All-American as a "bruising tackler. He can smell a forward pass coming."

Another article on Schloredt during the week was entitled "Schloredt Relishes Bruising Grid Combat." He impressed the coaches and players as a blacksmith-type of player who couldn't be intimidated. He was reported to be his most articulate and at ease when discussing the joys of combat. He once said, "There's an art to being aggressive. We call it 'head-hunting' or 'hunting with the helmet.' The idea is that if you can soften the other guy up, he'll be thinking about you."

Sometimes, in football as in war, you lose a skirmish but later win the battle. Before more than 54,000 spectators, whose emotions during the game ranged from complete elation to gut-wrenching misery, Washington's battered band of brothers defeated UCLA 10–8.

The first period was scoreless. In the second quarter, Schloredt was injured when he went head-hunting. He took aim at UCLA's Earl Smith as Kilmer's pass fell off the Bruin's fingertips. Wanting Smith "to remember me," as he later put it, Schloredt lowered his head and attempted to drive his helmet into Smith's chest. Schloredt flew past his mark, caught Smith's legs with his hip, and toppled over on his side. His elbow struck the ground first, forcing his shoulder back and fracturing his collarbone. So Bob Hivner—who had injured his finger in the opening game of the 1959 season and was replaced by Schloredt—now had to carry the load. On Hivner's first offensive series, he directed a

Two-time Rose Bowl MVP Bob Schloredt (No. 15).

53-yard drive to the Bruins 19. With time running out in the half, Fleming kicked a 38-yard field goal.

Schloredt was in tears on the sideline, not from pain but from bitter disappointment. Gone were the dreams of another All-American season and a possible Heisman Trophy. Even more important, gone was his chance to lead the Huskies to another Rose Bowl. He was out for the rest of his senior season. The only chance for him to play again was if the Huskies won the conference title and got the Rose Bowl bid. The Huskies made a commitment to get him there.

One of the Greatest Comebacks in Husky History

The Huskies next traveled to Multnomah Stadium in Portland to face the 18th-ranked Oregon State Beavers on October 22, 1960. The Washington injury list was getting longer; several key starters were out. Some of the members of the alternate unit now were starters, including Pat Claridge, Stan Chapple, Dave Enslow, Sam Hurworth, and Dave Phillips across the front. Only two starting linemen—McKasson and Meyers—had been starters in the 1960 Rose Bowl, an event that seemed so long ago.

McKeta was concerned. "There were guys in the line who went down that I thought would make a difference. You had younger, less experienced guys coming in and we didn't know if they were up to it. But they played like men," he said.

Meanwhile, Tipps appealed to the injured linemen's inner strength and desire: "You guys have to get well. We cannot finish this season with all of you on the sideline." Because of the number of injuries, Owens planned to send in individual substitutes rather than an entire unit. He was trying to keep a nucleus of battle-tested players in the game at all times.

Against Oregon State, the Huskies needed all their courage, determination, guts, and physical toughness. They battled to a 30–29 victory in one the greatest comebacks in team history.

Sophomore Terry Baker, the Beavers' tailback in Coach Tommy Prothro's single-wing formation, scored twice in the first period. His two-point pass attempts twice failed— plays that would loom large at the end—and the Huskies trailed 12–0. Baker, showing the brilliance that would earn him the Heisman Trophy in 1962—the first awarded to a West Coast player—set an Oregon State single-game record of 302 total yards.

The Huskies retaliated in the second quarter when Fleming sped 38 yards through a lane for a touchdown. His perfect kick followed. Oregon State matched that and then some before the intermission. Three points came on a 19-yard field goal, seven came at the end of a 79-yard drive, and the Beavers led 22–7 at the intermission. Baker had accounted for almost all of the yards with his running and passing. Mitchell remembered one of the coaches saying to his team at halftime, "You completely embarrassed us. You knocked on their dressing room door on the way out to start the game, you challenged them at halftime, and then you go out and play like wimps."

Mitchell got the message. He returned the second-half kickoff 34 yards. He finished the job on a trap play that gave him room to speed past the Beavers secondary with little more than three minutes gone. The situation called for a two-point attempt to get the Huskies within seven. After a delay-of-game penalty, Hivner set up and found McKeta for the critical two points.

The Huskies gave seven right back just minutes later. Another sophomore, Bob Monroe, fumbled, and Oregon State took over on the Husky 25. Baker took the Beavers most of the way, with Bill Monk scoring from three yards out. The kick was good, and the Corvallis crew led 29–15. With 30 seconds remaining in the third stanza, Washington pulled to within six after an 80-yard drive capped off by a 12-yard Fleming scamper. Owens again elected to go for two. This time Hivner hit Folkins, and Washington trailed 29–23 at the close of the third quarter.

Washington started its last drive at their own 36 with less than nine minutes remaining. Calm and cool, Hivner called a marvelous mix of plays, including his own rollout run into the end zone on third-and-1. One of the key plays on the drive was Mitchell's 13-yard sweep around the left end to the Beavers 9. "As I was spinning for extra yards, I got hit in the back and head. I suffered a concussion. I didn't even know who won the game. I stayed overnight in Portland for observations," Mitchell said. (Two years later in his senior season, Mitchell got cracked ribs in the Oregon game in Multnomah Stadium. He was happy to be done playing in that place.) During the Huskies' drive, Oregon State was waging a war of attrition. At one point, three Beavers were prostrate. They wearily pulled themselves to their feet in a vain effort to meet the desperate Washington charge.

With the score tied at 29, thousands of Husky fans who had journeyed to Portland crossed their fingers and held their loved ones tight as Fleming zeroed in and kicked Washington's 30th point. Fleming then squelched the Beavers' hopes by stealing Baker's last-gasp throw and returning it to the Washington 48. And so ended a saga of sweat, blood, tears, and triumph. Owens was proud of his players: "A team has to be great to come back like my team did today. The boys kept their poise. We just seemed to know we could pull it out."

The game provided an interesting contrast in coaching styles. Coach Prothro sat in the coaches' box. He quarterbacked his team by remote control 100 feet above the field. "You can see the patterns much better up here. The bench is an awful place to watch a game from," he said. A dangling preposition aside, Prothro wasn't able to

Charlie Mitchell burst onto the Husky scene as a speedy running back in 1960, leading the team in rushing with 467 yards. His 6.3-yards-per-carry average was the best among all AAWU running backs. In 1961, he received many honors, including first-team All-Conference and second-team All-America by ABC-TV. He led Washington in kickoff returns in all three years that he played, averaging 32.4 yards per kick return—still the best average in Husky history.

He holds the distinction of being the first Husky named to a *Playboy* All-America squad (1962). He played in the East-West Shrine Game, the Hula Bowl, and he was the leading rusher on the College All-Star team that defeated the Green Bay Packers. He went on to play professional football in the AFL for six years.

He was inducted into the Husky Hall of Fame in 1992. He went on to serve as chancellor of the Seattle Community College system, which served more than 51,000 students during his tenure.

give a deserving player a pat on the back or offer words of encouragement from his perch.

Owens, on the other hand, was with his troops on the sideline and let his quarterback make most of the decisions, especially in the second half.

The new "wild card" substitution rule that went into effect in 1960 gave coaches the ability to send in all the plays with a substitute player. The rule change ostensibly permitted players to enter and leave the game at will. (Free substitution, when offensive and defensive platoons could be employed, would come in 1965.)

"Oh Shit"

On October 29, the 5–1 Ducks came to Seattle for another slugfest. Senior quarterback Dave Grosz was again at the helm of the Oregon offense. Unlike the Husky quarterbacks,

All-Conference running back (1961–62) Charlie Mitchell.

he went to the sideline on defense to talk with the coaches upstairs and to get a breather. The Ducks were focused on avenging the 13–12 loss from 1959 that had taken them out of the Rose Bowl race. The Oregon seniors had never beaten Washington. Oregon end Dale Herron summed up the players' feelings: "I'm getting tired hearing about last year's Washington team. I think our team is really ready for this one."

After more than 57 minutes, the Ducks led the Huskies 6–0. Oregon had scored in the third quarter when Bruce Snyder, who would later coach at California and Arizona State, reached the end zone on a five-yard run. The Ducks failed to make the extra-point attempt but got another chance when the Huskies were offside. The second kick was batted down by linebacker Ray Mansfield—a sophomore playing like a veteran—who climbed the backs of interior linemen to swat the ball away.

Late in the fourth quarter, Oregon reached the Husky 20. On third-and-4, Hivner picked off a deflected pass on the Washington 5. Once again, the Cardiac Kids took over. After picking up three first downs, the Huskies faced a fourth-and-6 on the Oregon 47. With less than three minutes to go, their time was running out; they elected to go for the first down. Hivner threw a short pass in the flat to McKeta. Slanting toward the north sideline, the Huskies' spiritual leader appeared to be heading out of bounds. At least that is what Oregon defender Dave Grayson—and most everyone watching—thought. But McKeta had no such intention.

His resolve was borne of the UCLA game, in which he felt he did not give enough effort after being tackled on a critical play. So when he caught Hivner's pass, he thought only of driving upfield or being knocked out of bounds. "I was lucky," McKeta said. "I was ready to go out of bounds if Grayson had come after me. I saw I had a step on him and so I turned the corner and ran.... I thought [for] sure I would be caught from behind."

He wasn't. As McKeta crossed the goal line, he had a great big grin. Georg Meyers, a noted sportswriter for the *Seattle Times*, asked him about that smile in the postgame interview. McKeta, with another big smile, replied, "As I cut back to go up the sidelines, I heard Grayson say 'Oh shit.'"

With the game again depending on his foot, Fleming kicked the ball squarely between the uprights. He gave a little jump for joy as he heard the thunderous salvo of cheers, picked up by the late October breeze, echo through the stadium and over Lake Washington.

Conference at Stake

The key to success in any conference race is what a team does in November. Two conference games remained, in addition to a final bout with Washington State. No game was bigger that the Huskies' battle with the Trojans. Both stood atop the Big Five standings. At the Sunday coaches' meeting, assistant coach Bert Clark gave his scouting report on Southern California. He described them as "the best team from the standpoint of physical bulk and experience that Washington will play all season. They are as strong as any team in the country."

The Huskies had traveled to the Los Angeles Coliseum at almost full strength. Allen, Gegner, and Kinnune returned as starters. Bullard would be ready for limited play but not without some extra help from the trainers and painkillers.

Stanford Coach Jack Curtice proclaimed, "USC will beat Washington easily." Owens readied his players to handle the largest linemen and backs in the conference. The USC line averaged 227 pounds, about 10 pounds more than the Husky front seven; the Trojans backs were also 10 pounds heavier than those in the Husky backfield. Under skies that cried a river, the Huskies took to the mud and rain and crushed the heralded Trojans 34–0. The blowout was a body blow to USC's hope for a Rose Bowl bid. It was the greatest margin of victory for the Huskies in the history of their series with USC, dating back to 1923. The Huskies climbed to sixth in the national polls.

California was next. The Bears' first-year head coach was Marv Levy. He would eventually coach the Buffalo Bills (1986–97) to six NFL division titles and four Super Bowl appearances. Facing the Bears, the Huskies were healthy again. Even Schloredt was suited up, the first time since his injury. The Washington fans cheered loudly as he sent booming punts far down the field in pregame warm-ups. It would be the last home game for 20 seniors—players who had given Husky fans some of the greatest gridiron moments they had ever seen.

The Huskies sent the homecoming crowd home with rosy thoughts, beating California 27–7. The game went according to script. Two long scoring drives and another keyed by McKasson's interception and 38-yard return to the Bears 4 helped put the Huskies up 27–0. Cal scored their only points late in the fourth quarter. The crowd loved every minute. For once, it was a nice, comfortable afternoon for the cardiacs in the crowd.

With a nostalgic sigh, almost 56,000 onlookers watched the conquerors disappear into the tunnel. The Husky faithful bid farewell to the seniors after singing the school's alma mater and its final ringing refrain, "All Hail! Oh Washington!" With a perfect conference record and a first-ever sweep of its California opponents, there was little doubt that Washington would have a repeat appearance in Pasadena. Particularly pleased was Schloredt. He flexed his mended shoulder and promised he'd be ready for the Rose Bowl. "There's no cast, no bandage—there's nothing on it but imagination," he said.

Kinnune, the great Husky guard, said he couldn't make up his mind "whether to be happy or sad. We have had four great years together here." McKeta, his teammate for three years, echoed Kinnune's sentiments: "It's almost the end of the line. They've been a perfect three years, playing under the greatest bunch of coaches you ever saw."

Owens described his seniors: "They were the kids who started with us, and there'll always be a special place for them. They had a lot of faith in the coaching staff, and they stayed with us when things were bad."

As always, Owens and his players were laser-focused on the next game—this one with archrival Washington State in Spokane's Memorial Stadium. The Cougars featured quarterback Mel Melin, who led the nation in total offense, and sophomore receiver Hugh Campbell. Washington State had the best passing game in the nation, and Campbell was nearing national records for both receptions and receiving yardage. Meanwhile, Washington's chief weakness had been pass defense. They had yielded more passing yards per game—154.3—than any major college team.

Blood, Sweat, and Another Conference Title

Before about 29,000 fans braving a very chilly day made colder by a bitter south wind, the Huskies returned to their heart-pounding ways. Shades of night fell as Owens' invincibles reached way down once again and won by a whisker. The first three periods were scoreless. On a field strewn with sawdust to ameliorate the muddy spots, the Cougars jammed the middle to combat Washington's traps and force the Huskies outside. They trusted the soggy field to slow Fleming and Mitchell. The Huskies fumbled six times and lost two. The Husky line and secondary tried to defend against the Cougars aerial game. Campbell broke the national records and scored the Cougars' touchdown early in the fourth period. All told, Washington gave up 188 yards in the air and only 92 on the terrible turf.

Early in the second period, McKeta suffered a gaping gash in his right leg. The players were wearing mud cleats with inch-and-a-half-long spikes. The cleat of one of the Cougars tacklers ripped into McKeta's leg. He collapsed in pain as he was trying to walk off the field to the locker room; two Husky reserves had to lift the Washington warrior and pack him off. Amazingly, with 10 stitches in a leg wrapped with bandages, McKeta came back for the second half. All he did was lead all ground gainers with 56 yards—67 for the game—and display once again his courage and commitment to play from the heart.

None of his yards were more important than on Washington's one scoring drive. It started with Mitchell receiving the kickoff and galloping for 38 yards; Bylan's touchdown-saving tackle knocked the speedy sophomore down on the Cougars 47. With backup quarterback Kermit Jorgensen at the helm, the Husky ship moved slowly down the watery passage. Except for a six-yard toss to McKeta for a first down on the 25, the remaining 15 plays were all just straight-ahead tests of strength and conditioning and an incredible will to win. Joe Jones, Jorgensen, McKeta, and Mitchell repeatedly mushed over the tackles and wings all the way to the Cougars 11.

Jorgensen went back to pass and then cut back over the middle for nine yards. On the next play, the Renton redhead dropped the ball while trying to stuff it in Jones' belly, but the QB recovered it on the 3. Jones clutched the ball on the next play and dove over the right guard to within inches, setting up Jorgensen's sneak. Washington was then within one.

Certain that Owens would go for two, the crowd stood tensely under the arc lights in dwindling daylight as Hivner came in to execute a short version of the Utah Special. McKeta forgot about the pain and pressure and slid off the left side; he was all alone in the end zone as he tucked Hivner's pass safely into his chest for the 8–7 lead and the victory.

Keith Jackson was in a hurry to interview the coaches. He remembered, "I did the broadcast by myself on a local basis. I had no help and no bathroom. I was drinking coffee because it was so damn cold. I did the first interview in the men's room."

The Husky locker room was subdued. The coaches and players knew they had played in a very tough game and they had high praise for their in-state rival. With another late game-winning drive complete down Cardiac Canyon, Coach Tipps said, "This team will be the death of me yet. We had it when we needed it, just like we have all year."

Owens felt the season had been even more satisfying than the year before. "We were under more of a handicap this year. Every school was pointing for us, particularly the schools from the Northwest," he said. Indeed, the margin

of victory in each of the three games against Northwest opponents was just one point.

Lineman Ben Davidson reflected on the several come-from-behind victories: "Even though we were down in the fourth quarter in those games, you say to yourself, 'This isn't a big deal. Somebody, somewhere, somehow is going to do something to pull this game out.' And, sure enough, it happens."

Schloredt thanked everyone for giving him a chance to play in one more game, saying, "I'll be ready to go on

Chuck Allen.

Chuck Allen, a member of Washington's 1960 and 1961 Rose Bowl–championship teams, stands as one of the greatest linemen in school history. Named to the Huskies' All-Centennial Team, Allen was a two-time All-Conference performer. He went on to play 12 years of professional football with San Diego, Pittsburgh, and Philadelphia. As a rookie with the Chargers in 1961, he was named to the All-AFL team.

He began his coaching career at Washington in 1973 and later served two decades as an executive with the Seattle Seahawks. He was enshrined into the Chargers' Hall of Fame in 1984 and named to the Husky Hall of Fame in 1994.

January 2." McKeta, gingerly walking on his injured leg, was among the last to reach the shower room. His heavily taped leg was mute evidence of the rages of battle. This courageous Husky, who seemed to thrive in the toughest moments, finally emerged to get dressed. "Does it hurt?" inquired a well-wisher who had wandered into the locker room. "Nothing hurts now," McKeta said quietly, "Nothing."

The final Associated Press and United Press International regular-season polls crowned Minnesota as national champions. The Gophers were followed by Mississippi, Iowa, Navy, Missouri, and Washington, at number five. Washington also finished fifth in the UPI poll, behind Minnesota, Iowa, Mississippi, and Missouri, consecutively. Navy's Joe Bellino, who had become an American football folk hero, won the Heisman Trophy. His vote margin over second-place Tom Brown, Minnesota's All-American guard, was one of the biggest in Heisman history.

Because the Big Five Conference could pick any opponent in the land, there was quite a bit of discussion about who that opponent should be. Washington players had different opinions. Some wanted to play Navy because they felt the Midshipmen had lucked out with their game-winning last-second field goal. Others felt the Big Ten Conference was the strongest in the country and wanted to play Minnesota. On November 22, Minnesota was given the invitation to face Washington in the 47th Rose Bowl. It would be the Gophers' first appearance in Pasadena.

Attendance swelled to 430,783 in 1960, and for the first time, Washington had a higher total attendance than any of the California schools (the Huskies also led each school in the old Pacific Coast Conference).

The other major bowl games were set. Number seven Arkansas would face 10th-ranked Duke in the Cotton Bowl. The Sugar Bowl would match No. 2 Mississippi against unranked and thrice-beaten Rice. Navy would go after fifth-ranked Missouri in the Orange Bowl. Two of the major polls—the Helms Foundation and the Football Writers Association—would choose a national champion after the bowl games were over.

Washington faced a much tougher Rose Bowl opponent this time around. Minnesota had a grinding, mobile line that averaged 223 pounds—almost 20 more than the

At 6'1" and 205 pounds, **Roy McKasson** was considered undersized, even by 1960 standards, when he piled up numerous honors as the Huskies' center. He earned All-American honors from five organizations. Owens, speaking for all the coaches, heaped on the praise: "Pound for pound, he's a real top-notch football player. He's not as big as college linemen go—especially a center. But he makes up for it by constantly trying to improve. He's a smart player. His defensive quarterbacking has been fine. And he has proved this season that he can carry an extra load, staying in there when others were hurt. Roy is a fine, stabilizing influence."

After one year with the Edmonton Eskimos in the CFL, he joined the staff of Young Life and was widely known for his Christian witness, friendliness, kindness, and generosity. He was inducted into the Husky Hall of Fame in 1987. He died in 1998 at the age of 58. At his memorial service, Don McKeta said, "Roy had all the things that make someone great: dedication, high values, and his conviction to Christ. He was someone everybody looked up to."

Husky front wall. The hub of the line was 243-pound Tom Brown, who was acclaimed as the best interior lineman in college football. He received not only a fistful of national awards, but also was crowned the Big Ten's Most Valuable Player, only the eighth lineman to receive the award in its 37-year history.

Despite size differences, the two teams matched up pretty well. Minnesota scored 221 points in nine games to Washington's 255 in 10 games. Minnesota gave up 71 points to opponents, Washington 100. The Gophers' big scoring quarter was the fourth—86 points to the Huskies' 51. One of the major differences between them was in the punting game: Washington allowed 3.75 yards per punt return to Minnesota's eight-yard average.

Forty Huskies took off for Long Beach on Saturday, December 17, after a rousing rally at Sea-Tac Airport. When the teams met in Disneyland, Jim Skaggs was asked by one

Roy McKasson, consensus
All-American in 1960.

of the Gophers, "I notice that most of your players have a healed-over cut on their foreheads. What's it from?" Skaggs explained that their coaches taught them to strike the first blow with their heads. "The repeated impact drives down the rim of the helmet and makes a sore spot which never heals." The Minnesota players, brows unmarred, stood in awe after the reply.

The Huskies were healthy. Schloredt was running with the second team and going through punting drills with Hivner. Owens said, "Defense would come first in the Huskies' preparation. We've got to figure out a way to stop Minnesota and then see if our kids can handle it... Then we'll go ahead strong with our offense."

Hivner deserved to start. He had done a masterful job of guiding the Huskies to six-straight victories after Schloredt went out for the season. Hivner was poised under pressure in engineering come-from-behind wins over Oregon State and Oregon and hitting McKeta for the two-point conversion in the 8–7 thriller over the Cougars. During the regular season, he completed 54.4 percent of his passes and led the Huskies in total offense and passes intercepted. Even so, Owens reported that Hivner and Schloredt would share the quarterbacking duties.

On the day before the game, the Huskies bused up to Pasadena to have a look at the empty Rose Bowl. Dressed in blue blazers, gray slacks, and rep ties, they walked up and down the green turf. Some climbed up the aisles in small groups and wandered amid the empty seats. Some climbed up the west side to the very last row and sat in the shade of the press box to see the perspective the media crews and sports columnists would have the next day. During the tour of the field, backfield coach Chesty Walker herded all the ball carriers into the end zone. As he had the previous year, he told each of the players to pluck a blade of grass and put it in his hip pocket. Harking back to the Wisconsin game, when five backs scored, he smiled and said, "That means you will score a touchdown."

Schloredt stayed down on the field, squinting down the length of the gridiron at the northern goal posts. "That's where we made our first touchdown against Wisconsin, up there. And we made another up there in the third quarter," he said. Finishing his reflections, he added, "I'm

more nervous about this game than I was for Wisconsin. Minnesota's better than Wisconsin. You can see that in the movies. There's nothing complacent about this team."

A National Championship

In its long history, the Rose Bowl probably had never been shaken by such passion from the stands. Two hours before kickoff, 12,000 had already filled the student section. By game time, nearly 30,000 Washington fans had assembled in the stands. Another 300-plus students with tickets stood outside the bowl throughout the whole game, unable to crowd themselves into the tiers of seats. The Gophers fans, meanwhile, put on a display of maroon and gold so vast that it gave the impression that everyone was in the bowl to cheer for Minnesota.

Their pom-poms soon fell limp as Washington got off to a fast start. The Huskies' speedy running back Charlie Mitchell took the kickoff on his 8-yard line, near the right sideline, and cut initially upfield. As he reached the 25, Mitchell raced diagonally to his left, past and around his defenders, to the Washington 33.

Washington immediately went into their new Red Eye formation. McKasson started to execute his blocking tactics on Brown. McKeta gained eight over left tackle and then, breaking away from four Gophers tacklers, willed his way for another six over the same side and a first down. Kinnune remembered that he pulled out left from his right guard position to hit Bobby Bell, the Gophers' right tackle. "It was like hitting a cement wall. I muttered 'Oh boy.' He was tough," he said.

Many of the Huskies felt Bell was the best Minnesota player. (Their opinion was shared by the Kansas City Chiefs, who drafted him two years later. He later became the first Chiefs player elected to the Pro Football Hall of Fame.) Bell, from Shelby, North Carolina, had been advised to go to Minnesota by Jim Tatum, the Tar Heels coach. Bell could not enroll at the segregated University of North Carolina.

According to Schloredt, the play "set the tone of the victory. McKeta crashed through them and they knew exactly what he was going to do. They couldn't stop him. They saw they couldn't do anything about it. You could see the funny looks on their faces."

On fourth-and-4, Hivner punted. The Gophers' Dave Mulholland decided not to catch the ball on the 17 and watched it bounce and roll dead on the 6. The Gophers' punt receivers did not try to catch or run with a Washington punt for the entire first half.

On its first defensive series, Washington set up in its new 5-3 scheme. It worked perfectly on the first two plays. Roger Hagberg was stuffed by Pat Claridge and lost ground. On the next play, Kinnune stood up Brown, and Enslow straightened up Larson. Allen and McKeta filled the gap to hold Hagberg to three yards. Brown's wrist was slightly sprained. The Husky interior was winning the battle in the trenches.

On third down, Stephens initially set up over his center and then dropped back five yards into the end zone. He booted the ball to Fleming, who took it at midfield and danced between several defenders to the Gophers 34. Four plays later, on fourth-and-3, Fleming marked the spot from which he would attempt the field goal on the Minnesota 34. He said that some of the Minnesota players started laughing and saying "No way" about his kicking a field goal from that distance. They shut up as he swung his leg perfectly into the ball, sending it sailing through the uprights for a 3–0 lead. "I got back there and just boomed it. It went about 60 yards," he said. His 44-yard field goal was then the longest one in Rose Bowl history. It was also a personal best for Mr. Automatic.

Early in the second quarter, the Huskies scored a touchdown. Starting from their own 38, the Huskies drove to the Gophers 18 before the first quarter ended. Then Mitchell dashed for 11. On fourth-and-goal on the 3, Brent Wooten initially set up on the left side, then went in motion in an arc to the right. He kept on running after the snap and was wide open when Schloredt hit him with a short toss on the 1 and he went untouched into the end zone. "We were in a double-wing," said Wooten. "I'm sure Minnesota hadn't seen it before because when I caught the pass, God, there wasn't anybody close."

Fleming's kick made it 10–0, and it was beginning to look like the previous year's Rose Bowl all over again. With about four minutes to play before halftime, the Huskies scored after a 68-yard drive in nine plays. From inches out,

Schloredt followed a host of linemen into the end zone— Washington 17, Minnesota 0.

At the beginning of the second half, Minnesota drove to the Husky 35. On fourth-and-inches, Chapple, crashing in from the left tackle position, met Hagberg head-on and dropped him for a one-yard loss. There was no chest thumping, no pointing to the sky; the Husky senior simply trotted off the field with the satisfaction of having done his job.

The Huskies set up to put the game away early in the third quarter, as they had a year before. But not this time. On the first play of the possession, Hivner backed away from the center a wee bit early and fumbled the exchange; Minnesota's Bob Deegan recovered on the Husky 32. In three plays, the Gophers reached the end zone and pulled within 10 points.

Near the end of the third quarter, Stephens' punt rolled out of bounds on the Husky 11. The next Washington series took away Minnesota's momentum and ate up precious minutes.

The Gophers set up in an eight-man front. Schloredt knew that if he got past the first wave, he would pick up a lot of yards. He momentarily set up for a handoff, then busted through the left side. The hole was widened by McKeta, trying to get there ahead of him. The two hit the gap together. McKeta joined Folkins on his left side to take care of the cornerback and make it difficult for the safety to get a good shot at Schloredt. Finally, help arrived from the other side to bring the Husky quarterback down on the Washington 42 after a gain of 22 critical yards.

Minnesota then turned the tables. They forced the Huskies into third-and-19. Schloredt punted 47 yards to put the Gophers 76 yards away from making the game much tighter. In eight plays, they reached the Washington 26, where they faced fourth-and-2. Hagberg fumbled, and Husky sophomore Ray Mansfield recovered. Unfortunately, Washington had jumped offside, so the Gophers had new life on the 21. After Stephens rolled around the right end for six and Judge Dickson plowed over the right guard for a first down on the 11, Minnesota reached the 6. On third-and-5, Stephens dropped straight back to pass. As he turned to throw, he found McKeta blitzing. "It was just a gut feeling to get near the line of scrimmage," McKeta recounted. "I just knew Stephens was coming my way. I had to go in and cut him off." Stephens was dropped on the 18. Coach Tipps would later call the play one of the keys to victory.

With the crowd standing and all the coaches and players on the sidelines encouraging the men on the field, Minnesota set up for a field-goal attempt on the 25. Stephens, the holder, caught the snap, rose, and rolled right, right arm cocked. He continued running down to the 20, where three Huskies were converging on him. He then threw toward the goal line, where a column of four Huskies had the passing lane to the lone Gophers receiver covered. McKeta was the third one in the phalanx and in front of the receiver. He stepped up to catch the underthrown pass on the 1 and returned it out to the 9. McKeta would later say that he didn't want to catch it. "But I was afraid if I batted it into the air, a Minnesota player might grab it and we really would be in trouble. So, I caught it and ran as far as I could. My terrific speed," McKeta laughed, "carried me all the way to the nine."

McKasson had neutralized Brown early on. By the end of the devastating, destructive, and decisive first quarter, the Minnesota All-American guard was out of the game. He later returned, but he was never very effective. Jackson, on the other hand, was the ironman. He gained 60 yards and played every minute of the game except for the few plays when Jones replaced him.

For Schloredt, Hollywood couldn't have scripted it any better. From a broken collarbone in October to standing by and watching all those gut-wrenching one-point victories to get to the Rose Bowl, Schloredt got his reward. He had played a large part in another Rose Bowl victory. Back on the big stage, his flair, his ability, and his bruising style led the Huskies to a stirring victory over the regular-season national champions. He had gained 68 yards and averaged 13.6 yards per carry. He scored one touchdown and threw for another. For the second year in a row, he was voted the game's Most Valuable Player (he shared it with Fleming in 1960). He was the first player in the bowl's 47-year history to receive the award twice.

It was the second-straight time the Huskies, as the underdog, had stepped up and smashed a Big Ten opponent

Bob Schloredt was a key player in the Huskies' back-to-back Rose Bowl victories in 1960 and 1961. After a childhood accident left him limited vision in his left eye, the "one-eyed quarterback" went on to a dazzling football career. In addition to his quarterback duties at Washington, he was one of the best punters in the nation and a tough defensive back. He was named the Associated Press' first-team All-American quarterback in 1959. He also set a school record with his punting average (40.0 yards in 1959) and for the longest punt (70 yards in 1958). He still holds the Husky record for average punting yards in a game—57.0 yards in the Colorado game in 1959. He is 10th in Husky history for the longest punt and second in number of punts for 60 yards or more in a season (five in 1958).

Following his senior season, he played in the Hula and All-American Bowls and then in two seasons for the British Columbia Lions in the CFL. He was inducted into the Husky Hall of Fame in 1981, the College Football Hall of Fame in 1989, and the Rose Bowl Hall of Fame in 1991.

with a decisiveness that left only the size of the score, never the winner, in doubt. It was the first time in the continuous series with Big Ten teams that a West Coast team had won two Rose Bowls in a row.

In the final analysis, it was Owens' philosophy and system for success that was clearly in evidence on the battlefield—fast and lean linemen, speedy backs, two heady and confident field generals, vicious tackling, the kicking game, and finely conditioned athletes who had become a band of brothers in battle

Over the two-year period—1959 and 1960—the Huskies had forged the second-best record of any collegiate football team in America: 20 wins and two losses. With 20 victories, one tie, and one defeat, only Mississippi had a slightly better résumé. The evidence showed that both teams deserved a piece of the national championship. However, in 1960, the system of selecting a national champion was seriously flawed. Most polls made their final selections *before* the bowl games were played. Controversy reigned as much in 1960 as in the early 21st century. Imagine it—some were even calling for a national playoff system!

At that time, there were just two polls that selected a national champion after all the evidence—regular-season records and bowl-game results—was in. The Football Writers Association of America selected Mississippi; the Helms Foundation selected Washington. As a result, Washington laid claim to the national title, or at least to a shared title with the Rebels.

It is easy to forget where the program stood just a few years earlier. Owens and his staff and their band of football brothers had taken a program on probation and won back-

to-back Rose Bowl games and a national title. Washington's football program had risen from the ashes to a national championship.

Another Rose Bowl

In 1963, legendary *Los Angeles Times* columnist Jim Murray wrote, "I won't say Owens gets the hungriest football players in the West each year, but if they were in the Roman Coliseum, the lions wouldn't come out."

After the second-consecutive Rose Bowl victory, Owens went on to coach for 14 more seasons. In 1961 and 1962, the Huskies finished second in the conference. They began the 1963 season 0–3 but then won six of their last seven games to win the conference title and a Rose Bowl bid. It was the first time a team advanced to the bowl with more than three defeats. Led by Junior Coffey, Bill Douglas, and Rick Redman, it would be Owens' last team to go to a bowl game.

The Huskies faced third-ranked Illinois in Pasadena. The Illini, coached by Pete Elliott, featured Jim Grabowski at fullback and Dick Butkus at linebacker. Butkus was a consensus All-American in 1963 and 1964 and finished

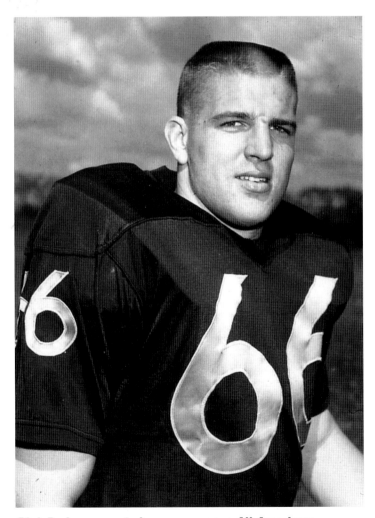

Rick Redman was twice a consensus All-American.

Coming out of Blanchet High School in Seattle after being selected to the All-America High School Football Team, Husky fans could not wait for **Rick Redman** to join the Washington lineup. Playing from 1962 to 1964, he was one of Washington's most decorated football players. He was a consensus All-American in 1963 and 1964, the only player in UW history to receive those honors. He also was a great punter. In the 1965 East-West Shrine Game, he was honored as the best lineman of the game.

He joined the San Diego Chargers in 1965 and played for nine seasons, the last two as player-coach. Redman then went on to become CEO and then chairman of Sellen Construction, one of the largest contractors in the Northwest. He was inducted into the Husky Hall of Fame in 1982 and the College Football Hall of Fame in 1995.

sixth in 1963 in the Heisman Trophy balloting and third in 1964. Grabowski was an All-American selection in 1964 and 1965. The Huskies, in turn, were led by All-American linebacker and offensive guard Rick Redman, end Jim Lambright, quarterback Bill Douglas, running backs Dave Kopay and Ron Medved, and fullback Junior Coffey.

Early in the game, Coffey was sidelined with a foot injury. Douglas then suffered a game-ending knee injury after moving the Huskies to the Illini 15. A few plays later, the Huskies lost a fumble on the 6-yard line. The Huskies later scored in the second stanza on Kopay's six-yard scamper. Illinois answered with a field goal to trail 7–3 at halftime.

The Huskies were shut down in the second half and could not hold their opponents from scoring two touchdowns. The final score was 17–7. The loss was the only blemish on Owens' bowl records. He had played on three bowl winners as a player at Oklahoma, was an assistant to Bear Bryant when Kentucky won the Cotton Bowl in 1952, and of course coached the Huskies to victory in the 1960 and 1961 Rose Bowls.

Owens' teams had thrived in the one-platoon era. When free substitution became legal in 1965 and two-platoon football was implemented, it had a very significant impact on Husky football. Owens did not like the new rule. He believed that one-platoon football was how the game should be played. The change undermined the foundations of Washington's success in the eight seasons he had been the head coach. The stress on defense and physical conditioning that enabled the Huskies to punish its opponents, particularly in the fourth quarter, was not so important with players going only one way and having significant sideline "breathers." Two-platoon football required a change in the recruiting process. Owens said he and his coaches were slow to select high school and junior college players who focused on just offense or defense. "Looking back on it, we made some mistakes. We should have picked some people who were more specialized. But we hadn't been experienced in that type of football," Owens reflected.

Another major change came in the mid-to-late '60s. It was a time of much campus unrest brought about

All-American defensive end Tom Greenlee.

Tom Greenlee graduated from Garfield High School and began his Husky football career as a running back on the freshman squad. In his sophomore year, he moved to the defensive secondary and also returned kicks. With a penchant for making big defensive plays, he played defensive end as a senior.

Greenlee was twice selected to the All-Conference team and earned consensus All-America honors in 1966, his senior year. He participated in the East-West Shrine Game and the Hula Bowl. He was inducted into the Husky Hall of Fame in 1987.

They say that records are meant to be broken. It will take a Herculean effort to break the mark that **Al Worley** etched into the college football annals in 1968, his senior year. He intercepted an NCAA-record 14 passes at a time when the Huskies played only 10 games. Worley also set a Husky single-game record with four interceptions against Idaho. No wonder the Wenatchee native was known as "the Thief."

Worley finished his Washington career with 18 interceptions. He still holds the all-time Husky records for most interceptions in a career, season, and a single game. He was a consensus All-America selection in 1968. He ended his collegiate career participating in the Hula Bowl—yes, he intercepted a pass—the East-West Shrine Game, and the All-American Game. Worley was named Washington's outstanding athlete of the year for 1968–69. He was inducted into the Husky Hall of Fame in 1992.

Consensus All-American Al Worley.

by the war in Vietnam, the civil rights movement, and other social issues in the country. The attributes of discipline, commitment to pay the price, and team unity that characterized the 1959 and 1960 teams were no longer embraced by college athletes to the same degree. Many students and some athletes also began to challenge the "authority" of leaders in business, government, universities, and coaching staffs. To add to difficulties, the Huskies simply were not winning.

In early 1968, 14 African American student-athletes demanded the hiring of an African American coach or administrator, alleging discriminatory practices in the athletic department. In August of that year, Carver Gayton, a member of the 1960 Rose Bowl team, joined the staff as an assistant football coach. Individual and group counseling sessions were initiated. A wide variety of community events took place to connect the student-athletes with the local African American community. Although the 1968 team ended with a 3–5–2 record, Gayton felt that things were moving in a positive direction.

Then Washington lost the first six games of the 1969 season. The coaches and players became frustrated. At the end of October, several days before the UCLA game in Los Angeles, Coach Owens met with university officials to discuss the situation. After the meeting, he decided to present a loyalty oath to each of the 80 players. Owens talked with each player and asked each of them to pledge 100 percent unconditional loyalty to him, the team, and the university. Four players refused and were suspended. All of them were African American. Gayton, who did not know about the loyalty oath, resigned in protest because he felt that the process, and the result, undermined his relationship with the athletes.

Tension, fear, and rage became pervasive in the black *and* white communities of Seattle. A University of Washington Human Rights Commission was appointed in 1970 and issued its report in late January 1971. The report contained many recommendations, including the firing of Coach Owens and athletic director Joe Kearney—who had replaced Owens as AD in 1969—and the hiring of a black assistant coach and a black assistant athletic director. The board of regents rejected the recommendation to dismiss Owens and Kearney.

Reflecting on the situation, Gayton said, "The irony of the situation was that the same qualities that had led to the success in the late 1950s were part of what led to the difficulties ten years later. The players began to question authority and a strong, disciplined approach. Some could not accept pledging loyalty to the coach and the university. And Owens, who personified the qualities of discipline, hard work, team unity, and paying the price, was not the type of person who would sit down and say 'let's talk' or apologize for his treatment of the players—for example, the death march."

Mitchell saw the explosion coming. Reflecting later, he said, "Did racism exist when I played [1960–62]? Yes. Was it different than in other programs? No. Does that necessarily make it right? No. We didn't have that many black ballplayers on the 1960 team. And all of us were playing and we were winning. And, it was before the time of the civil rights movement. We didn't have a lot of episodes. All the episodes started after that. I don't believe Washington coaches were prepared to handle what came later."

Dr. Charles E. Odegaard, president of the university, remarked in a staff meeting that he didn't believe Owens was racist; he thought Owens and some of the coaches were colorblind. He felt that the situation required a different approach. University officials had to understand what was happening to African Americans around the country. They had to discuss and evaluate the demands of organizations such as the Black Student Union, meet with their leaders, and determine what changes were required to ease the tension.

When the 1970 season started, the turmoil had subsided somewhat. Coming off a 1–9 season in 1969, Husky fans had little hope for the new season with an inexperienced sophomore quarterback at the helm. What they got instead was a legend. Sonny Sixkiller's debut was one of the most stunning in the annals of the program. Directing a wide-open passing attack, Sixkiller led Washington to a 42–16 victory over Michigan State in the season opener. He was honored as national "Back of the Week" by the Associated Press after his first game. His exploits helped the Huskies to a 6–4 record in 1970, their best since the 1966 season. Washington was acclaimed the most improved team in the country. The Huskies finished tied for second in what then had become the Pacific-8 conference after the addition of Washington State in 1962 and Oregon and Oregon State in 1964.

"Stay Cool and Score"

September 18, 1971, marked one of the wildest games ever played in Husky Stadium. The game featured two of the nation's top passers—Sixkiller and Purdue's Gary Danielson. Washington lit up the scoreboard first when Sixkiller connected with wide receiver Tom Scott on a fourth-down play. Early in the second quarter, Danielson faked a handoff and pitched the ball to wideout Darryl Stingley for a 17-yard scoring run. With 5:30 left in the half, Purdue picked off a Sixkiller pass and Danielson gave the Boilermakers the lead when he scampered 43 yards for a score. Several plays later, Scott took a handoff on a reverse and raced 60 yards to tie the game. With nine seconds remaining in the half, UW's Steve Wiezbowski gave the Huskies a 17–14 halftime lead with a 32-yard field goal.

The seesaw battle continued into the third quarter when Purdue's outstanding running back Otis Armstrong scored on a 39-yard run. Washington regained the lead on Jerry Ingalls' dive into the end zone. Sixkiller made four long passes on third down during the series to keep the scoring drive alive. Late in the quarter, the Boilermakers reclaimed the lead 28–24 on the power of Armstrong's running. Once again, the Huskies responded with another touchdown run by Ingalls, with 13 minutes to play.

With Washington holding a 31–28 lead, each team's defense finally managed to hold each other scoreless for about 10 minutes. Then, with 3:39 to play, Danielson found

Stingley open behind the Washington secondary. Stingley raced 80 yards for the score to put Purdue ahead 35–31.

Washington had one last comeback left. Heeding the advice of Coach Owens to "stay cool and score," Sixkiller needed just five plays to get the Huskies back in the end zone. The final play was a 33-yard pass to Scott. The game remained in doubt until Husky linebacker Rick Huget picked off a Danielson pass right before the final whistle.

In 1972, with a veteran team surrounding him, Sixkiller had every reason to believe that his final game would be in the Rose Bowl. They started the season with five-straight wins. Then Stanford shut out the Huskies 24–0 in Palo Alto. The next week at USC, the Trojans trounced the Huskies 34–7. The Huskies rebounded with three-straight wins over California, Oregon State, and UCLA but ended the season with a 27–10 loss to the Cougars in Spokane. USC got the Rose Bowl bid, and with that, the Sixkiller era was over.

Off the field, changes were being made to improve the relationships between the coaches and student-athletes. In January 1971, former Husky fullback Ray Jackson became an assistant coach. Later that month, Don Smith was named assistant athletic director. In the ensuing months, Smith worked tirelessly to heal wounds, to develop better relationships between the various factions, and to gain the confidence of all parties that the racial tension would be improved.

Smith also selected Gertrude Peoples, a member of the newly created Office of Minority Affairs' Black Student Division, to establish an outreach program for student-athletes, especially African Americans. "I provided a friendly voice for the athletes," she remembered. "I was kind of like a mom, a good friend." She and her small staff started an academic counseling program that provided a host of services to those who needed help in what, for some, was a very different environment. "The Athletic Department became a lot more sensitive," she concluded. As a result of the changes, the Black Athletes Alumni Group, led by another former Husky fullback, Joe Jones, reversed its stand discouraging black athletes from attending Washington.

Owens continued to coach for two more seasons. In 1973, his team went 2–9 overall and 0–7 in the conference. In 1974,

Sonny Sixkiller graduated from Ashland High School in Oregon, where he was a three-sport star. As a collegian, he did not receive any All-America or All-Conference awards, but he had one of the greatest romantic names ever linked with college football.

He joined the Husky varsity team as a sophomore in 1970, leading his team to a 6–4 record after the varsity had gone 1–9 in 1969. He led the nation in passing that year, a mark that was based on completions per game (he had 18.6). That season, he set five Husky single-game records and six season marks. He quickly became an idol in the Northwest. There was even a hot-selling record: "The Ballad of Sonny Sixkiller." There were "6-Killer" T-shirts and a "6-Killer" fan club sponsored by a local radio station. Of course, he wore jersey No. 6.

As a junior and senior, he guided the Huskies to back-to-back 8–3 records and third place in the conference both seasons. He finished his Washington career as the all-time passing leader with 5,496 yards, 811 passing attempts, 385 completions, and 5,288 total offensive yards. Sixkiller was featured on the October 4, 1971, cover of *Sports Illustrated* and also in *Boys' Life*. After graduation he became involved with football television. He also appeared as a player in the Burt Reynolds movie *The Longest Yard*. He was inducted into the Husky Hall of Fame in 1985.

the team improved, finishing 5–6 and fifth in the conference. On November 23, 1974, what would be Owens' last game as coach, the Huskies beat Washington State 24–17 on the road. In that game, quarterback Dennis Fitzpatrick set a Husky record for rushing yards by a quarterback—249 in 37 attempts. That record still stands. All told, he rushed for 697 yards in the season. Fitzpatrick stands third in Husky history for career rushing yards by a QB.

On November 27, 1974, at the football team's annual postseason banquet, Owens announced his retirement from coaching. Before he spoke, athletic director Joe Kearney remarked:

Today marks the end of an era—the Jim Owens era. All who have shared this span of football history can take pride in the past 18 years. The Owens years included more drama, change, and excitement than any comparable span of time in Washington athletics. Many shared in the halcyon years when the Purple gang terrorized the nation's best in Pasadena. During some of those years, controversial issues swirled around the football program but in the final analysis, what was evident was the stature of the man. Jim Owens has been a credit to the university, the state of Washington, and to the coaching profession. He has conducted the Husky football program in an ethical manner and has exemplified the highest ideal of the coaching profession. Today, we mark the end of an era. But it most certainly marks the beginning of a legend that will grow from this day on. The legend of Jim Owens the coach and Jim Owens the man.

During Owens' own remarks, he quoted Ralph Waldo Emerson: "We are the sum of our days, and should look sharp at how they pass. Of our days, they come and go like muffled and veiled figures sent from a distant friendly party; but they say nothing, and if we do not use the gifts they bring, they carry them silently away." He ended with, "Heaven Help the Foes of Washington."

Owens finished his 18-year Husky tenure with 99 wins, 82 losses, and six ties for a .545 winning percentage. Owens was inducted as a charter member into the Husky Hall of Fame as a player in 1979. He was inducted into the College Football Hall of Fame as a player in 1982 and into the Rose Bowl Hall of Fame as a coach in 1992. On October 25, 2003, a statue of Owens was placed in front of the northwest entrance to Husky Stadium. Because of the events in 1969 and 1970, some in the African American community were angry over the erection of the statue. Owens helped heal the wounds when, in his acceptance speech before 72,000 Husky fans, he gave a heartfelt apology to his players for the pain he may have caused them. For Gayton and others, Owens' apology ended one of the most excruciating sagas in Husky history.

After Owens left coaching, he entered the private sector before retiring to Big Fork, Montana, with his wife, Martha. Owens passed away at his home on June 6, 2009, at the age of 82.

Many football seasons have come and gone since the 1959 and 1960 teams rose to the top of collegiate football. When you talk today about the Husky tradition—endurance, passion, pride, tenacity, and toughness—it all started with them. Don James, who followed Owens as the Husky football coach in 1975, remarked, "Those teams laid the foundation for Husky football."

For example, in 1999 the 1959 team was honored at the end of the third quarter of the Stanford game on October 30, 1999, in Husky Stadium. The modern-day Huskies were behind. Quarterback Marques Tuiasosopo looked out at the gray-haired men as they spread across the field at the west end of the stadium. He later said, "I thought to myself, *Those are the real Dawgs. They are the ones who turned it around in the first place... We can't lose in front of these guys.*"

After the older generation was given a thunderous applause from the fans, the Huskies huddled up at midfield, turned to wave to the legends leaving the field, and then came from behind to beat the Cardinal 35–30 in the fourth quarter. Tuiasosopo ran for 207 yards and passed for 302, the first time a collegiate player had ever put together a 200/300 game.

The legacy of the 1959 and 1960 teams still lives on in the minds of coaches, players, fans, and historians. Those Husky teams picked up an entire state and region. People were drawn to the teams because of their commitment, sacrifices, courage, and focus. The coaches and players provided an example of what people with those attributes can achieve. They were heroes, and they provided hope to thousands—not just then, but for many decades to come.

Dave Enslow, one of the members of the 1960 team, penned a poem in 1992 that included these lines:

As athletes we once were the best
Models for all of the rest

His words are just as true today.

CHAPTER 8

The James Gang

It would be very difficult to find a college football coach who was better prepared to be a head coach than Don James. The third of four sons, he was born on New Year's Eve 1932 in a garage that served as a "temporary" family home until his father completed the family's house some years later. Thomas worked two jobs—one in a steel mill and the other as a bricklayer—to provide money for daily living and also to build a fund for the college education of his four sons.

James' oldest brother, Tommy, played for the legendary Paul Brown at Massillon High School, one of the most outstanding high school football programs in the country. Brown went on to coach at Ohio State and with the Cleveland Browns, which were named after him. At Ohio State, his team won the school's first national championship in 1942. Tommy then played professionally with the Browns for most of his eight years in professional football.

Don James followed in his brother's football footsteps and was Massillon's starting quarterback on two state championship teams. It was then that he decided to be a football coach. At the University of Miami, he elevated his goal to being a *college* football coach. He was Miami's starting quarterback in his last two seasons—1952 and 1953—and established five passing records while there.

After graduating in 1954, he served his two-year ROTC commitment in the Transportation Corps, then he received a master's degree in education psychology and secondary-school administration at the University of Kansas, where he was also a graduate assistant for the Jayhawks. Two years later, he got his first full-time college coaching position as assistant defensive coach at Florida State in 1959. "I think I was the only coach I knew who went from an assistant high school coach to an assistant coaching position in college. It was primarily because my college coaches supported me, pushed me, and recommended me," James later said.

After seven years at Florida State, four of them as defensive coordinator, he became the defensive coordinator at Michigan under Bump Elliott in 1966. Elliott had coached the Wolverines to a 34–7 victory over Oregon State in the 1965 Rose Bowl. His stay in Ann Arbor was short-lived; because of potential changes in the coaching staff and in the athletic director position, James left to go to Colorado in 1968 as defensive coordinator. Three years later he got his first head-coaching position, at Kent State.

Don James observes the action from the sideline.

For James and his family, it was a wonderful experience because it meant they were back in Ohio, near their extended families. It was, however, a tumultuous time at the school. Just seven months earlier, a confrontation between students and the Ohio National Guard had resulted in the death of four students and the wounding of nine.

At Kent State, he had the opportunity to put together his first coaching staff; they quickly became known as the "James Gang." One of the players on James' roster at Kent State was Nick Saban who, after playing for three years, joined the James Gang as a graduate assistant in 1974. James also established a longstanding relationship with Mike Lude, then the Kent State athletic director. When James became Washington's head football coach in 1975, Lude soon followed, replacing Joe Kearney as AD in Washington.

In his autobiography *James*, coauthored by Virgil Parker, the coach gives credit for his gridiron success to his mentors. He attributes the overall organization of his football program to Bill Peterson at Florida State, who had in turn learned it from LSU coach Paul Dietzel. Dietzel, who won a national championship in 1958, had been an assistant coach under three of the greatest minds in college coaching—Army's Colonel Earl "Red" Blaik, offensive-minded Sid Gillman at Cincinnati, and Bear Bryant. From Bryant, Dietzel learned about hard-nosed aggressive play with great speed and quickness. From two coaches in the Southeastern Conference—Georgia Tech's Bobby Dodd and Tennessee's General Robert Neyland—Dietzel was schooled about field position, the kicking game, and defense.

James learned about compassion for players from Elliott at Michigan. From Eddie Crowder at Colorado, James came to understand the coaching philosophy of Bud Wilkinson. Crowder had been an All-American quarterback at Oklahoma on Wilkinson's 1950 national championship–winning team.

James brought the accumulated wisdom of all of these coaches with him to Seattle. He also brought with him four assistant coaches from Kent State: Ray Dorr, Skip Hall, Dick Sesniak, and Bob Stull. Jim Mora joined the staff from UCLA (James and Mora previously coached together at Colorado). James also kept Jim Lambright from Owens' staff.

With his staff in place, James introduced a system that was unlike any before used in the history of Husky football. The system had two underlying attributes. The first was his scripting of almost every phase of the year for his players. He said, "I told each player that came to Washington that 'I will tell you what you are going to do in the various segments of your year at Washington and what is expected of you.'" He provided each of them a "player book," which included a schedule of each phase of the football year—spring practices, weight lifting, preseason practices, season practices, games, and scheduled meetings. It also provided information on academic activities and requirements, the academic-year schedule, summer activities, and work schedules.

The reason for the book was simple. James believed that if a player knew what was expected, the player had a chance to get it right. Assistant Coach Hall, who kept journals of James' practices for more than 10 years, summed up James' strengths: "What Don always tried to do was take any guesswork or vagueness or waste of time out of the system. He was very efficient with time. We had meticulous organization and planning. We critiqued everything, and we used those critiques to get better... The other thing, he hired good people. He had a good plan and he managed people well. He had the ability to motivate and get the most out of people." Chuck Nelson, a Husky All-American kicker, put it succinctly: "You knew exactly what was expected of you and when it was expected."

The second attribute of James' system was the deft management of his staff. He said, "I felt my job was to coach the coaches, who in turn coached the players. In my opinion, the number one role of the head coach is to tie the whole package together and get the coaches and players going. Get the coordinators going... Many head coaches at the major college level take on a specific coaching responsibility. If the head coach is to coach a position or try to coordinate the offense or defense, he will lose something that I didn't want to lose in the overall scheme. That is why I wanted to be a 'tower' coach. Bryant was best known for using that style of coaching."

James continued, "First, if you are down on the field with either the offense or the defense, you can't know what is going on with the other side of the ball. Secondly, if an assistant coach is working with his position players, it would be easy to step in and say, 'No, that is not the way I want it done. I want it done this way.' That could be perceived by the players as putting the assistant down. I wanted the players to have total respect for their position coach."

So to the tower James went. When he was in the tower, he took lots of notes. Then, in his daily staff meetings, he would coach the coaches about what he saw. Then the assistants would in turn talk to the players. "That's when I could say to the assistant, 'I don't want it done that way or that's not the way to coach the players.' I also made some decisions about players from being able to see the whole field during practice," James said.

One of those players he evaluated from the stands was freshman Jacque Robinson, then playing on the scout squad. James said, "I went to the next morning staff meeting and said, 'Hey, our freshman running back is looking better than anybody we've got at the other end of the field with our offensive unit.'" Just a few months later, Robinson was the Rose Bowl MVP.

James' system worked, indeed. As most Washington faithful know, in his 18 years of coaching, he won more games than any other coach in Husky history in the Pacific Coast Conference. His teams won six conference titles and went to 14 bowl games—including six Rose Bowls—winning 10 of them. But his career at Washington did not start very well. After his first two seasons, the Huskies were just 11–11 and started 1977 with one win and three losses. With such a weak beginning, fans and the media started to get restless.

On the bus trip to Oregon for game five of the season, things got prickly. James sat in the front seat of the lead bus—Bus 1—which was to be followed by Bus 2 (the coach's attention to detail extended to bus trips). James was going over game plans, and when he looked up he saw that the second bus had changed lanes and passed them. James then told the driver of Bus 1 to get back in front, but he refused, saying, "I am going at my own speed." James was concerned for several reasons. One, he had hired the bus company. Second, only the driver of Bus 1 knew where

the lead bus would stop on the way down to Oregon, how the buses would get to the Oregon stadium, and where the visitors' locker room was. When the buses reached their first stop, James was furious. "I am renting this bus, I am the boss, and you are going to do what I say. You are going to drive us to Eugene in the lead bus and you are not going to drive us home," he said. The driver got as far as the Portland bus station and said he would not drive any further. James got a new driver. "That was the last time I used that bus company," James said.

The coach's anger carried over to the players, galvanizing the floundering team. The next day, they completely dominated the Ducks (54–0)—and it could have been a lot worse. When the two coaches met at midfield after the game, Oregon's coach, Rich Brooks, actually thanked James for not running up the score. The Huskies won at home against Stanford and Oregon State and lost 20–12 to UCLA in Los Angeles. Next, Washington traveled to Berkeley and beat California 50–31 to stay in the race for the Rose Bowl. For the Cal victory, James received national Coach of the Week honors.

Warren Moon's Long Touchdown Run Tramples the Trojans

Before the largest Husky Stadium crowd in five years, Washington faced 14th-ranked USC in a game that opened the door for the first Rose Bowl in the James era. The Huskies and the Trojans entered the stadium tied with UCLA for the conference lead. USC's powerful offense featured tailback Charles White, the nation's leading rusher, and quarterback Rob Hertel. They had also just come off a 49–0 blowout of Stanford, a game in which they gained 592 yards of total offense.

The Huskies' special teams and defense created turnovers that prevented USC from getting its high-powered offense in gear—forcing six Trojan fumbles and recovering three, intercepting three passes, and blocking two punts. Junior linebacker Michael Jackson made two of the interceptions, smothered one fumble, and led the Huskies in tackles. With about four minutes left in the first half, Washington faced a fourth-and-goal at the USC 2. Quarterback Warren Moon faked a handoff to tailback Joe

Quarterback Warren Moon drops back to pass.

Steele and darted around the drawn-in linebackers for the touchdown. The Huskies took a 7–3 lead to halftime.

Washington sprang to life in the second half as heavy rains and strong winds pelted the field. Moon found Spider Gaines in the end zone for a 19-yard score. Linebacker Mike Rohrbach blocked a Trojans punt to set up Joe Steele's one-yard plunge, which gave the Huskies a commanding 21–3 lead. Trying to run out the clock later in the game, Moon, on third-and-5, kept the ball and went around right end, found a crease, and cruised 71 yards to pay dirt and a 28–10 victory.

The next week the Huskies beat Washington State 35–15, but they had to wait six days for the outcome of the UCLA-USC game, which would determine who won the conference title. Husky fans were cheering for a Bruins defeat that would send Washington to Pasadena. In a classic matchup, USC's Frank Jordan kicked a 38-yard field goal with two seconds remaining that gave his team a 29–27 victory.

Don't Make the Dawgs Mad

About six weeks later in Pasadena, the Husky marching band put on a show-stopping performance at the Rose Bowl. So did the Huskies.

The Huskies finished the regular season 9–2–0, 6–1 in the conference. The Huskies' Pasadena appearance was their first since the 1963 season. The Huskies, ranked 13th, faced Bo Schembechler's fourth-ranked Michigan. Building up to the game, there were several incidents that made the Huskies growl. For a week or more, the *Detroit News* ran a full-page ad in the *Los Angeles Times* that read: EVERY DOG HAS HIS DAY. UNFORTUNATELY FOR THE HUSKIES, JANUARY 2 ISN'T THE DAY. GO MICHIGAN! Even more disturbing to the Washington players was another message, which took up a full page of the official Rose Bowl program. This ad read: LOST. ONE TEAM OF HUSKIES IN THE VICINITY OF PASADENA ON JANUARY 2, 1978. CALL "BO" SCHEMBECHLER FOR CONGRATULATORY MESSAGES. If that wasn't enough to rankle the team, Michigan quarterback Rick Leach committed a serious breach of etiquette when he refused to have his picture taken with Warren Moon. The stage was set for an all-out war.

In 1929, the first Washington marching band was formed under the direction of Walter Welke. Welke's bands were the first on the West Coast to march through formations while playing. Bill Cole replaced him in 1956. In 1965, he hired an assistant director, **Bill Bissell**, who became band director in 1970. Halftime shows at Husky Stadium have never been the same. Bissell believed the band should be both entertaining and fun, and halftime routines became "theater in the round." Theme shows and outrageous costumes were commonplace. "Tequila" and "Louie, Louie" became so popular they took on the status of school songs.

Popular Husky band director Bill Bissell takes charge.

The Huskies took out their anger by just playing hard-nosed, smart football to beat the Wolverines 27–20. Michigan took the opening kickoff down into Husky territory. On fourth down, after John Anderson set up in punt position, he reached for a low snap and his knee touched the ground. And with that, the Huskies had first-and-10 on the Michigan 49. Moon finished off the Huskies' first drive with a two-yard run to give Washington a 7–0 lead.

Early in the second stanza, the Huskies added three more points after Moon's pass reached speedy Spider Gaines for a 62-yard gain. Michigan's defense stiffened, but Steve Robbins' perfect kick put the Huskies up 10–0. Before the half ended, Moon snuck over the middle for the last yard of a 60-yard drive, giving the Huskies a 17–0 lead.

Early in the third quarter, Moon tossed a 28-yard touchdown strike to Gaines, and it seemed like the rout was on. But two plays later, the Wolverines awoke from their slumber when Leach found Curt Stephenson for a 76-yard touchdown. Washington got another field goal to close out the third quarter up 27–7.

Then Michigan made the fourth quarter nerve-racking for Husky fans. Two Wolverines touchdowns left the Huskies with a seven-point lead. With 2:46 remaining, Michigan took over on its own 42 and advanced to the Husky 8—first-and-goal. Both Washington and Michigan

fans began to envision a Wolverines go-for-two to win it all. But Washington outside linebacker Michael Jackson never let it happen. Leach drifted around in the backfield and then lobbed a little pass in the direction of tailback Stanley Edwards. It hit the back on the shoulder pad and bounced in the air. Jackson said, "I felt I had a chance for the ball, especially after it rolled over Edwards' head and down his

As a senior at Washington, **Warren Moon** completed an athletic questionnaire by answering the "Career plans?" question with "Professional football." He sure had that right.

A native of Los Angeles, Moon transferred to Washington after a year at West Los Angeles College, where he had been a record-setting quarterback. He became the Huskies' starting quarterback in his junior year and led the Huskies to victory in the 1978 Rose Bowl in his senior season. As a senior he completed 125 of 222 passes (56.3 percent) for 1,774 yards and 12 touchdowns. He was selected as Co–Player of the Year in the Pac-8 in 1977 (along with Stanford quarterback Guy Benjamin) and was MVP of the 1978 Rose Bowl.

He began his professional career with Edmonton in the CFL. During his six years with the Eskimos, he guided them to five Grey Cup titles. He joined the NFL in 1984 and spent 10 seasons with the Houston Oilers, three with the Minnesota Vikings, two with the Seattle Seahawks, and two with the Kansas City Chiefs. During his NFL career, he was named to nine Pro Bowl games.

He was elected to the Husky Hall of Fame in 1984, the Rose Bowl Hall of Fame in 1997, and the Pro Football Hall of Fame in 2006. During his professional career, he threw for more than 70,000 yards. His 49,325 NFL yards rank him fifth all-time.

Warren Moon in a publicity shot for the 1978 Rose Bowl.

back. I took it away from him as we fell to the ground." And with that, Washington came away with the win.

The 1977 campaign marked the beginning of a remarkable run for the Husky program that extended for another 15 seasons and included five more conference titles and nine more bowl victories.

Those teams were stacked with remarkable talent. Blair Bush, the center on the 1978 Rose Bowl–winning team, was a three-year letter winner at Washington.

He was a first-team All-Pac-8 selection in 1977. That season, he was a second-team All-American and was honored with an NCAA postgraduate scholarship. He also earned the Seattle 101 Club Scholarship for academic excellence. He was the fourth player in Husky history to be selected in the first round of the NFL draft when the Cincinnati Bengals made him the 16th overall pick. He played 17 seasons in the NFL with the Bengals, the Seattle Seahawks, the Green Bay Packers, and the Los Angeles

Rams. Bush was named to the Huskies' All-Centennial Team and was elected to the Husky Hall of Fame in 2008.

Michael Jackson was a four-year letter-winner at Washington and another Huskies' All-Centennial Team member. He established several Husky defensive linebacker records in tackling, including totals for single game (29), single season (219), and career (578). He was selected All-Pac-8 linebacker in 1977 and All-Pac-10 in 1978. In 1979, he was selected in the third round of the NFL Draft by the Seattle Seahawks and was the team's starting linebacker for eight seasons. He was elected to the Husky Hall of Fame in 2000.

The fourth member of the 1978 Rose Bowl team to be elected to the Husky Hall of Fame was Joe Steele (1996). Steele played from 1976 to 1979 and set the Huskies' single-season and career rushing records (1,111 in 1978 and 3,168, respectively). He is still third all-time in career rushing yards. In 1979, he was a first-team All-Pac-10 running back.

The Eyes of Texas Teared Up

When the Pacific Coast Conference expanded to the Pac-10 in 1978, the Huskies finished tied for second. The following season, with a 9–2–0 regular-season record, Washington again took second place in the conference. The 13th-ranked Huskies were invited to the Sun Bowl in El Paso, Texas, to meet the 11th-ranked Texas Longhorns on December 22, 1979.

Washington pulled ahead in the second quarter on two quick scores off Texas turnovers. Defensive end Stafford Mayes jumped on a fumble on the Texas 47. Washington quarterback Tom Flick led the offense to a third-and-11 on the Texas 18. Coach James decided to set up a special formation that put split end Aaron Williams wide right and freshman flanker Paul Skansi in the slot. When tailback Vince Coby went in motion to the right, that side became flooded with three very fine receivers who put great pressure on the Texas secondary. Skansi went straight downfield and then cut right and caught Flick's pass in the corner of the end zone. Mike Lansford kicked the extra point.

Two plays after Texas returned the kickoff, Texas halfback Darryl Clark muffed a pitchout and strong safety

Thanks to the efforts of the University's Alumni Association, the Big W Club, and the athletic department, a **Husky Hall of Fame** was started in 1979. It was created to honor and preserve the memory of those athletes, coaches, and members of the athletic department staff who have contributed in an outstanding and positive way to the distinction of the Washington athletic program. The first Hall of Fame class was Steve Anderson (Track, 1928–30), Chuck Carroll (Football, 1926–28), Hiram Conibear (Crew, 1907–17), Gil Dobie (Football, 1908–16), Hec Edmundson (Basketball, 1921–47; Track and Field, 1919–54), Bob Houbregs (Basketball, 1951–53), Hugh McElhenny (Football, 1949–51), Jim Owens (Football, 1957–74), Al Ulbrickson (Crew, 1924–58), and the 1936 Olympic Gold Medal–Winning Men's Eight-Oared Crew.

Greg Grimes recovered on the Texas 23 to set up another Husky touchdown. After Lansford's kick, the Huskies led 14–0.

On Washington's next possession, Flick was blindsided and fumbled; the ball was recovered by the Longhorns on the Husky 44. Texas stayed on the ground until they reached the Husky 5. On third down, quarterback Donnie Little pitched a short pass to halfback Brad Beck in the right corner of the end zone. John Goodson's kick was good, and the score was 14–7 at halftime.

The second half was characterized by mostly "push-and-shove" as the two teams played tough defense and could not muster any significant offensive drives or scores. Washington came away with the victory, and Skansi was named the game's MVP.

A Day of Rose-Colored Smashes

On November 15, 1980, the Huskies journeyed into the dreaded land of Troy and came out smelling like a rose. In a memorable performance, Washington clinched the conference title and a return to the Rose Bowl when they upset second-ranked USC 20–10. It was the first

On October 31, 1981, former Husky cheerleader **Rob Weller** was the guest yell king during the homecoming football game against the Stanford Cardinal, who were led by junior quarterback John Elway. He instructed the Husky fans in the northeast section of the stadium to stand up as he ran past them on the track below. He continued all around the stadium, creating the now-familiar stadium staple known as "the wave." Seattle was the first place to routinely perform the wave, at both Husky Stadium and in the Kingdome at Seattle Seahawks games. It is now a part of athletic contests throughout the world.

Washington win over the Trojans in Los Angeles since 1964 and USC's first loss at home since 1977.

The Trojans had eight turnovers—four recovered by the Huskies—and had four passes picked off by Washington defenders. The game was won during a span of less than three minutes early in the third quarter. Washington's Ray Horton fielded a Trojans punt and sprinted 73 yards for a touchdown. Just three plays later, Husky defensive back Tony Caldwell intercepted his second pass of the day, setting up Paul Skanski's leaping touchdown catch. Trojans tailback Marcus Allen decreased the gap to seven late in the third quarter, but Chuck Nelson's field goal in the fourth quarter put the game away for good.

In the final game of the regular season, the Huskies beat Washington State 30–23 and won the Pac-10 Conference title. Once again, they met Michigan in the Rose Bowl. This time, Bo Schembechler's fifth-ranked Wolverines were ready; they beat the Huskies 23–6.

The Apple Cup: Another Disappointment for the Cougars

In 1981, the Husky faithful had plenty to cheer about as the season ended. The team had lost only to Arizona and UCLA, entering the Washington State game with an 8–2–0 overall record and 5–2–0 in the conference. The Cougars came to Husky Stadium with an overall 8–1–1 record and were 5–1–1 in conference play. Fans were intent to hear the result of the UCLA-USC contest, which started 40 minutes before the Husky game. They needed the Trojans to beat the Bruins to clear the way for the Rose Bowl bid.

The Cougars were ranked 14th in the nation to the Huskies 17th. Washington's defense was the best in the league, while the Cougars ranked high in offensive categories. With the Huskies trailing 7–3 late in the second quarter, sophomore quarterback Steve Pelluer fired a low pass toward wide receiver Paul Skansi. Cougars cornerback Nate Bradley looked as if he would smother the ball when Skansi dove over the defender for an amazing catch in the end zone.

Washington State evened the score with a field goal to open the second half. From that point on, the Huskies, behind the great effort of their offensive line, took control. Ron "Cookie" Jackson capped an 80-yard march by running 23 yards to put the Huskies up 17–10. Following a Cougars turnover, Chuck Nelson booted his second field goal to

When it came to catching footballs, few Washington players did it better than and with as much flair as **Paul Skansi**. As a prep player at Peninsula High School in Gig Harbor, Skansi had a hard time convincing the Husky coaches he was worthy of a scholarship. However, after five games in his freshman season, he became a very important part of the Husky offense. He earned Most Valuable Player honors in the Huskies' 14–7 Sun Bowl win over Texas in 1979. In his senior year, he was named to the All-Pac-10 team. He appeared in four bowl games in his Husky career. Skansi is third all-time in Washington history with 161 catches.

At just 5'11", he was not the prototype college receiver and was considered even more of a long shot as a professional player. He again proved the critics wrong. After being cut by the Pittsburgh Steelers after one season, he played for eight seasons with the Seattle Seahawks.

increase the lead to 20–10. With less than three minutes to go, Nelson kicked three more points to put the game away. When it was announced that USC had upset the Bruins, the Huskies were off to the Rose Bowl.

"He's Only a Freshman?"

Iowa shared the Big Ten title and came to the 1982 Rose Bowl ranked 13th in the country against 12th-ranked Washington. The Hawkeyes had given up less than 90 yards rushing during the season and featured one of the most outstanding punters in the nation in Reggie Roby. Iowa was a three-point favorite. Before the game, Husky freshman running back Jacque Robinson told the press that he was going to win the game's Most Valuable Player Award.

After initial changes of possession, Roby booted the ball 56 yards, but he outkicked his coverage. Ray Horton caught the ball and broke out to the far side, racing 48 yards before Roby made a touchdown-saving tackle on the Iowa 29. Unfortunately, the Huskies were not able to move the ball, and on fourth down Chuck Nelson attempted a 50-yard field goal, but it tailed off to the left.

After several more exchanges, Roby sent the ball deep to the Husky 8. Horton again noted plenty of room to run, and he returned the punt to the Husky 40. Freshman Jacque Robinson—who had been on the scout team at the beginning of the season—entered the game and carried three times for a first down. Pelluer then hit Allen for 21 yards. Robinson did most of the rest, gaining 34 yards on a 60-yard drive, and ultimately scored with more than 10 minutes left before halftime.

At the Washington 39 and with only 1:35 left in the half, Iowa elected to go for it on fourth-and-7, believing they could contain the Husky offense if they failed to convert. The Huskies stopped Iowa for a one-yard loss, and 11 plays and 60 yards later, Washington scored. The Huskies went into halftime up 13–0.

Washington put increasing pressure on Iowa in the second half and held them scoreless. Near the end of the third quarter, the Huskies struck with vengeance. After another one of Roby's skyscraper punts, Washington started on its own 31. Robinson then took over. He ran for 15 yards and then another 17 to the Iowa 37. After

Coby punched three yards closer, Robinson broke over the middle, evaded the swarm of oncoming Hawkeyes defenders, and broke out of the grasp of a tackler at the 8 for the score. Pelluer connected with Skansi under the shadow of the goal posts for two points and a 21–0 lead.

After Washington recovered an Iowa fumble on the Iowa 29, Tim Cowan came in the game to relieve Pelluer at quarterback. He was returning to the lineup for the first time after suffering a thumb injury in the second game of the season. Showing no signs of the injury, Cowan faked a handoff, circled wide to the near side, and entered the end zone untouched, a worthy return. With the score 28–0 and with 7:47 left, the Huskies stopped Iowa the rest of the way.

Robinson's prediction was right; he was voted the game's MVP after rushing for 142 yards and two touchdowns on 20 carries. After the game, reporters bombarded Coach James with questions about the running back. "Is he only a freshman?" was one. With a big grin on his face, James quipped, "I just introduced myself [to him]. I'm glad he's a freshman. I just checked the program."

The Huskies entered the 1982 season ranked second in the preseason polls. After a convincing 23–13 win at Arizona in the second game of the season, they were ranked No. 1. And for the first time in school history, Washington played a home game as the nation's top-ranked team. The Huskies lived up to their ranking by beating Oregon 37–21. They reeled off four more victories before being upset 43–31 by Elway and Stanford in Palo Alto.

The Huskies ended the season with close wins over UCLA and Arizona State and a tough road loss to the Cougars, 24–20. The loss kept Washington out of its third-straight Rose Bowl. Many years later, James would say, "That loss hurt me more than any other in my career."

Too Bad, Boomer

Rose Bowl dreams dashed, the ninth-ranked Huskies instead accepted a bid from the Aloha Bowl in Honolulu to play 16th-ranked Maryland on Christmas Day 1982. The Terrapins were led by quarterback Norman Julius "Boomer" Esiason. The Huskies boomed first. At about the 10-minute mark in the first quarter, the Huskies went on an 80-yard drive that ended with a 27-yard touchdown pass

Two-time bowl MVP Jacque Robinson (No. 28).

Chuck Nelson was a unanimous All-American place-kicker in 1982.

from Tim Cowan to split end Anthony Allen. Chuck Nelson's kick was good. Maryland scored later, but their point after was missed. The Huskies increased their lead with 5:21 left in the half on a 71-yard pass play from Cowan to Allen. The quarterback threw a short sideline pass, and the Maryland defender, going for the interception, missed the ball; Allen sped upfield for the remaining 63 yards. Nelson again hit the point after, and the Huskies took a 14–6 halftime lead with them into the locker room.

In the second half, Maryland scored early but missed the two-point conversion. At 10:44 in the fourth quarter, the Terrapins took the lead 20–14 on a two-yard run followed by a two-point conversion. With 3:49 left, the Huskies mounted a drive for the victory. With time running down, Cowan found Allen in the end zone. Almost lost in the drama of the final seconds was the snap from center; injured quarterback Steve Pelluer came in to hold for

Nelson. The snap was low, but the ball was retrieved by Pelluer, who managed to get it to the kicking tee in time for Nelson to put the crucial 21st point on the scoreboard.

Tim Cowan received the Most Valuable Player trophy, which the sportswriters had already voted to give to Esiason before the final Husky drive was over.

There were many fine players on that bowl-winning squad, including Mark Stewart, one of the finest linebackers in Husky history. Playing from 1979 to 1982, he was selected All-Conference and consensus All-American in his senior season. During his career, he established Husky game records for quarterback sacks (5), fumbles caused (5), and solo tackles (15). He was inducted into the Husky Hall of Fame in 2008.

Huskies Go for the Win and Get the Glory

The fifth-largest crowd in Washington history witnessed one of the greatest comebacks in Husky history on September 17, 1983, against Michigan. The Huskies had lost 34 lettermen from their talented 1982 outfit. With less than 14 minutes left in the game, the Wolverines led 24–10. Up to that point, Michigan had played a near-perfect game.

After receiving Michigan's kickoff, Washington went to work. Wide receiver Danny Greene caught two passes for 31 yards, and Mark Pattison hauled in one for nine yards on the drive to put the ball on the Wolverines 22. Pelluer then hit Greene, slicing across the middle to the 4, and then fullback Walt Hunt rushed into the end zone from the 3. No mistakes, seven points, and the Huskies were down by just seven, with 9:09 left. Michigan then launched a drive to try to put the game away. The Wolverines methodically moved to a first down on the Husky 20. Three downs later they were on the 15. Michigan then set up for a field goal. Todd Schlopy, who had successfully kicked one from 35 yards in the first quarter, sent this one just wide right from the 32. "From where I stood, I thought it was good," said Coach James. The scoreboard clock read 3:40 as the Huskies set up on their own 20.

First a nine-yard pass from Pelluer to tight end Larry Michael, then for 15 over the middle to flanker Dave Stransky, and another to Michael for nine yards. Pelluer was on a roll, but on the next play he was rushed hard and

At the age of nine, **Chuck Nelson** finished sixth in the national Punt-Pass-Kick competition—a very auspicious beginning. In 1982, Nelson, a place-kicker on the Washington football team, booted 30 consecutive field goals over his last two seasons, crushing the old record of 16. As a senior, he made 25-straight field goals, missing the last one of his career against the Cougars. He scored 112 points as a senior to give him 282 in his career—a mark that is still third in Husky history. He was the Huskies' leading scorer in 1980–82. He capped a terrific Washington career by being named a unanimous All-American and the owner of eight NCAA records, 14 Pac-10 records, and 14 Washington records.

Nelson also excelled in the classroom, where he earned Pac-10 All-Academic honors for three years and was an Academic All-American in 1981 and 1982. He was a recipient of an NCAA postgraduate scholarship in 1983. Nelson spent five seasons in the National Football League and was elected to the Husky Hall of Fame in 1998.

had to eat the ball. On third down with 1:09 left and still 40 yards away, Stransky made a clutch first-down catch at the Michigan 28. Greene then ran to the 7, and Pelluer completed a pass out of bounds to stop the clock with 47 seconds remaining.

Mark Pattison lined up with single coverage, and Pelluer felt that if his wide receiver could get a step on the defender, he might be able to score. Pelluer threw high, ensuring that the ball be caught or go out of the end zone. It was caught. Pelluer had completed 13-straight passes—27-of-33 for the day—when he brought his team to the line for the two-point-conversion attempt. The Huskies set up with two tight ends. Michael was on the right side and ran a crisscross pattern with Greene. Pelluer was on target for the 14th-straight time. He later said, "I saw their safety line up across from Larry. I didn't know if they'd bring everything but the kitchen sink after me, and they did. I saw them coming and knew Larry would be single-covered. I thought he could get a step on the defender and I just tried to get the ball to him. The rest is history."

The Sooner Schooner

In 1984, quarterback Hugh Millen engineered another great game. Growing up in Ann Arbor, he dreamed about playing for the Wolverines. Well, he realized *some* of his dream by playing in Michigan Stadium when he led Washington to a 20–11 victory. He completed 13-of-16 passes for 165 yards and a touchdown. He was the first walk-on quarterback to start for a Don James team.

That season, Washington lost only to USC in the Los Angeles Coliseum (16–7). The Huskies finished second to the Trojans in the conference and played second-ranked Oklahoma in the Orange Bowl. Washington was ranked No. 4 going into the bowl game.

The Oklahoma Sooners were a very cocky bunch, from their coach, Barry Switzer, to linebacker Brian Bosworth. The Huskies were no slouches—led by All-American Ron Holmes and a tough defensive unit. It was smash-mouth football, and the Huskies ended up doing the smashing against an opponent that led the nation in defense. Coach James devised a system of trap plays that capitalized on the Sooners' aggressive defense to pull off the victory.

Washington took control early in the game when it scored twice, once on a 72-yard march ending with Jacque Robinson's one-yard scoring run. Oklahoma rallied for a pair of second-quarter touchdowns, including a 61-yard pass play at the end of the half to tie the score.

The turning point in the closely contested game happened in the third quarter with the score still tied. Oklahoma seemingly took the lead when Tim Lashar kicked a field goal to put the Sooners up by three. After the successful kick, two white horses and a covered wagon rolled onto the painted turf to celebrate Lashar's points. The referee threw the flag on the Sooner Schooner. Switzer was livid. "We've been doing that for 50 years. It's a tradition," he said. But in this case, the ref thought it was unsportsmanlike (some said unhorsemanlike). Backed up 20 yards, the Sooners were forced to rekick. Lashar's second attempt was blocked by Washington free safety Tim Peoples.

Later, Oklahoma took a 17–14 lead when Lashar kicked a 35-yard field goal with 6:15 to go in the game. At that point, Hugh Millen entered the game to replace starting quarterback Paul Sicuro. He marched the Huskies 74 yards downfield in seven plays, the last a well-timed 12-yard touchdown lob to his former Roosevelt High School teammate Mark Pattison. Seconds later, after Buster Rhymes fumbled the kickoff return out of bounds at the 2, All-American defensive tackle Ron Holmes tipped a forward pass and the ball fell into the arms of Husky linebacker Joe Kelly at the Sooners 10, and he hustled to the 6. Fullback Rick Fenney scooted into the end zone to put the Huskies firmly in control 28–17.

Robinson received his second bowl game MVP honor after a 135-yard rushing effort. After the game ended, the only question was whether the Huskies would be voted No. 1. BYU, with a 13–0 record, had claim to the title as well. Many felt BYU had played a weaker regular-season schedule than the Huskies, and the Huskies had defeated the second-ranked team in the country. After the game, Coach Switzer said Washington would get his vote for sure. However, when the two major wire polls—AP and UPI—released their votes, Washington was second to BYU.

One of the most outstanding defensive linemen in Husky history was **Ron Holmes**. Playing from 1982 to 1984, he was named to the All-Pac-10 first team in each of his last two years and was a consensus All-American in 1984. That same year, he won the Morris Trophy, awarded annually to the best offensive or defensive lineman in the Pac-10. He still stands at the top or near the top in quarterback sacks—first in single-game totals (5), second in a single season (13), and second in a career (28).

Holmes was drafted eighth in the first round of the 1985 NFL Draft and played for four years with Tampa Bay before joining Denver on its run to Super Bowl XXIV. He was admitted to the Husky Hall of Fame in 2001. He passed away on October 27, 2011, at the age of 48.

Consensus All-American defensive lineman Ron Holmes in 1984.

Whew!

After a 6–5 regular-season record in 1985, the Huskies received a bid to play in the Freedom Bowl in Anaheim, California, on December 30, 1985, against the Colorado Buffaloes. It was the Huskies' seventh-straight postseason appearance and eighth in nine years. With Husky quarterback Hugh Millen on the sideline with an injury, sophomore Chris Chandler was starting in only his third game.

A Colorado field goal had tied the score at 10–10 early in the third quarter. A 36-yard kickoff return by flanker Dave Trimble gave the Huskies excellent field position, and Washington scored to go ahead 17–10. The Huskies then scored on their next possession, moving 67 yards on 11 plays. Stalling out at the 1, Washington opted for a field goal at fourth-and-goal to put them ahead by 10.

Colorado had Husky fans on the edge of their seats midway through the fourth quarter when Barry Helton passed 31 yards to Jon Embree for a touchdown and the Buffaloes cut the lead to three (20–17). Colorado held the Huskies on their next possession and marched to the Husky 7. But linebacker Joe Kelly forced a fumble, and David Rill pounced on it, preserving the Washington win.

Husky Stadium Symmetry

The symmetry arrived in 1987 when the upper deck and roof were added to the north side of Husky Stadium. From the top of the roof to the field below, the stadium was the height of a 16-story building. Its capacity grew to 72,500 with the addition of 13,000 seats at a cost of $17.7 million. At the time, the renovation made Husky Stadium the largest college facility in the nation. And with 70 percent of the seats located between the end zones, it had also become one of the loudest.

Consensus All-American place-kicker Jeff Jaeger in 1986.

Just as Chuck Nelson had, **Jeff Jaeger** missed his first Husky field-goal attempt. But he did not miss many more. During his four years (1983–86), Jaeger went on to set an NCAA record with 85 career field goals. He also finished his Husky career as the school's all-time leader, with 358 points. Jaeger was named a consensus All-American in 1986 after connecting on 19-of-23 field-goal attempts and making 42 of 43 extra-point attempts. He was drafted in the third round of the 1987 NFL Draft and played for 12 seasons. He was admitted to the Husky Hall of Fame in 2004.

Completion of the upper deck in time for the September 5, 1987, dedication game against Stanford became a huge concern when, on February 25, several sections of the steel framing collapsed in a heap. Thanks to an accelerated construction schedule, inspectors gave final approval to the north deck the morning of the game.

From 1986 to 1988, the Huskies had winning seasons but fell out of the top 10 national rankings. They appeared in two more bowl games in that span, losing 24–12 to Alabama 28–6 in the 1986 Sun Bowl and defeating Tulane in the 1987 Independence Bowl.

Shutting Down Emmitt Smith

In 1989, the Huskies finished 8–4 and played Florida in the Freedom Bowl on December 19, 1989.

The Huskies put a 34–7 thrashing on the Florida Gators. After the game, All-American running back Emmitt Smith said, "This game was myth. Everything that went on seemed like a mirage. We didn't play like we should. We never got into the game."

He was spot on. The Huskies simply destroyed the Florida Gators. The Huskies held the ball for almost 42 minutes, gained 433 yards—242 of them passing—and gave up just 231 yards. Quarterback Cary Conklin was at his best. He completed 16-of-24 passes for 184 yards in the first half to lead the Huskies to a 27–7 lead and put the game out of reach. Greg Lewis rushed for 97 yards in 27 carries and was

named the game's Most Valuable Player. It was Coach James' eighth bowl victory in 11 bowl appearances.

The Road to a National Championship

The 1990 season was the centennial season for Washington football. Great moments and great players were discussed, and a centennial team was selected. Don James began his 16th season as the Huskies' head football coach, including a very successful decade in which the Huskies were frontrunners in the Pac-10 Conference in several major categories. In the 1980s they had 10 winning seasons, 84 wins, and nine bowl appearances.

In 1990, James welcomed back 39 lettermen and 13 starters from the 1989 season. With offensive coordinator Keith Gilbertson, James had successfully employed the one-back offense that stretched out defenses by land and by air. Jim Lambright, defensive coordinator and assistant head coach, had implemented defensive schemes that provided lots of headaches to opponents.

The season started with lackluster wins at home against San Jose State (20–17) and at Purdue (20–14). Next up was fifth-ranked USC, who had started the season with impressive wins over Syracuse and Penn State. The Trojans were led by quarterback Todd Marinovich and tailback Ricky Ervins. A staggering 72,617 fans nestled into Husky Stadium on a gorgeous sunny day, the temperature reaching 92 degrees.

"I Just Saw Purple"

The winner of the USC-Washington game had gone to the Rose Bowl 10 of the previous 13 seasons. While this game was an early season affair, it would prove to substantiate that trend. Greg Lewis gained 126 yards and Mark Brunell threw for 197 yards as the Huskies rolled to a 24–0 halftime lead. The Husky defense, led by All-American lineman Steve Emtman, stopped everything the Trojans attempted. During the first half, USC had a measly two first downs and 43 yards of total offense. Of its 22 plays, 13 of them produced no gain or a loss of yardage.

In all, the Husky defense held USC to 163 total yards and seven first downs. They recorded three quarterback sacks and intercepted three passes. They put so much pressure

1991 Rose Bowl MVP Mark Brunell.

on Marinovich that after the game and having been shut out 31–0, he said, "I just saw purple. That's all. No numbers, just purple."

The Huskies' All-Centennial Team

The capacity crowd at the halftime of the USC game gave thunderous applause to the Huskies' All-Centennial Team in celebration of 100 years of Husky football (1889–1989). The team was selected by alumni, members of the media, and longtime season-ticket holders.

Position	Player	Years Played
Wide Receiver	Paul Skansi	1979–82
Wide Receiver	Lonzell Hill	1983–86
Offensive Guard	Max Starcevich	1934–36
Offensive Guard	Chuck Allen	1958–60
Offensive Tackle	Vic Markov	1935–37
Offensive Tackle	Arnie Weinmeister	1942, 1946–47
Center	Blair Bush	1975–77
Quarterback	Don Heinrich	1949–50, 1952
Running Back	George Wilson	1923–25
Running Back	Hugh McElhenny	1949–51
Running Back	Joe Steele	1976–79
Place-Kicker	Chuck Nelson	1980–82
Defensive Lineman	Paul Schwegler	1929–31
Defensive Lineman	Doug Martin	1976–79
Defensive Lineman	George Strugar	1955–56
Defensive Lineman	Ron Holmes	1982–84
Linebacker	Rick Redman	1962–64
Linebacker	Michael Jackson	1975–78
Linebacker	Joe Kelly	1983–85
Defensive Back	Nesby Glasgow	1975–78
Defensive Back	Ray Horton	1979–82
Defensive Back	Calvin Jones	1970–72
Defensive Back	Dick Sprague	1950–52
Punter	Rich Camarillo	1979–80

Among them, 12 of the 24 team members had played on Don James' teams.

Greg Lewis was a Husky tailback from 1987 to 1990. As a senior, he rushed for 1,407 yards, a school record at the time (he is now fifth), and was named the Pac-10 Conference Player of the Year. He also received the inaugural Doak Walker Award, given to the nation's top junior or senior running back. He finished seventh in the Heisman Trophy voting, the highest-ever finish for a Husky offensive player at the time. He was named to several All-America teams in his senior year. After rushing 1,197 yards as a junior, he became the first UW running back to rush for 1,000 yards or more in two consecutive seasons. His 15 career 100-yard games are still third-most in Husky history. Lewis held the Husky record for consecutive games with 100 or more rushing yards, compiling a streak of 10 such games during the 1989 and 1990 seasons.

After his college career, he played for two seasons with the Denver Broncos before returning to his alma mater to complete his degree in political science. He spent five years in the UW athletic department as the head of the Big "W" Alumni Club and one year as the special assistant to the athletic director. In 2006, he became the director of advancement for diversity and minority affairs, a position he held for six years. Lewis became the senior director in the same department in 2012. He was inducted into the Husky Hall of Fame in 2006.

Pac-10 Champions for the First Time Since 1981

The Arizona Wildcats came into Husky Stadium ranked 23rd in the country to play the seventh-ranked Huskies. The Huskies mauled them 54–10. Washington gained 429 yards to the Cats' 272. Arizona's coach, Dick Tomey, was impressed. "They did all the things that good teams do... They're as good a team as any in the country," he said. The Huskies jumped to No. 2 in the polls after the game, when four of the teams ahead of them lost.

Greg Lewis won the first-ever Doak Walker Award.

In the team meeting room after the game, they were greeted by Roy Coats, president of the Pasadena Tournament of Roses. He formally invited Washington to the Rose Bowl and handed Coach James a bouquet of long-stemmed red roses. It was their first Rose Bowl bid since 1981. "It's a great feeling," James said. "It's a good group of guys who prepared well and hung in there week after week and put up some numbers that are absolutely incredible."

Bruins Baffle the Huskies

However, the chance for a national championship died the following week. The Bruins entered the stadium with a 4–5 record. Led by quarterback Tommy Maddox, a redshirt freshman, the Bruins gained 394 yards, the most yielded by Washington in the season. Maddox threw for 239 yards and two touchdowns. His counterpart, Mark Brunell, completed 10 passes in 34 attempts for 137 yards, and running back Greg Lewis was held to 50 yards on 12 carries, the first time during the season that he had not rushed for more than 100 yards.

Washington took the lead late in the third quarter on a 61-yard drive that featured a 47-yard pass from Brunell to Orlando McKay. The Bruins regained the lead early in the fourth quarter on a 30-yard touchdown pass. After the extra-point kick failed, UCLA led 19–14. After a Husky fumble on the Washington 14, a Bruins field goal increased the lead to 22–14. With 3:18 to play, the Huskies got a big break when the Bruins' Scott Miller muffed a wind-buffeted punt and Husky Jay Barry recovered on the Bruins 37. Four plays later, Brunell threw a cross-field pass into the wind and through the rain; Mario Bailey caught it and fell backward in the end zone. Brunell ran for the two-point conversion to tie the score at 22.

With 2:03 to play, the Huskies started on their own 30. On second-and-3, Brunell tried to get his pass to Bailey, but it was intercepted at midfield by Eric Turner. Four plays later, the Bruins had a field goal and the game, at 25–22. After the game, Washington dropped to No. 10 in the polls.

The Huskies closed out the regular season in Pullman, taking out their frustrations on the Cougars, 55–10.

1991 Rose Bowl

In the 1982 Rose Bowl, the Huskies recorded a 28–0 shutout against the Iowa Hawkeyes. In the 1991 Rose Bowl, it was a shootout, not a shutout, against Iowa. Washington's 46–34 victory was the highest-scoring game in Rose Bowl history, and the Huskies' 46 points were the second-highest by a Rose Bowl team (topped only by Michigan's 49–0 shutout of USC in 1948).

The Husky victory was engineered by sophomore quarterback Mark Brunell, who threw for two touchdowns and ran for two more. He was named the game's Most Valuable Player, the fourth time a Husky QB had won the award. Former recipients Warren Moon, the 1978 MVP, and Bob Schloredt, the MVP in 1960 and 1961, were both on hand. Schloredt presented the trophy to Brunell after the game.

The young Washington team had the upper hand from the start of the game and led 33–7 by halftime. The Hawkeyes came out in the second half and made the game more exciting. They went 80 yards to open the second half to pull within 19. Trailing 39–14 with fve minutes to go in the fourth quarter, Iowa struck for two more touchdowns but missed both two-point conversions. Washington 39, Iowa 26. Brunell quickly struck again. Just 24 seconds after the Hawkeyes scored, he found Bailey in the end zone from 31 yards out to increase the Huskies' lead to 20. Iowa scored another touchdown and a two-point conversion late in the quarter. The Huskies came away the victors, 46–34.

In 1990, Washington ended a highly productive 10–2–0 season ranked fifth in the final poll and with lots of players coming back. The Rose Bowl victory over Iowa provided great enthusiasm for the 1991 season. "I think the guys next year should be able to…go undefeated and get a national championship," predicted Lewis.

The Greatest Season in Husky History

The Huskies entered the 1991 season ranked fourth in the preseason polls. By that time, most of the coaches had worked together for many years. Don James was starting his 17th year as head coach. He had built a consistent, nationally prominent, winning program. During his previous 16 seasons, the Huskies had been invited to a record nine-straight bowl games (1979–87), 11 in the past 12 seasons. He had led his Husky teams to victory in eight of them, including two Rose Bowls.

His seasoned group of assistant coaches was led by assistant head coach and defensive coordinator Jim Lambright, who joined the staff in 1969 and had built nothing less than one of the strongest defensive units in the nation. His pressure defense attracted coaches from many parts of the country to talk to him about the way he ran the defense. Keith Gilbertson was the offensive coordinator and offensive line coach. He introduced a wide-open offense. In 1990, he quipped, "Before, you could cover the Husky offense in a phone booth. Now, you are going to see players spread out all over the field." Randy Hart was the defensive line coach, starting his fifth season in that role. The tight ends coach was Myles Corrigan, also in his fifth season. Matt Simon had spent eight seasons as the

Huskies' running backs coach. Larry Slade had coached for five seasons as the secondary coach. Outside linebacker coach was Chris Tormey, entering his eighth season and the fifth with OLs. In his ninth year on the staff, Jeff Woodruff was the quarterbacks coach. It was his first year in that role, but he had been with the Huskies previously, working primarily with wide receivers. Bill Wentworth, the incoming wide receivers coach, was the only rookie. Finally, Dick Baird was the recruiting coordinator, a position he had held since 1985.

The coaches were a close-knit group, a quality fostered by spending many, many hours together as a coaching staff. They became "family," as Baird described them. Don and Carol James made that happen. For example, the coaches, their spouses, and their children spent many Christmas holidays together as they prepared for a bowl game and spent much time together throughout the season and year. That "family" atmosphere transferred to the Husky football team.

The 1991 team had 14 returning starters—nine on defense and five on offense. Mark Brunell, 1990's starting quarterback, injured his knee in spring practice and appeared to be out for the season; he was replaced by

The 1991 Pac-10 Offensive Player of the Year and consensus All-American Mario Bailey.

sophomore Billy Joe Hobert. The leader of the defense was Steve Emtman, the conference Lineman of the Year in 1990 and a second-team All-America selection. The Huskies began the 1991 season in Palo Alto, where they overwhelmed Stanford 42–7.

Huskies Overpower the Cornhuskers

On September 21, 1991, a crowd of 76,304 assembled in Lincoln, Nebraska, to cheer mightily for the ninth-ranked Cornhuskers. Nebraska had reeled off 20-straight home wins against nonconference opponents. Through the first three quarters, it looked as if it would be 21 in a row. Nebraska took a 14–6 lead into halftime. Early in the third quarter, the Huskies' Beno Bryant fumbled a punt on his own 2-yard line; Nebraska's Mike Anderson recovered it. On first down, Derek Brown ran for the touchdown to put the Cornhuskers up 21–9. James was concerned. "We had adversity and then when we fumbled the punt and fell further behind that's the time when a team can hang it up and quit," he later said.

Then Hobert took over. With about five minutes left in the third quarter, the Huskies' quarterback engineered a 76-yard scoring drive. On one play, Hobert completed an apparent touchdown pass of 33 yards to Orlando McKay, but a holding penalty nullified the play and left the Huskies with third-and-27. Hobert admitted he was angered by the penalty but reflected, "There are two things about being a quarterback: you've got to keep your composure and you've got to show that you have the leadership to take the team to victory." On third-and-27 on the Nebraska 49, he ran for 19 yards. On fourth-and-8, he hit Orlando McKay for 15 yards and the all-important first down. Bryant went the rest of the way to close the gap to five: 21–16.

The Huskies owned the fourth quarter. Their defense did not give up a point and simply wore the Cornhuskers offensive line down. The one-back offense was working. The Huskies came with the pass, spreading the field, forcing Nebraska to expend a lot of energy on the pass rush. Then Washington came back with the run. Against one back and three receivers, Nebraska tried to get by with just one linebacker in the middle of the field. It did not work. Early in the fourth quarter, Washington took the lead. The

Mario Bailey was the Pac-10 Conference Offensive Player of the Year and a consensus All-American in 1991. He played a key role on the 1991 national championship team. His career receptions mark (141) is still fifth in Husky history. He ranks seventh in single-season receptions with 68.

Huskies went 69 yards in six plays and just more than two minutes. Three of the plays were passes—22 yards to tight end Aaron Pierce, 20 yards to fullback Matt Jones, and eight yards to McKay for the go-ahead touchdown. The two-point conversion failed, and the score was 22–21.

Nebraska started its next possession on their own 40. On second down, Jaime Fields rushed in from his linebacker position and forced quarterback Keith McCann to fumble. The Huskies recovered on the Nebraska 33. Six plays later, Hobert ran three yards for the score and Travis Hanson kicked the extra point for a 29–21 lead with seven and a half minutes to go. Less than two minutes later, Jay Barry cruised 81 yards up the right sideline for the knockout punch, and with Hanson's kick, the game was over, 36–21.

Week 3 brought undefeated Kansas State (3–0) to Husky Stadium. The Huskies thrashed the Wildcats 56–3, then followed with shutouts of Arizona (54–0) and Toledo (48–0). On October 19, third-ranked Washington traveled to Strawberry Canyon to face seventh-ranked California. Both teams were 5–0, and the winner would have the inside track to the conference title and a bid to the Rose Bowl.

Down to the Final Play

For the first time since the third quarter of the Nebraska game, the Huskies fell behind when Cal quarterback Mike Pawlawski hooked up with wide receiver Sean Dawkins for a 59-yard touchdown in the first quarter. The Huskies answered quickly, going 80 yards in five plays, featuring Jay Barry's 15- and 32-yard runs and ending with a 35-yard pass from Billy Jo Hobert to Mario Bailey. The teams traded field goals to again tie the score. The Huskies then went 56 yards in four plays. After a 24-yard pass to Beno Bryant, the Husky running back raced the final nine yards into the end zone in the final minute of the half to put the Huskies up 17–10.

Late in the third quarter, Cal evened the score when running back Lindsey Chapman sped 68 yards for a touchdown. Then on the third play of the fourth quarter, Bryant broke up the middle, where he was confronted by a Cal defender. Beno broke to his right, toward the sideline, and took off on a 65-yard scoring scamper. He never was touched. He later called it the biggest touchdown of his career. That it was at a time when he was not completely healthy made it even more remarkable.

With the Huskies ahead 24–17, the Bears battled to win the game right up to the final play of the contest. With five seconds to go, Cal was on the Washington 22. Pawlawski threw over the middle for Mike Caldwell, who was between two Husky defenders. The ball sailed just off his fingertips and time expired. The clock was then reset to five seconds after Washington was penalized for being offside. With one more chance, the Bears elected a pass to their best receiver, Brian Treggs. He ran a corner route to the left—but he was well defended by Walter Bailey and he never had a chance. The ball was batted away and bounced on the ground.

Hobert was on the sideline as Bailey denied the touchdown. "My heart was racing," Hobert said. "It was fun to watch. I'll bet ABC loved it."

Washington returned home for its next two games. They beat Oregon 29–7. Next was Arizona State. The Huskies scored the first 41 points on their way to a 44–16 win. On the road again, they had all they could handle from USC. But the Huskies won 14–3 and went on to thrash Oregon State 58–6, clinching the conference title. Washington closed out the season in Seattle with a 56–21 victory over the Washington State Cougars.

The Huskies finished the regular season having scored 461 points and given up only 101. They were the No. 2 team in the nation, behind only the University of Miami. The Hurricanes played in a Big East Conference that had only two teams win more than six games. By comparison, the Pac-10 had four teams win more than six games, and each was ranked in the top 25 in the final polls.

With a shot at the national title, Washington faced fourth-ranked Michigan in the 1992 Rose Bowl. The Wolverines had a star-studded lineup that included Heisman Trophy winner and wide receiver Desmond Howard; All-Big-10 quarterback Elvis Grbac, who led the nation in passing efficiency; and Butkus Award winner and linebacker Erick Anderson.

Coach James always gave his pregame speech 48 hours before game time, and it was always 30 minutes long. By doing so, he felt that the players had more time to "lock in" and focus on what they needed to do to win the upcoming game. None of his speeches were more important than the one he gave on December 30, 1991.

He first commented on the strength of Michigan's coaching staff and their offense and defense. He next reminded the Huskies of what Michigan had achieved and what was on the line in the Rose Bowl. He repeated the five ingredients of being a good team player.

1. 100 percent physical preparation and performance
2. Courage—11 tough football players on the football team at all times
3. Mental preparation
4. Care—we all owe each other everything
5. Loyalty—keep the great team unity

He then told them to get their game faces on: "Get it on as soon as possible. This is the time we cannot be bothered by others. Our total focus is our preparation for Michigan. We stop the levity. The entertainment is over. We will soon be the entertainers. We will be the performers in the biggest game of all of our lives. I mean every man in here. We have to be mentally prepared and not make dumb mistakes... Now is the time to set a personal record. A PR will get us the greatest prize in all of college football. You will be marked forever in the eyes of the football fans in the state of Washington. You will cherish this honor for a lifetime."

A National Championship

Nestled in the foothills of Pasadena in the Arroyo Seco Park, on a somewhat dewy field warming in the bright sun, television announcers Keith Jackson and Bob Griese

Steve Emtman was the most decorated football player in Husky history.

welcomed millions of viewers on ABC while 103,566 fans inside the bowl readied for the kickoff.

Michigan kicked off, with freshman Napoleon Kaufman and junior Jay Barry set to return. Kaufman, showing speed that the Wolverines had not encountered in the Big Ten, raced up a lane in the middle of the field where he was tripped up by Michigan's last defender at midfield. Hobert came out throwing. He found Bryant over the middle beneath the defensive linebackers for four yards. Bryant rushed over the right side to the Michigan 41. On third down, Bryant tried the right side again but was stuffed for no gain. Despite the quick start and great field position, Washington was stalled.

Punter John Werdel sent the ball 47 yards and into the end zone. Michigan lined up on its own 20. Ricky Powers found a hole on the left side and went for seven yards. Powers tried the left side again and was greeted by linebacker Dave "Hammer" Hoffmann. On third down, Andy Mason pressured Grbac, and the quarterback threw high and out of bounds. The Michigan punt was short and out of bounds on the Husky 25. Even though the game was scoreless, the Huskies were winning the battle in the trenches.

On the next series, the Huskies ended up punting to the Michigan 22, where Howard caught the ball and ran it back to the 37. On the next play, Grbac threw a long pass toward Howard that was intercepted by Walter Bailey on the Husky 8. After an exchange of punts, Washington started on their own 46. Pierce set up underneath the coverage and Hobert zipped the ball to him for a gain of eight. An illegal procedure penalty set the Huskies back to their own 49. Hobert then looked deep and threw short to Pierce up the right sideline for a first down on the Wolverines 40. Two Husky passes intended for Orlando McKay were broken up and the Huskies faced third-and-10. Then a breakthrough: Mario Bailey went deep and made a leaping catch at the 6-yard line.

Hobert started the second stanza with a two-yard touchdown run. The snap was mishandled on the ensuing conversion and kicker Travis Hanson had to hesitate. He lifted the ball high with a pooch kick, and the ball barely went over the crossbar to put Washington up 7–0.

Howard quickly helped erase the deficit. After Washington was penalized for interfering with a fair catch on a very short kickoff, Michigan set up on the Husky 44. Four plays later, the Wolverines knotted the score. The big play was a 34-yard pass to Howard on the Washington 9. Howard made a great catch in traffic on an up-and-out route. Hall had good coverage, but Howard leaped higher for the underthrown ball. After Michigan gained three, Tommie Smith came thundering in from his strong safety position, completely took out the blocker, and threw Powers for a loss at the nine. Michigan took a timeout to set up an excellent scoring play. Yale Van Dyne came into the game to set up as the tailback in the Wolverines backfield. He went in motion right to left. Grbac finally had great protection as he looked first to the right to Howard and then threw to the wide-open Walter Smith coming on a slant from the left into the middle. The conversion was good.

Jay Barry returned the kickoff to the Washington 40. Mark Brunell came into the game for the first time to take over the quarterbacking duties. He took the Huskies 60 yards in 13 plays, a drive that featured a 26-yard pass to Pierce and a 14-yard throw to Barry for an apparent touchdown. It was nullified by offensive holding. Brunell then hit Bryant and McKay to get to the Michigan 5. On fourth-and-2, Hanson kicked a 24-yard field goal to put the Huskies up by three with less than seven minutes to play in the half. Another Hanson field goal put the Huskies up 13–7 at halftime.

Michigan received the kickoff to open the second half and went four-and-out. After an exchange of punts, Michigan took over at its own 8-yard line. A pass in the flat to Tyrone Wheatley, Michigan's fastest running back, netted 18 yards. Wheatley picked up 19 more on a sweep around the right side. On fourth-and-10, Michigan tried a fake punt. The Huskies stuffed the play for a five-yard loss, but Washington was guilty of defensive holding. On the next play, Michigan was assessed a delay-of-game infraction and punted into the end zone.

On the next possession, the Huskies began their run for the roses. From their own 20, Bryant picked up six, then two more. After a fake sweep, Hobert found Pierce over the middle to the Washington 49 and a first down. Hobert then fired a quick pass to Curtis Gaspard down to the Michigan 36, followed by another first down on the 26. On third-and-3, Hobert rolled right and ran to just behind the line of scrimmage and then fired a rope to Bailey on the 3. Bryant got slammed to the ground by Anderson for a loss of two.

Then true freshman tight end Mark Bruener set up on the left side. Hobert ran right. Bruener broke to the left and then turned back to the right, behind the Michigan defender. Billy Joe threw back across the grain to Bruener, tiptoeing along the end line. Touchdown. Pierce caught a pass for two more points, and the score was 21–7 Huskies.

Michigan began to unravel. With an unsportsmanlike-conduct penalty after the successful two points, the Huskies kicked off from the 50 rather than their 40. Wheatley could only get back to the 5. On second-and-8, Emtman drove right through the center and forced Grbac back to the 1. Facing a fierce rush, he had to throw high and out of bounds.

Michigan punted to Bryant on the 43, and he tried to run back away from the coverage and was tackled on the Michigan 48. On third-and-5, Bailey sprinted for about six yards, turned to catch the pass, and raced to the Michigan 32. On fourth-and-1, Hobert dove over the right side to the 20 and another first down. On third-and-4, the Husky quarterback found Pierce coming right to left in the back of the end zone. Hanson missed the conversion, but the Huskies lead 27–7.

After the kickoff, Michigan began on the 29. On third-and-1, Grbac ran out of the pocket and was absolutely leveled by Jaime Fields. He fumbled but was able to recover the ball. On fourth-and-1, Grbac tried again for the first down. Emtman stuffed him and the Huskies took over on the Wolverines 38.

On the ensuing play, Brunell found Bailey for a diving catch into the end zone. Bailey quickly got to his feet and struck the Heisman Trophy pose, perhaps to show Desmond Howard that he was a very good receiver as well. In this game, Bailey caught six passes for 126 yards and Howard had one catch for 35 yards. (In the regular season, Bailey had 62 catches for 1,037 yards and 17 touchdowns and Heisman winner Howard caught 62 for 985 yards and

Quarterback Billy Joe Hobert was a co-MVP, with Steve Emtman, of the 1992 Rose Bowl.

19 TDs). With 13:12 to go in the game, the Huskies had put the game out of reach. Michigan scored one more time and the game ended 34–14. Washington had racked up 404 total yards to Michigan's 205 and had dominated every other phase of the game.

Both Hobert and Emtman were named Most Valuable Players of the game. Grbac remarked, "Give them credit. I don't think Miami could ever handle them. They're the best in the nation by far. We played Notre Dame and Florida State and this team is ten times better." Howard concurred, "Washington is a great team. They should be national champions."

A few hours later, Miami beat Nebraska 22–0 in the Orange Bowl, leaving Miami and Washington each with a 12–0 record. The Huskies had entered the Rose Bowl

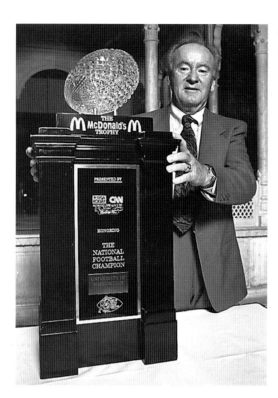

National champions.

ranked number two behind the Hurricanes, who had a 37–23 edge in first-place AP votes and a narrow 31–28 margin in the Coaches Poll votes. After the spectacular Rose Bowl win, Coach James quipped to the media, "I know who I'm voting for."

In the wee hours of January 2, Coach James fell into an uneasy sleep. He had already been informed that the Associated Press had chosen Miami as national champion in a very close vote. At 6:30 AM (9:30 on the East Coast) James told his wife, Carol, "We haven't won it. Nobody's got the nerve to call and give us the news." Finally, a call came from Bob Roller, a representative from the advertising agency managing the Coaches Poll trophy. He said that the Huskies were number one in the Coaches Poll. Carol immediately started calling family and friends. Don called Mike Lude and Don Heinrich, the Husky All-American quarterback some 40 years prior who was dying of cancer. By 8:00 AM, most of the players knew. In the meeting room at the Marriott in Pasadena, James met with reporters and coaches. The normally stoic coach wept.

"Tears," James said, as if disbelieving it himself. "It's so difficult to express the feeling I have for these kids. I don't

If Washington was the best team in the country, **Steve Emtman** was the best defensive player in the country. He grew up on a farm in Cheney, Washington. As a recruit, Washington State told him that Washington had too much depth at his position and that he would never get much playing time there. Emtman was insulted and elected to go to the Husky program, where he proved WSU scouts dead wrong. Emtman's emergence as the nation's best defender was aided by his dedication and hard work and the coaches' decision to retool the Husky defense after a disappointing 6–5 season in 1988.

Emtman played sparingly as a redshirt freshman in 1989 but became the focal point on Washington's new "attack-style" pressure defense as a sophomore. He had 55 tackles in 1990 and helped the Huskies lead the nation in rushing defense, allowing only 1.9 yards per rush. In Emtman's junior year, his last at Washington, he drew plenty of national attention. He was a unanimous All-America selection, finished fourth in the Heisman Trophy balloting (the highest ranking in Husky history), and won the Lombardi and Outland Trophies, presented to the nation's top lineman. He was also the Pac-10 Defensive Player of the Year in 1991. He anchored Washington's All-Star-laden defense that allowed only 67.1 rushing yards per game and 9.6 points per game.

Emtman was selected as the No. 1 choice in the 1992 NFL Draft by the Indianapolis Colts and went on to play with the Miami Dolphins and the Washington Redskins. Unfortunately, his professional career was marred with injuries, though his exceptional determination enabled him to play through lots of pain. His playing career ended after the 1997 season at the age of 27.

Emtman was the co-MVP in the 1992 Rose Bowl and was inducted into the Rose Bowl Hall of Fame in 2006. He was inducted into the Husky Hall of Fame in 1999 and into the College Football Hall of Fame in 2007.

mind sharing it [the championship]. For them not to get a piece of this...I don't know what more our guys could have done."

The Huskies were also picked first by the UPI / National Football Foundation, Football Writers, and *Sports Illustrated* polls. Only the AP gave the Hurricanes the top spot.

Certainly, the other Pac-10 Conference head coaches felt the Huskies deserved to be the national champion.

Dick Tomey, Arizona: "Their defense is dominant. Steve Emtman has to be the most dominant lineman in the country. Nobody blocks him and the folks around him are great football players. Washington is as good a team as the Pac-10 has ever had."

Rich Brooks, Oregon: "I said it before the game that Washington is the best team I've seen in this league, ever, and I still stand by that. I thought we made them work for it [in the 1991 regular-season matchup]. The main problem was that we couldn't move the football against them."

Bruce Snyder, California: "Against that good of a football team, a team that motivated and that skilled, you need to play a perfect game."

Larry Smith, USC: "There is no question in my mind that Washington is the best team in the country. They've got a balanced offense, a fantastic defense, and they're strong in the kicking game. In my years of experience, I haven't seen a better overall team."

A Night to Remember

Many fans were looking forward to the 1992 season with hopes of another conference and national championship season. They became even more hopeful after the Huskies won their first eight games, including an early season home win over Nebraska. Coach Gilbertson had resigned after the 1991 season to take the head-coaching position at California, but otherwise the coaching staff remained intact. The Huskies returned 12 starters—six each on offense and defense.

Ranked No. 2 in the nation, the Huskies faced ninth-ranked Nebraska in a rare night game on September 19, 1992. Nebraska clearly was looking for revenge for the loss they suffered at home in the 1991 season. Nationally televised on ESPN, the game promised to be a bruiser.

Running back Napoleon Kaufman shows off his speed.

Late in the first quarter, a Husky punt pinned Nebraska on its own 3-yard line. Crowd noise caused the Cornhuskers linemen to jump offside on consecutive plays; players simply could not hear their quarterback's signals. And with each offside call, the crowd grew louder. As Nebraska quarterback Mike Grant dropped back to pass in his own end zone, everyone in the stands watched with glee as strong safety Tommie Smith raced in untouched to hit Grant on his blind side, dropping him for a safety. The deafening roar reverberating off the twin roofs literally had the stadium rocking. An ESPN sideline reporter, armed with a noise meter, reported that the clamor had reached 130 decibels—equivalent to sound vibrations 30 meters away from a four-engine jet aircraft readying for takeoff.

Holding a 9–7 lead, the Husky offense went into quick-strike mode near the end of the first half. Kaufman ended an 80-yard drive with a one-yard touchdown run. After the kickoff, Walter Bailey intercepted Grant's pass and the Huskies went for the kill. Quarterback Billy Joe Hobert threw a 24-yard scoring pass to a diving Joe Kralik, increasing the lead to 23–7 after the point after. Travis Hanson booted a pair of field goals in the second half as the Huskies posted a 29–14 win and jumped to No. 1 in the polls the following week.

The Huskies remained top-ranked for all but one of the next five weeks. They won most of their games by a wide margin, including a 41–7 victory over 15th-ranked Stanford.

The Husky Program Unravels

After beating Stanford on Halloween, the Huskies had regained their No. 1 ranking. Next up was 12th-ranked Arizona in the Grand Canyon State. Two days before the game, the *Seattle Times* broke the headline: HUSKIES' HOBERT GOT $50,000 LOAN. Hobert actually received three loans totaling $50,000 from Charles Rice, a wealthy Idaho scientist. The article reported that Hobert went on a spending spree that included a car, golf clubs, and wild weekends with his friends. The money was exhausted within a few months. Fans began to speculate on the potential penalties for Washington. Hobert was suspended by Washington's athletic director, Barbara Hedges, and extensive internal and external investigations soon began. Hedges' decision ended Hobert's Husky career.

In Tucson, the Huskies faced the fourth-ranked defense in the nation. The Wildcats did not lose any ground in the polls after beating Washington 16–3. The Huskies did not play like the No. 1 team in the country. They lost three fumbles and threw one interception and rushed for only 90 yards in the 16–3 defeat.

The next week, having fallen to six in the rankings, the Huskies beat Oregon State 45–16. They ended the season losing to Washington State 42–23 in the snow and icy turf of Martin Stadium. Cougars quarterback Drew Bledsoe seemed to have no problem with the conditions; he had a brilliant passing performance.

1993 Rose Bowl

The ninth-ranked Huskies attempted to make history by winning their third-straight Rose Bowl.

The Wolverines grabbed an early lead in the game on a 41-yard field goal. Washington answered with a one-yard run by fullback Darius Turner at the end of an 80-yard drive to go ahead 7–3. The seesaw first half continued, with Michigan taking a 17–7 lead before the Huskies pulled within three on a 64-yard touchdown pass from Brunell to freshman Jason Shelley. Brunell's pinpoint passing continued on Washington's next possession, when he again connected with Mark Bruener, this time in the corner of the end zone to put the Huskies ahead 21–17 at halftime.

On the first play of the second half, Tyrone Wheatley busted up the middle, broke free, and raced 88 yards for the score—Michigan 24–21. Napoleon Kaufman returned the kickoff 47 yards to the Wolverines 46. Seven plays later, Kaufman dove over the top to regain the lead, 28–24. On the Huskies' next possession, Travis Hanson kicked a 44-yard field goal to increase the score to 31–24.

With less than two minutes left in the third quarter, Michigan recovered a Kaufman fumble that led to a

Lincoln Kennedy received many honors for his outstanding performance as an offensive tackle from 1989 to 1992. In 1991 and 1992, he received the Morris Trophy as the Pac-10 Conference Lineman of the Year and is the only Husky to receive the award twice. He was a unanimous All-America selection in 1992 and was inducted into the Husky Hall of Fame in 2004. A first-round pick of the Atlanta Falcons in the 1993 NFL Draft, he enjoyed an 11-year career in the NFL before retiring after the 2003 season.

Lincoln Kennedy had a successful career with the Huskies before going on to the NFL.

Michigan touchdown to tie the score. Then, with more than five minutes left in the game, Michigan quarterback Elvis Grbac threw 15 yards to tight end Tony McGee for a touchdown. Michigan held on to the lead and won 38–31. The loss spoiled a fine performance by Brunell. He completed 18-of-30 passes for 308 yards and two touchdowns.

Over the three-year period, from 1990 to 1992, the Huskies won 31 games and lost five. It was the finest three years in Husky football (in an era when the team played a full schedule against major college teams). Those three teams boasted an array of great players who won awards in their college careers and went on to excel professionally.

On August 11, 1993, after many months of investigations into the Hobert affair, the Pac-10 Compliance and Enforcement Committee voted to ban the Husky football team from going to a bowl game for one year, to ban television revenue for two years, to cut 20 football scholarships—10 in each of the next two seasons—and to reduce the number of recruiting visits coaches could make. The committee later decided to reduce the ban on TV revenue to one year and increase the ban on bowl games to two years.

On August 22, James resigned, citing several reasons. He strongly believed that the sanctions the Pac-10 Conference placed on Washington were not appropriate for the cited violations. He also believed that the university administration had betrayed him in their discussions with the committee.

James later told this author that his main reason for leaving was to keep the Husky coaching staff in place. "Well before the 1993 season had started and before the penalties were finalized, I thought about coaching for several more seasons. If I coached a few more seasons and then resigned, my whole coaching staff would have been replaced by a new head coach from a different program and he would bring in a whole set of new assistant coaches. If I resigned before the 1993 season started, I knew my existing coaching staff would stay in place. I told [athletic director] Barbara Hedges that Lambright should be immediately appointed head coach and that the other coaches should remain as well."

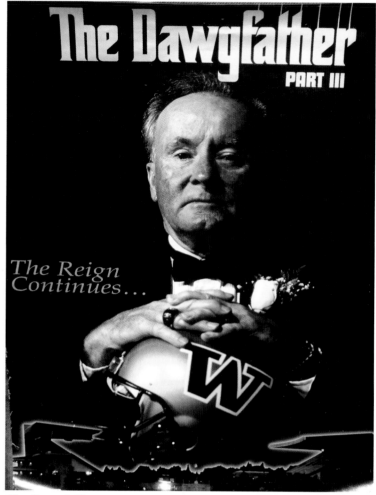

The Dawgfather.

After 18 years at Washington, James ended his career with a record of 153 wins, 57 losses, and two ties, a .726 winning percentage. When *Sports Illustrated* once named the top three then-current coaches in collegiate football, their list was: Don James, Don James, and Don James. In the August 20, 2012, issue of *Sports Illustrated*, Nick Saban, the highly successful Alabama coach and James' former player and graduate assistant at Kent State, credits James with the criteria for evaluating recruits. The article also reports that Saban implemented another piece of James' philosophy—an academic support system for the players. Saban said, "He [James] really was into the personnel, motivational, [and] and moral development. There was

James Gang Standouts

Player, Position	Years Played at Washington	Major Honors Received	Professional Career
Mario Bailey, WR	1989–91	Pac-10 Conference Offensive Player of the Year (1991), Consensus All-American (1991)	Houston (1992–94)
Mark Bruener, TE	1991–94	All-Pac-10 (1993, 1994)	Pittsburgh (1995–2003) Houston (2004–08)
Mark Brunell, QB	1990–93	1991 Rose Bowl MVP	Green Bay (1993–94), Jacksonville (1995–2003), Washington (2004–07), New Orleans (2008–09), and New York Jets (2010–11); member of the Super Bowl XLIV–champion New Orleans Saints
Beno Bryant, RB	1989–92	All-Pac-10 (1990)	Seattle (1994)
Ed Cunningham, C	1988–91	All-Pac-10 (1991)	Phoenix/Arizona (1992–95), Seattle (1996)
Steve Emtman, DT	1989–91	All-Pac-10 (1990–91), Pac-10 Conference Defensive Player of the Year (1991), unanimous All-American (1991), Lombardi and Outland Trophies for Best Lineman in America (1991), 1992 Rose Bowl MVP, Heisman Trophy voting (4th, 1991), No. 1 selection in the NFL 1992 Draft, Husky Hall of Fame (1999), Rose Bowl Hall of Fame (2006), College Football Hall of Fame (2007)	Indianapolis (1992–94), Miami (1995–96), Washington (1997)
Chico Fraley, LB	1988–91	All-Pac-10 (1991)	
Dana Hall, CB	1988–91	All-Pac-10 (1991)	San Francisco (1992–94), Cleveland (1995), Jacksonville (1996–97)
Billy Joe Hobert, QB	1990–92	1992 Rose Bowl MVP	Los Angeles/Oakland (1993–96), Buffalo (1997), New Orleans (1997–2000), Indianapolis (2001)
Dave Hoffmann, LB	1989–92	All-Pac-10 (1991–92), Conference Defensive Player of the Year (1992), All-American (1991–92), Husky Hall of Fame (2012)	Pittsburgh (1993)
Donald Jones, LB	1988–91	All-Pac-10 (1990–91)	New York Jets (1992–93), Indianapolis (1994)
Napoleon Kaufman, RB	1991–94	All-Pac-10 (1992–94), Husky Hall of Fame (2004)	Oakland (1995–2000)
Lincoln Kennedy, OG	1989–92	All-Pac-10 (1992), unanimous All-American (1992), Husky Hall of Fame (2004)	Atlanta (1993–95), Oakland (1996–2003)
Dean Kirkland, OG	1988–90	All-Pac-10 (1990)	Buffalo (1991)
Greg Lewis, RB	1987–90	Pac-10 Conference Offensive Player of the Year (1990), All-American (1990), Doak Walker Award for the nation's best running back (1990), Husky Hall of Fame (2006)	Denver (1991–92)
Charles Mincy, CB	1989–90	All-Pac-10 (1990)	Kansas City (1991–94), Minnesota (1995), Tampa Bay (1996–98), Oakland (1999–2000)
Jeff Pahukoa, OT	1989–92	All-Pac-10 (1990)	Los Angeles Rams (1991–93), Atlanta (1995–96)
Travis Richardson, DE	1987–90	All-Pac-10 (1990)	

a belief there that who you are mattered in terms of how successful you were going to be or how you played."

James ended his career with an extensive list of honors and the admiration of his Kent State and Washington coaching staffs, coaches throughout the nation, his players, and a legion of fans. Here are the major accomplishments he achieved at Washington:

- National champions in 1991
- Pacific Coast Conference Coach of the Year (1977, 1980, 1990, 1991)
- National Coach or Co–Coach of the Year (by several associations and publications, 1977, 1981, 1982, 1984, 1991)
- President of the American Football Coaches Association (1990)
- Most wins in Husky history (153)
- Most wins in the Pacific Coast Conference (98), tied with UCLA's Terry Donahue
- Winner of six Pacific Coast Conference championships
- Appeared in 14 bowl games, winning 10
- Appeared in six Rose Bowls, winning four
- In 1991, received the Paul "Bear" Bryant Coach of the Year Award, the Eddie Robinson Coach of the Year Award, and the George Munger Coach of the Year Award
- Retired with the 10th-best winning percentage of all active coaches, eighth-most victories, the third-best bowl winning percentage, and the 12th-most bowl appearances
- Inducted into the University of Miami Athletic Hall of Fame in 1992, the Husky Hall of Fame in 1994, the Rose Bowl Hall of Fame in 1994, and the College Football Hall of Fame in 1997

The Lambright Era

Jim Lambright grew up in Everett and played football for Everett High School. He entered the University of Washington in 1960 and played defensive end for Jim Owens' teams in the early 1960s. He played in the 1964 Rose Bowl and earned All-Coast and All-Conference honors in the 1964 season. He started his coaching career as an assistant coach at Fife High School, followed by a coaching position at Shoreline Community College. In 1969, he joined Jim Owens' coaching staff.

He joined Coach James' staff in 1975. Eventually, Lambright became the Huskies' defensive coordinator and designed the "Purple Reign" defensive schemes that enabled Washington defensive teams in the late 1980s and early 1990s to hold opponents to very low scores. He was a Husky through and through. Dave Mahler, a sports talk host who has covered the Huskies since 1994, said, "If you opened up Lambright, purple blood would spill out."

In Lambright's six seasons as Husky head coach, his record was 44–25–1 (.664) and his teams appeared in four bowl games. His 1995 team tied for first with USC for the conference title, and his 1996 team finished second.

Tribute to Don James

The 1993 season opener was against Stanford. Earlier in the week, Cardinal coach Bill Walsh had called the Huskies a bunch of "mercenaries" and questioned the Husky football program's graduation rates. Before the game, Coach Lambright walked across the field to introduce himself to Walsh. "There is a way to marshal emotion and a way to use what you're given—and we were given a lot by Don James' retirement, by the Pac-10 penalties, and by Bill Walsh," Lambright said. "But there is also a way to retain control of what you do, and to win with class."

The Huskies beat Stanford 31–14. The game was impressive in many ways. Before the game, the team paid a tribute to Coach James. Lambright said it was the team captains who formulated it. "I sat down with them and asked what would be appropriate. They said, 'Coach, how about walking four abreast coming down the tunnel, holding hands?' I said great. They said, 'How about taking a knee and pointing to the press box [where Don and Carol James would be sitting]?' To me it seemed appropriate for what Don had done," Lambright said. James later said it was one of the most emotional moments of his life. The players' tribute caught James and his wife by complete surprise.

The Huskies' defense was a major factor in the victory. Stanford's quarterback Steve Stenstrom was sacked six times. After leading 10–7 at the intermission, Washington scored 14 in the third quarter and seven more in the fourth. Mark Bruener proved that grace and speed can come in big packages. He caught five passes for 101 yards and two touchdowns, including a 66-yarder from quarterback Damon Huard. Napoleon Kaufman rushed for 195 yards on 24 carries. The Lambright era was off to a good start.

The Huskies went 7–4–0 for the season with losses to Ohio State in Columbus, to UCLA and Arizona State away, and a late-season loss to USC at home 22–17.

Whammy in Miami

After losing 24–17 to USC in the 1994 season opener in Los Angeles, 16th-ranked Ohio State came to town with its outstanding running back Eddie George. The Huskies scored three touchdowns in the first 10 minutes, before a nationally televised audience, on its way to a 25–16 victory. Kaufman rushed 32 times for 211 yards.

The Huskies had a bye week to prepare to meet the fifth-ranked Miami Hurricanes in Miami on September 24, 1994. They were certainly a formidable foe. They had won a record 58 straight at home and were led by sophomore linebacker Ray Lewis and All-American defensive tackle Warren Sapp. Before the game, Miami coach Dennis Erickson jokingly suggested the losers of the game relinquish their national championship rings from 1991, when both teams went undefeated and split the AP and Coaches Poll decisions.

Ahead 14–3 at halftime, Miami appeared to be on their way to another victory. Then, in a span of about four minutes at the start of the third quarter, the Huskies scored 22 points. There were three plays that put the Huskies

Coach Jim Lambright.

Quarterback Damon Huard looks downfield for a receiver.

ahead 25–14. First, Husky fullback Richard Thomas caught a short outlet pass from Damon Huard, cut inside, and ran 75 yards untouched to the end zone. Huard hit flanker Dave Janoski in the back of the end zone for two more points. Then cornerback Russell Hairston intercepted a Hurricanes pass and returned it 34 yards for another touchdown. Finally, Husky strong safety Tony Parrish hit Jammi German on the kickoff return, forcing a fumble. Jerry Jensen recovered at the Miami 23 to set up another touchdown. Napoleon Kaufman also gained 80 yards in the game, breaking Joe Steele's career rushing record by three yards—3,094 in total.

After the Huskies won 38–20, Lawyer Milloy walked off the field shouting, "Take the rings back."

It was a crucial game for everyone, including the Husky coach. "No game has meant more to me," Lambright said afterward.

Senior wide receiver Eric Bjornson said, "We won at Nebraska in 1991 because we were a great team. We won here because we had to. There had been so much going against us. We'd lost a coach, we'd lost our chance to be in a bowl game, and we lost many of our players who had transferred. This is just unbelievable. It feels as if we've gotten a lot back."

It was an energizing win for the Huskies, who went on to finish the season 7–4 for the second time in two years.

A Conference Tie and Back in a Bowl

The Huskies ended the 1995 regular season playing for the Apple Cup and the Pac-10 Conference title. USC was 6–0–1 in conference play. The only blemish on its record was a 7–7 tie with Washington in Husky Stadium in late October. The Huskies were 5–1–1 and Oregon was 5–2–0. For the Huskies, the game went down to the wire. When it was over, Damon Huard had set a Washington career record for passing and total offense. The Cougars' quarterback, redshirt freshman Ryan Leaf, received wide acclaim for his outstanding performance. Leaf completed 22-of-33 passes for 291 yards and rushed for two touchdowns.

But the day belonged to Damon Huard and his Husky teammates. Huard threw for 276 yards, breaking Sonny Sixkiller's 23-year-old record. Sophomore running back

In 1995, yell leader **Barry Erickson** started to perform in various costumes. At one game, the Husky Band was doing a halftime musical tribute to the Superman movie. Erickson said to Band Director Bill Bissell, "Hey, you can't do the routine without Superman, and it can't be Superman, it's got to be super Husky man." After Erickson graduated, his friends challenged him to change into a costume and lead spell-outs in the third quarter. And with that, Captain Husky was born. From then until the last game of the 2011 football season, Erickson wore a superhero cape over his big "W" sweater and got the Husky crowd to spell out H-U-S-K-I-E-S. It was always entertaining and inspirational.

Rashaan Shehee scored three touchdowns on 26 carries and 212 yards.

In a game like this, there were many big plays—but none bigger than a 42-yard pass reception by split end Dave Janoski. With the Huskies trailing 22–15 in the fourth quarter, Huard needed to make something happen. After scrambling, he threw over the middle to Janoski, who was double covered. Both Cougars cornerback Brian Walker and Janoski reached skyward, but it was Janoski who wrested the ball away and fell to the ground in the end zone.

Late in the game, the Huskies had forged a 30–22 lead. When the Cougars scored a touchdown and a two-point conversion to tie the game, only 2:17 remained. Jerome Pathon returned the kickoff 30 yards, and the Huskies drove 42 yards in 75 seconds to set up the winning field goal. John Wales booted it through from 21 yards out, and with that the Huskies were cochampions of the Pac-10 Conference (thanks to UCLA's 24–20 defeat of USC). Based on the Trojans' overall record of 8–2–1 and Washington's 7–3–1 record, USC got the invitation to the Rose Bowl. Washington gladly accepted the bid to the Sun Bowl but lost 38–18 to Iowa.

In 1996, Brock Huard replaced his brother Damon as Husky quarterback. In the season opener at Arizona State, he entered the game with Washington down by 21 points.

A unanimous All-American in 1995, Lawyer Milloy was a dominant defender for the Huskies.

Lawyer Milloy had the reputation as a big hitter for the Huskies. He was also a solid hitter on Washington's baseball team, on which he earned three letters. Milloy's football career got off to a rough start in his freshman year (1992) when a broken foot forced him to redshirt the season. As a sophomore, he became the starting free safety and earned first-team All-Pac-10 honors, the only sophomore in the conference to be so honored. He led Washington with 106 tackles, placing him third among Pac-10 defenders.

Milloy had 115 tackles as a junior to again lead the Huskies in that category. He became the first Husky defensive back to lead in tackles in back-to-back years. A unanimous All-America selection in 1995, he was named the nation's Defensive Back of the Year by the Touchdown Club of Columbus and was one of the three finalists for the Jim Thorpe Award as the nation's top defensive back. He was named to the All-Pac-10 team for the second consecutive season.

After the 1995 season, Milloy declared himself eligible for the NFL Draft and was chosen by the New England Patriots in the second round. As a rookie, he started in the 1997 Super Bowl.

He was also drafted in the 19th round of the Major League Baseball Draft in 1995. He hit a home run in his first at-bat as a Husky freshman, and in his final Husky baseball game, he blasted two three-run homers to help defeat the Cougars. He was a member of the 1993 Husky baseball team that finished 16th nationally and reached the NCAA regional final. He played for 15 seasons in the NFL—New England (1996–2002), Buffalo (2003–05), Atlanta (2006–08), and Seattle (2009–10). He was elected to the Husky Hall of Fame in 2012.

In the huddle, center Olin Kreutz stated that Washington needed to get in the end zone by the seven-minute mark. Huard said, "You make your block and we'll be there in seven seconds." He then threw a 67-yard touchdown pass to Gerald Harris and rallied the team to a 42–42 tie. Late in the game, the Wildcats kicked a field goal for the victory. Arizona went on to finish the regular season 11–1 and take the conference title. (They lost 20–17 to second-ranked Ohio State in the Rose Bowl.)

In Washington's next-to-last game of the season, tailback Corey Dillon ran for 222 yards—all in the first quarter—as the Huskies raced to a 25–0 lead. Thanks to a screen pass in the quarter, he amassed a total of 305 all-purpose yards during just 15 minutes of play. Although Dillon was on pace to break Hugh McElhenny's single-game rushing record of 296 yards, Coach Lambright pulled Dillon out after the first stanza to avoid embarrassing San Jose State. Washington finished the season second in the conference with a 7–1 record and an overall 9–2 regular season. They lost to eighth-ranked Colorado in the Holiday Bowl.

"Hawaiian Punch-Out"

Washington won seven of its first eight games in 1997. The Huskies were ranked No. 2 in the nation as they faced off with No. 7 Nebraska in Week 3. They lost 27–14 to the Huskers. The game may be best remembered for the appearance of backup quarterback Marques Tuiasosopo, who came in for injured Brock Huard.

Down the stretch, with a 7–1 record, the Huskies lost their last three games—at home against Oregon, at UCLA, and at home against Washington State. Washington State won the conference title. The Huskies met Michigan State in the Aloha Bowl.

Hawaiian Punch-out. That headline started the *Seattle Post-Intelligencer* article covering the Huskies' 51–23 win over Coach Nick Saban's Spartans. The game was practically over before it began. On the first play from scrimmage, Spartans quarterback Todd Schultz fumbled, Chris Campbell recovered, and on the second Husky play, Rashaan Shehee ran 33 yards for a touchdown.

The Huskies never looked back. On defense, Washington stuffed Michigan State's running game, allowing only 47

In 1996 and 1997, the Huskies had two of the best offensive linemen in the nation. Center **Olin Kreutz** was a consensus All-American in 1997 and Morris Trophy winner as the best lineman in the conference. **Benji Olson** was a consensus All-American in 1996 and earned other All-America recognition in 1997. They were selected to the Pac-10 Conference teams in 1996 and 1997. Olson was inducted into the Husky Hall of Fame in 2010.

Olin Kreutz was a consensus All-American lineman in 1997.

Benji Olson was a consensus All-American in 1996.

rushing yards. The Huskies had 298 rushing yards and a total of 477. Shehee racked up 193 yards on 29 carries and was named the game's Most Valuable Player.

In 1998, the Huskies were unable to sustain their winning ways. They finished in fifth place in the conference with a 6–5 regular-season record and an invitation to the Oahu Bowl to play 16th-ranked Air Force. The Fighting Falcons bombed the Huskies 45–25.

Five days after the Oahu Bowl, Lambright was fired by AD Barbara Hedges. The 1998 season was the first time in 22 years that the Huskies failed to have a winning season. Lambright was reportedly surprised, shocked, and hurt by Hedges' decision. His 44 wins as a head coach ranked him sixth among the many coaches who had guided the Husky football program. With Lambright gone, the James-related era had finally come to an end.

CHAPTER 10

Demise, Resurrection, and Renovation

Shortly after firing Coach Jim Lambright, AD Barbara Hedges hired Colorado head coach Rick Neuheisel. Hedges felt she needed to make a quick decision because the recruiting season was in full swing. Neuheisel was almost 38 when he arrived in Seattle.

A walk-on at UCLA, he became the Bruins' starting quarterback in 1983, his senior season. UCLA had a dismal start with Neuheisel at the helm, and soon he was benched. He came back after his replacement, Steve Bono, was injured. He culminated the season with a win over USC that, combined with Washington State's upset of Washington, gave UCLA the Pac-10 title and sent the Bruins to the 1984 Rose Bowl. Neuheisel led UCLA to a smashing 45–9 victory over fourth-ranked Illinois in the Rose Bowl and was named the game's MVP. He was admitted to the Rose Bowl Hall of Fame in the class of 1998.

He graduated from UCLA in 1984 with a BA in political science. He received a JD from USC Law School in 1988, and during his time in law school, he was a graduate assistant coach at UCLA. From 1988 through the 1993 season, he was a full-time assistant coach for the Bruins, and then he moved to Colorado as an assistant coach under Bill McCartney. When McCartney retired after the 1994 season,

Neuheisel was named head coach at age 34. He coached the Buffaloes for four years.

When Neuheisel was hired at Washington, reports had his annual starting salary at $1,000,000, which at the time was reported to be one of the five highest in the country. While an astounding sum, there were many proponents who felt he was worth the price. He was bright, a great speaker, easy to like, very close to his players, and friendly with fans and major boosters.

An NCAA Record

Neuheisel was fortunate to begin as Husky coach in 1999, with junior quarterback Marques Tuiasosopo leading the way. On October 30, Washington beat Stanford 35–30, a victory that put Washington in the lead for the Rose Bowl race. The big story in this game was Tuiasosopo's running and passing performance. He led the offense with 207 rushing yards and 302 passing yards as the Huskies rolled up 670 total yards and controlled the clock for more than 36 minutes. Afterward, a check of the NCAA record books revealed that no player had ever put together a 200/300 game. In the week following, Tuiasosopo garnered numerous national honors and acclaim for his exploits. His

Rick Neuheisel's Washington tenure lasted only four seasons.

509 yards of total offense ranked as the fourth-highest single-game effort in Pac-10 history.

The Huskies finished the season 7–4 and second in the conference, missing the Rose Bowl bid.

Caning the 'Canes

On September 9, 2000, the 15th-ranked Huskies battled the fourth-ranked Hurricanes. Washington got off to a great start when Miami's Santana Moss fumbled a punt return and the Huskies recovered. Tailback Braxton Cleman quickly scored to give the Huskies an early lead. The Huskies took a huge 21–3 lead to halftime.

In less than four minutes in the third quarter, Miami scored 19 points to Washington's six, bringing the score to 27–22. The Huskies held off the surging Hurricanes and held on to win 34–39. Perhaps the most crucial score came in the second half. After a quick Miami score to open the second half, Washington scored on a 50-yard gallop by freshman Rich Alexis from Miami. Neuheisel had put him in the game "just so his parents in Florida knew he was doing okay." Just a few weeks earlier, Alexis was the fourth-string tailback and desperately homesick; he was even considering leaving school and returning to Florida.

After a 17–14 win over Colorado in Boulder, the sixth-ranked Huskies traveled to Eugene. The Ducks won 23–16. Fortunately, it was the only loss Washington suffered in the 2000 season.

Paralyzed for Life

On October 28, 2000, the Huskies beat Stanford 31–28—but there was no joy in the locker room following the comeback victory. Every coach and player was subdued because of a very serious injury to senior safety Curtis Williams. With just more than two minutes left in the game, Kerry Carter, Stanford's 235-pound running back, cut into the line and Williams came flying in. His head dipped just a little, and the two collided helmet-to-helmet. Williams bounced off backward, his body already rigid, and just lay there. Then his body started to shake and his eyes started to roll. For about 15 minutes, a medical team attended to Williams on the field. He responded only with his eyes. Teammate Anthony Kelly remembered that Curtis mouthed the words,

Curtis Williams in game action.

"I can't breathe." Williams was taken off on a stretcher, put into an ambulance, and taken to Stanford Medical Center, where doctors confirmed he was paralyzed from the neck down.

One of the wildest fourth quarters in Pac-10 history was rendered secondary to Williams' situation. With less than six minutes on the clock, the two teams combined to score four touchdowns. Down 24–6 after Husky tailback Willie Hurst scored the second of his two touchdowns at 5:57, Stanford came alive. After its first scoring drive of the period, the Cardinal recovered an onside kick and scored again to come within three points of the Washington lead. Stanford recovered another onside kick on the Washington 48 to set up the go-ahead touchdown with 53 seconds left—Stanford 28, Washington 24.

After the kickoff return, the Huskies started on their own 20, where Marques Tuiasosopo went to work. He threw a 27-yard strike on a deep post route to flanker Todd Elstrom—41 seconds to go. Next, Tuiasosopo drilled a pass to split end Wilbur Hooks down to the Cardinal 22—27 seconds left. On the third play of the drive, the Husky quarterback was flushed out of the pocket toward the sideline, where he bought some time. Freshman Justin Robbins was running a streak pattern down the left side. As he saw his QB running right, he drifted across the end zone, left to right, and separated himself from a Stanford defender. Tuiasosopo rifled the ball to the back of the end zone, and Robbins went up, briefly juggled the ball, and then held on for the winning touchdown with 17 seconds left.

Drew Brees Outplayed by Tui

In one of the many press conferences prior to the 2001 Rose Bowl, Coach Neuheisel observed that the team that keeps its offense on the field will win the game. Fourth-ranked Washington did just that and beat 14th-ranked Purdue 34–24.

Washington scored on its first two drives. Then Purdue quarterback Drew Brees directed the Boilermakers on a 90-yard scoring drive. A Purdue field goal near the end of the half made the score 14–10. Both teams scored quickly in the third quarter. Washington garnered a field goal and Purdue scored a touchdown to deadlock the score at 17–17.

Washington's John Anderson responded with another field goal from 42 yards out to give the Huskies a three-point lead.

Late in the third quarter, Husky fans became very concerned when they saw Tuiasosopo jogging with a trainer toward the tunnel leading to the locker room. The player was in pain after being slammed to the ground by Purdue's pass rushers. Backup quarterback Cody Pickett came in on the Huskies' next possession and filled in for

Marques Tuiasosopo did not win the Heisman Trophy. He did not make a single All-America team. But to observers of Husky football from 1997 to 2000, he certainly proved himself one of the great quarterbacks in the university's history. He was the heart and soul of Washington's offense during his senior year. In 2000, he guided the Huskies to an 11–1 record, a Rose Bowl win over Purdue, and a third-place ranking in the postseason polls—only Washington's fourth postseason top-five ranking.

Tuiasosopo differentiated himself from the great Husky quarterbacks by the number of things he could do so well. He was an efficient passer, an outstanding runner, a great field general, and an unsurpassed competitor. Tagged as a running quarterback, Tuiasosopo passed for 5,879 yards in his career—still the sixth-highest total in Husky history. He set 12 offensive records during his career at Washington and graduated as the all-time leader in total offense with 7,374 yards—more than 1,000 yards more than the next-closest player. His ability to scramble and orchestrate the offense put great pressure on all defenses he faced. His cool under pressure was invaluable.

He was named the Pac-10 Offensive Player of the Year in 2000 and the 2001 Rose Bowl MVP. He was also recognized as the best player on the West Coast when he was presented the 2000 Pop Warner Award. He finished eighth in the Heisman Trophy balloting that season.

Marques Tuiasosopo shows off his speed and agility in the 2001 Rose Bowl.

three plays. By the start of the fourth quarter, Tuiasosopo was back. A few minutes later, Washington scored to go up 27–17. The Boilermakers then scored to draw within three, but it wouldn't be enough. The Huskies put together a 66-yard drive to put the game away for good, 34–24.

Curtis Williams, the Husky player paralyzed weeks earlier, was driven by ambulance from San Jose to the Rose Bowl to watch the game. When he arrived, he asked to go to the locker room to see his teammates, who were en route from their hotel. Once in the locker room, he was moved into a wheelchair and was fitted with his Rose Bowl jersey, No. 25. Trainers and managers arrived first, the players next. None of them had any idea that Williams was waiting for them. Offensive lineman Matt Rogers later said, "It was emotional, it was tough in some ways seeing him but I said to myself, 'It's going to be bad for Purdue.' Seeing Curtis like that can get to your heart. It was a tremendous inspiration for us."

After the game, the Washington players ran to midfield, looked up to the press box from where Williams had been watching the game, raised their helmets, and chanted "C-Dub." It was an emotional moment for the team, who rallied behind their fallen player. Sadly, less than a year and a half later, Williams died from complications relating to his paralysis. The tragic loss rocked the Husky team and community.

Pickett Arrives

In 2001, Cody Pickett began to shatter Husky passing records with the help of wide receiver Reggie Williams. He ended his Husky career with 10,220 yards passing, the fourth-highest in Pac-10 history. Williams, meanwhile, finished with 3,598 receiving yards, also the best in Husky history.

However, their heroics were not enough to win the Pac-10 Conference title. In the final game of the regular season, the Huskies traveled to No. 1 Miami. The game was originally scheduled in September but had been shifted to the last game of the season because of delays after the September 11 tragedy. Whether the delay impacted the outcome is hard to know, but the 'Canes, led by junior quarterback Ken Dorsey, annihilated Washington 65–7. It

was the second-biggest margin of defeat in Husky history. (Only the 72–3 loss to California in 1921 was higher.) The Huskies finished tied for second and went to the 2001 Holiday Bowl to face ninth-ranked Texas. The Longhorns won in a shootout, 47–43.

Triple Overtime

On November 23, 2002, the Huskies faced No. 3 Washington State in Martin Stadium. The 9–1–0 Cougars, led by quarterback Jason Gesser, were clearly on a run for the roses. With 9:44 to go in the fourth quarter, the Cougars led 17–10. Gesser set off on a run to keep the drive alive and protect the lead. Washington defensive tackle Terry Johnson chased Gesser and grabbed him by the front of the jersey and jerked him. The Cougars star spread his legs, tried to keep his balance, but torqued his right leg and had to leave the contest. Matt Gegel replaced him. He led the Cougars into field-goal range, and the successful kick put Washington State ahead 20–10 with 4:14 left. On the Huskies' next possession, quarterback Cody Pickett hit wide receiver Reggie Williams with a 48-yard pass. It set up Pickett's seven-yard throw to another wide receiver, Paul Arnold, to pull within three with just a little more than three minutes left. About 30 seconds later, 5'9" freshman cornerback Nate Robinson made one of the biggest plays of the game. With his extraordinary leaping ability, he went higher than 6'5" receiver Mike Bush to intercept a pass that set up a 27-yard field goal by John Anderson and sent the game into overtime.

Each team kicked field goals on its first two possessions to keep the score knotted at 26. In the third overtime, Anderson kicked a 49-yard field goal to put Washington up by three and to set up a controversial ending. Husky defensive end Kai Ellis ended the game. He first batted Gegel's attempted pass, then caught it, fumbled it, and finally got the football back. After about a minute of deliberation, the officials ruled that Gegel's pass was a backward pass, a fumble, and Washington's possession. Game over.

Neuheisel Fired

Hedges fired Neuheisel on June 11, 2003. He had lied to the AD about a visit to San Francisco to interview for the

49ers' head-coaching job. And he lied again when he denied participating in a neighborhood March Madness pool.

Hedges swiftly named Keith Gilbertson as Washington's new head coach. He had rejoined the Husky coaching staff as assistant head coach in 1999. Considering that the late summer is no the time to do a national search for a head coach, Hedges had little alternative. Gilbertson had previous head-coaching experience at Idaho, where he was 28–9 from 1986 to 1988. He was the head coach at California from 1992 to 1995, compiling a 20–26 record there. Best known for his innovative offensive schemes, he was hired by Don James in 1989 as offensive coordinator.

Unfortunately, his head-coaching record at Washington in the 2003 and 2004 seasons was a dismal 7–16–0. Worse, the only win in 2004 was a 21–6 victory over San Jose State.

On June 19, 2004, Todd Turner was hired as athletic director. Turner had gained great respect nationally for his focus on compliance with NCAA rules and on academic and behavior reform. Clearly those strengths were sorely needed at Washington. In January 2008, a four-part series in the *Seattle Times* disclosed that during the Neuheisel period, there was a significant level of criminal conduct:

- Safety Curtis Williams had cut his wife's face, broken her arm, and broken her nose. He had already served jail time for choking her into unconsciousness.
- Linebacker Jeremiah Pharms was under investigation for robbing and shooting a drug dealer.
- Tight end Jerramy Stevens was under investigation on suspicion of rape of a fellow Washington student.
- At least a dozen members of the 2001 Rose Bowl team were arrested that year or charged with a crime that carried possible jail time.

The *Times* articles claimed that Hedges and Neuheisel demanded little discipline or accountability from their athletes. The article stated, "And other community institutions, including prosecutors, police, judges, and the media, went along." That was the legacy that Turner inherited in 2004.

In December 2004, Turner hired Tyrone Willingham as Washington's head coach. His primary task was to change the program's image, which had been seriously tarnished. His résumé looked very strong. From 1995 to 2001, he was the head coach at Stanford, where his teams were 44–36–1, won the Pac-10 Conference title (the school's first in 29 years), and appeared in four bowl games. In 2000, he received the Eddie Robinson Coach of Distinction Award, annually bestowed on "an outstanding college football coach and role model for career achievement."

In December 2001, Willingham became the head coach at Notre Dame. He began the 2002 season 8–0 and went on to become the only first-year coach in Notre Dame history to win 10 games. For his efforts, he was named the ESPN / Home Depot College Coach of the Year, the Black Coaches Association Male Coach of the Year, and the Maxwell Football Club Coach of the Year. However, in the last game of the 2002 season, there was some evidence that Willingham's teams might have some problems in the upcoming season. USC absolutely crushed Notre Dame 44–13 and outgained the Irish 610-to-109—the worst margin in school history.

Over the next two seasons, Notre Dame struggled to an 11–12 record, and after the last game of the 2004 season, Willingham was fired. Many Husky supporters wondered why Turner wanted Willingham at all, given his poor showing with the Irish in the past two seasons. While they were pleased with Willingham's ability to ensure a "clean" program at Washington, they were not sure that he would be successful on the playing field. Their concerns were well founded. In Willingham's four-year tenure (2005–08) his teams won just 11 games, lost 37, and finished the 2008 season without a single win. It was the Huskies' first winless season in 119 years. Willingham's losing—not winning—percentage (.771) was the worst in Washington's history.

University president Mark Emmert realized the Husky football team was in dire straits. Not surprisingly, he received many e-mails about the football program, most of them negative. AD Turner resigned in mid-December. In a *Seattle Times* article on January 10, 2008, Emmert said, "An athletic department needs to succeed in four areas: the student experience, the business of athletics, the competitive area, and in relationships outside the university. Turner did fine with the first two [but] it was in the last two areas I was the most concerned." Coach Willingham, however, stayed on for another year before his contract was terminated.

Scott Woodward replaced Turner as athletic director. Woodward had served with Emmert when the latter was president at Louisiana State University and the former was the director of external affairs. Woodward also became Emmert's liaison with the athletic department. "There was some dysfunction because the outgoing athletic director and the head coach [Nick Saban] at that time did not have the greatest relationship," Woodward explained. "So I was there to troubleshoot and help do a lot of things to prepare for the next AD."

When Emmert came to Washington in June 2004, Woodward joined him as Washington's vice president of external affairs. At the beginning of 2008, he was appointed the athletic director on an interim basis. He then went through the selection process with a UW search committee and was installed on a permanent basis.

Woodward said, "We had a cultural problem—not a bad one—when I came in. It was just a little off kilter. This place is so special and so wonderful that people don't want to leave. With that, you can become stale and complacent." He felt that his first major task was to fix the complacency issue before fixing the problems within specific sports. He felt that the department had to be accountable. "Our first goal is to give the student-athletes the best possible chance to succeed in the classroom and to succeed in the sport in which they are participating," he said.

Emmert and Woodward conducted the search for the new football coach together. They started with an analysis of four environments where a new football coach could be found: football coaches with NFL experience; current collegiate head coaches in BCS-eligible schools; top assistants at BCS schools; and current collegiate head coaches at non-BCS schools.

"Mark and I talked to lots of coaches to determine who would be the best fit for the program," Woodward said. "I didn't want a quick fix. I wanted someone with a solid foundation." But an assistant coach? "With a head coach, you sometimes get guys who don't have a lot left.... We wanted someone who had the energy, the need, and the

ability to do a sustainable turnaround. We also wanted someone who had overcome adversity," Woodward said.

Resurrection

The coach Woodward picked to lead the resurrection was 34-year-old Steve Sarkisian. After a standout baseball and football career at West High School in Torrance, California, Sark began his college athletic career in 1992 as a non-scholarship middle infielder on USC's baseball team. After struggling on the baseball field at USC, he transferred to El Camino College, a two-year community college in Torrance, where he played baseball and restarted his football career. In 1994, he was named a junior college All-American after setting a national junior college record by completing 72.4 percent of his passes.

In 1995, he transferred to Brigham Young University, where he was coached by Norm Chow, a great offensive coordinator under head coach LaVell Edwards. As a junior, Sark passed for 3,437 yards and 20 touchdowns, earning All-Western Athletic Conference honors. In BYU's last regular-season game in 1995, he set a new NCAA record by completing 31-of-34 passes for 399 yards and three touchdowns in a 45–28 triumph over Fresno State.

In 1996, Sark had a remarkable season, leading the Cougars to a 13–1 regular season and a 19–15 win over Kansas State in the Cotton Bowl. BYU was No. 5 in the nation in the final polls. Sarkisian passed for 4,027 yards and 33 touchdowns during the regular season, and his 173.6 passer rating led the entire NCAA. He was named the Western Athletic Conference Offensive Player of the Year, a second-team All-American, and received the Sammy Baugh Trophy as the nation's best passer. His 162.0 career passing rating is third all-time on the NCAA list.

After playing for three seasons (1997–99) with the Saskatchewan Roughriders in the Canadian Football League, he started his coaching career as the quarterbacks coach at El Camino College. The following season, he joined Chow at USC. Chow was hired as the Trojans offensive coordinator by new head coach Pete Carroll. In 2001, Sarkisian worked as an offensive assistant and then as quarterbacks coach in 2002 and 2003. After a brief stint with the Raiders in the NFL, he returned to USC and

Coach Sarkisian changed the direction of the Husky program after his arrival in 2009.

eventually became the assistant head coach, offensive coordinator, and quarterbacks coach. By the end of the 2007 season, Sarkisian had become a top head-coaching candidate. On December 8, 2008, he was introduced as Washington's head football coach, calling the offer a "no-brainer."

He felt he had a pretty good chance to turn the football program around. "Once a program has found greatness, like Washington had under Don James, sometimes it is a little easier to find your way back when the path has already been paved," he said. "I felt that Washington was a good place to recruit. It provides a tremendous education, it had a real history and tradition of football, and it had tremendous players. There were too many positives to think I could not turn the program around. The one key to a turnaround is that you have a great quarterback. With Jake Locker here, we felt that we could come in and work with Jake and buy some time until we could build up the rest of the roster."

In the Last Second

In 2009, the Huskies climbed out of the basement of the Pac-10. With Jake Locker at the helm, the Huskies lost to LSU at home in the season opener, 31–23, followed by a 42–23 home victory over Idaho. Next up was third-ranked USC in Husky Stadium.

On September 19, 2009, Coach Sarkisian shocked his mentor by defeating Pete Carroll's Trojans 16–13 (an opponent that had beaten Washington 56–0 in the previous season). USC was a 19-point favorite going into the matchup. The Trojans moved easily down the field in their first two possessions to take a 10-point lead. Then the Huskies dug down deep and started to play tough defense. Meanwhile, they played a grind-it-out offense. With just 11 seconds left in the first quarter, the Huskies scored on a 68-yard drive. They evened the score with 4:09 left in the second stanza on a 28-yard field goal by Erik Folk. About midway through the last quarter, Folk drilled a 46-yard kick to put the Huskies up 13–10. The Trojans tied the score with a field goal with about four minutes left.

Washington then mounted a 63-yard drive to the Trojans 14. On third-and-15, Locker found Jermaine Kearse

open for 21 yards and a first down on the Husky 49. At 1:48, Locker scrambled for four yards on third-and-2 to the USC 39. On second-and-6, Locker threw to Kearse for 19 yards down to the Trojans 16 with 41 seconds left. A roughing the passer call on the play gave the Huskies first-and-goal at the 8. Chris Polk then picked up four yards to advance the Huskies to the 4. As the clock ran down, Folk went through his sideline preparation, trotted onto the field with three seconds to play, and calmly kicked the winning field goal.

Despite some close games, the Huskies lost six of their next seven. They lost three in the final minute of the game, including a 37–30 loss to Notre Dame in South Bend in triple overtime. They finished the season in strong fashion—first

Jake Locker was one of the most admired athletes in Husky history. He was revered for his leadership, unselfish behavior, and his community service. He wasn't a bad football player either. A standout football player and baseball pitcher and outfielder at Ferndale High School in northwestern Washington, he led Ferndale to a 14–0 record and a state title in his senior season. He was named 3A State Player of the Year and earned first-team All-American honors from *Parade* magazine.

As a Washington Husky, he hit the ground running and was named Pac-10 Freshman of the Year. He leads all quarterbacks in single-season (986 in 2007) and career (1,939) rushing yards. His career offensive yardage (9,578) is the second-best in Husky history behind Cody Pickett's 10,103.

During the summer of 2008, Locker played in the outfield for the Bellingham Nells of the West Coast Collegiate Baseball League. He signed with the Los Angeles Angels of Anaheim in 2009 and received a $300,000 signing bonus. The Angels retained Locker's rights for six years. Locker was selected as the eighth overall pick in the 2011 NFL Draft by the Tennessee Titans and earned the starting quarterback position at the beginning of the 2012 season.

Jake Locker is one of the most beloved players in Husky history.

dominating the Cougars 30–0 in the Apple Cup and then upsetting 19th-ranked California 42–10 at home.

Bears in Hibernation

The Huskies racked up 463 total yards and held California to 296. Jake Locker completed 19-of-23 passes for 248 yards, threw three touchdowns, and had no interceptions. On his first pass, he faked a handoff to Chris Polk, set up in the pocket, and arced a 40-yard scoring pass to Jermaine Kearse. Cal answered with a field goal later in the quarter. In the second quarter, Washington scored on its first two possessions. They went into the locker room with a 21–3 lead at the half. The Huskies roared into the second half, scoring 21 more points and holding the ball for more than 20 minutes en route to a decisive victory.

Defensive tackle Daniel Te'o-Nesheim had three sacks in the game to increase his total to 30 and set a new Husky record. By finishing the season 5–7 a year after the worst year (0–12) in Husky history, the Huskies' turnaround seemed afoot. At the end of the game, fans were yelling, "One more year." "I was chanting too," said Coach Sarkisian. Every Husky soul wanted Locker to return for his senior season. Many people speculated that Locker would decide to go to the National Football League after his junior year. After discussing the situation with his family and close friends, he decided to play for one more season.

Before Almost 83,000 at the Coliseum

The Huskies started the 2010 season slowly, losing at BYU, beating Syracuse, but then losing 56–21 to eighth-ranked Nebraska. Locker had a dismal day in Lincoln, completing only four of 20 pass attempts.

Then on October 2, USC and Washington staged a back-and-forth contest (there were seven lead changes) that went right down to the final seconds. The two teams scored 63 points and combined for 1,020 yards of offense.

Early in the fourth quarter, the Huskies led 29–28. The Trojans regained the lead after their drive ended with a field goal. With 6:02 remaining, Washington failed on a fourth-and-8 on the USC 38. USC then mounted a drive deep in Husky territory but was forced to try a field goal. The attempt bounced off the right goal post.

With 2:34 remaining, Washington began a drive on its own 23. On fourth-and-10, Locker moved around in the pocket to see someone clear and found D'Andre Goodwin breaking over the middle for 18 yards to the Washington 41. Chris Polk, who rushed 92 yards for the game, got 26 of them on the next play. Locker ran for eight more to the 20. Washington then managed the clock and called timeout with three seconds left. Erik Folk set up on the Trojans 32 and kicked the winning field goal as time expired.

After beating USC, the Huskies lost four of their next five games. With a 3–6 record, fans wondered if they would be bowl eligible at season's end. They would have to win all three of their remaining games: UCLA, Cal, and Washington State. Happily, they did just that and were invited to the Holiday Bowl to once again face Nebraska.

A Much Different Outcome

The Huskies looked forward to playing Nebraska again. After beating Washington at home 56–21 early in the regular season, Nebraska did not. They expected to play a better opponent, and they did.

In the regular season, the Cornhuskers had averaged 259 rushing yards per game—fifth-best in the nation. But their offense in the bowl was woeful; the Washington defense dominated the game, holding Nebraska to 91 yards rushing and 189 total yards. Washington also forced two turnovers, one of which led to a first-quarter touchdown.

Chris Polk earned All-Pac-10 honors as a running back in 2011. During his three-year career at Washington (2009–11), he established many rushing records—most rushing attempts in a career (799), career average rushing yards per game (101.2), most 100-yard games in a career (21), and most rushing yards as a freshman (1,113 in 2009). He is second in Husky history for rushing yards in a game (284), season (1,488), and career (4,049). He is one of only two Huskies ever to rush for 1,000 yards in three different seasons; Napoleon Kaufman is the other.

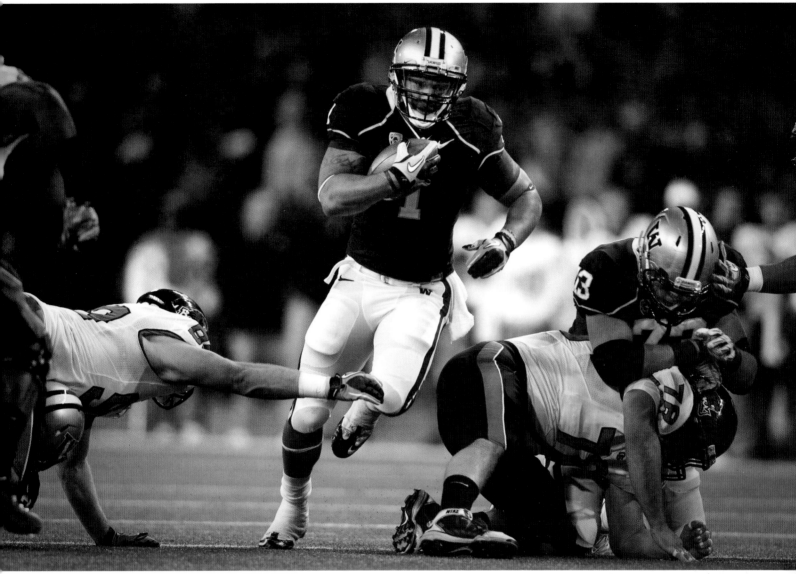

Chris Polk rushed for 1,000 or more yards in three seasons, making him one of only two Husky running backs to do so.

Chris Polk rushed for 177 yards on 34 carries and was the Offensive Player of the Game. He finished the season with 1,415 total rushing yards to put him second on the Husky all-time single-season rushing total.

Nebraska closed to within three midway through the second quarter, but that was as close as they would get. On Washington's first possession of the second half, the Huskies went 53 yards in four plays. On the Nebraska 25, Locker raced through the line before upending two defenders for a touchdown. Washington won 19–7, vindicating themselves after their early season shellacking.

After the game, Locker, who had a quiet day, said he was happy to play a supporting role in the victory. His biggest goal was to lead Washington to a winning season, its first since 2002. As he left the field for the last time in a Husky uniform, the crowd showed their appreciation for the outgoing quarterback, chanting "Locker, Locker, Locker."

Remember the Alamo

After the 2010 season was over, Coach Sarkisian signed a new five-year contract. The Huskies started the 2011 season with senior Chris Polk, sophomore quarterback Keith Price, and some outstanding receivers. They won five of their first six games and were ranked 22nd in the country. In the second half of the season, they barely held on to qualify for a bowl game. They lost four and won two, including some lopsided losses to Stanford (65–21), Oregon (34–17), USC (40–17), and Oregon State (38–21). After the home game with Oregon, the renovation of Husky Stadium began. The Huskies ended the regular season with a 38–21 victory over the Cougars at CenturyLink Field.

They matched up against Baylor in the Alamo Bowl in San Antonio on December 29, 2011. The Bears had one of the most exciting and talented players in the nation: Robert Lee Griffin III, who had won the Heisman Trophy earlier in the month. The game was a track meet. Baylor ran 85 plays for 777 total yards; the Huskies totaled 620 yards in 74 plays.

The Huskies led 35–24 at halftime, but Baylor ultimately won 67–56, scoring 43 points in the second half.

Link-ed In

Washington opened the 2012 season with a "home" game in CenturyLink Field in downtown Seattle, which would be their home field for the rest of the season while Husky Stadium was renovated. They beat San Jose State 21–12 in the opener and then traveled to Baton Rouge to play third-ranked Louisiana State, a perennial powerhouse in the Southeastern Conference and in the nation. The Huskies lost 41–3. On September 15, they played their last pre-conference opponent, Portland State University. The Vikings were the victims of the Huskies' explosive offense and stiff defense and lost 52–13.

After a bye week, eighth-ranked Stanford came to town. College athletics had, by that time, reached new levels of support from television networks. As such, this game was scheduled for Thursday night, September 27, 2012, in order to be nationally televised on ESPN. The Huskies rose to the occasion.

Stanford held a comfortable 10-point lead with less than three minutes left in the third quarter. Then, as the quarter ended, Washington sophomore tailback Bishop Sankey raced 61 yards on fourth-and-1. With the conversion, the Huskies pulled within three.

Midway through the fourth quarter, with less than nine minutes remaining, Washington started a drive at its own 35. After getting down to the Cardinal 35, sophomore wide receiver Kasen Williams caught a screen pass from junior quarterback Keith Price. He broke a tackle near the line of scrimmage and sprinted into the end zone. The Huskies led 17–13.

Stanford almost won the game three minutes later when their quarterback, Josh Nunes, fired a pass to Ty Montgomery on the 5; luckily for Husky fans, he dropped the ball. On fourth-and-4 on the Husky 34 and with two minutes left, Nunes threw a pass on a fade route down the sideline to Levine Toilolo, his 6'8" tight end. Husky safety Desmond Trufant intercepted the poorly thrown pass at the 8 and held on for the win. It was Washington's first victory over a top-10 opponent since it upset third-ranked USC in 2009.

At Oregon the next week, the Huskies faced the second-ranked Ducks in Eugene but just could not match their speed and hurry-up offense. They were buried 52–21. On October 13, USC came to the Link and beat the Huskies 24–14. Then, in one of the most disappointing outings of the season, Arizona seemed almost to score at will to defeat the Huskies 52–17 in Tucson.

The up-and-down Huskies returned to Seattle to welcome Oregon State for another night game. For the second time in October, the Huskies faced a top-10 team. Unbeaten Oregon State came north on October 27 ranked seventh in the country. The Huskies won 20–17. Because of outstanding play of the defense, four Beavers passes were intercepted. The victory was one of the most crucial in Coach Sarkisian's tenure. Had they lost the game, it would have been very difficult for the Huskies to have mounted a winning season and been eligible for a postseason game.

The victory seemed to put a little wind in the Huskies' sails. Washington increased its winning streak to four

The most beautiful stadium setting in the nation, but it was 91 years old in 2011.

after beating Cal 21–13, Utah 34–15, and Colorado 38–3. They had a 7–4–0 season record going into the game at Pullman on November 23, the day after Thanksgiving; the Cougars were 2–9–0. By the end of the third quarter, the Huskies led comfortably, 28–10. Then the Cougars came back strong, and Andrew Furney tied the game when he booted a 45-yard field goal with 1:59 left. The Huskies had a chance to win after quarterback Keith Price completed three passes to move the ball to the WSU 15. A penalty moved the ball back to the 20. Travis Coons lined up for a 35-yard field goal attempt to win the game with

five seconds left, but the ball started wide right from the moment he made contact.

In the overtime session, Washington got the ball first, on the 25. Price dropped back to pass. Under heavy pressure he was grabbed, and rather than keeping the ball and going to the ground, he tried to flip the ball to running back Bishop Sankey. Unfortunately, the ball went straight into the hands of defensive lineman Kalafitoni Pole, who took off downfield before being stopped at the 5. The Cougars went on to win the game when Furney kicked a clinching 27-yard field goal.

Sophomore Austin Seferian-Jenkins set new Husky season records for receptions (69) and receiving yards (852) and career records for receptions (110) and yards (1,388). The Huskies finished the season with a 7–6 overall record—the third 7–6 record in a row. Their final record earned them a bowl invitation, and they headed to the Maaco Bowl in Las Vegas on December 22, 2012, against 20th-ranked Boise State (10–2). The Huskies lost 28–26 despite sophomore running back Bishop Sankey's 205 rushing yards (a Husky record for bowl games). For his exploits, he was voted the Most Valuable Player of the game, despite being on the losing end.

Renovation

On November 7, 2011, two days after Washington played Oregon in a night game, the renovation of Husky Stadium began. Built in 1920, the stadium was acclaimed for its innovative design and unique setting with the mountains and the water. With its two cantilevered roofs, it was one of the loudest football venues in the nation. But by 2011, it was showing its age.

Chip Lydum, the associate athletic director for operations and capital projects, had sounded the alarm: not only did the stadium require substantial annual maintenance, but there were parts of the stadium that could become hazardous to the fans. It was time to do some major renovations. A stadium renovation committee, chaired by former Washington governor and U.S. senator Dan Evans, was formed in 2006. Some of the members were initially skeptical that the athletic department had to spend a lot of money on renovation. Lydum took them on a tour of the facility. What they found were a number of places in the lower stands where the concrete was crumbling. Worse, a section on the north side had collapsed because the dirt underneath had washed away, causing the concrete stairs to drop about six feet. (Fortunately, the stadium had been empty at the time.) The press box was woefully outdated. Soon after, the committee agreed that major renovation had to be done—not only because of the structural problems, but also because the existing stadium was not up to the level of newer stadiums in the Pac-12 schools and other parts of the country.

Jon Runstad, chairman and CEO of Wright Runstad, a Seattle development firm, and a member of the committee, said, "It is like an arms race. To see some of the facilities on other campuses, you get a sense of what Washington's program needed for recruiting and the football operations facilities to show recruits. These factors and others made a pretty compelling case for something to be done. However, what we had to do was not so clear."

So the committee hired HOK, a global design, architecture, engineering, and planning firm, to get some ideas about what the major renovations might include. In the spring of 2009, the committee made a decision to use a "developer" concept—one that was quite unique for a major stadium project. This concept included the selection of a development firm, a major contractor, and an architectural firm, all of them with experience in large-scale projects. The selected firms proposed to the committee a plan that, if implemented, would cost more than $300 million. After a review of the plan, the committee determined that the athletic department could not afford $300 million. Even though Husky Stadium was a state facility, no state funding was available.

In a January 2010 committee meeting, Runstad urged the development team to come up with any ways to reduce the price. As a result of the economic downturn, Runstad's own firm was seeing huge decreases in material costs on their own projects. Surely the development team would show similar decreases in their estimates. "The answer the committee got from the development team was 'No, our price is our price. Nothing has changed,'" Runstad said.

Runstad asked his own firm to come up with a second opinion about how much they thought the current design would cost. "We came up with a cost that was significantly less and we offered it to the committee. As a result, the committee decided to get some other proposals," he said. Since Wright Runstad wanted to provide a proposal itself, Runstad resigned from the committee to avoid any potential conflict of interest.

The committee then solicited new proposals from a number of firms. In August 2010, AD Scott Woodward announced the committee had selected a development

October 2012: The renovation of Husky Stadium is about halfway complete.

team for the renovation of Husky Stadium. He said the bid was $250 million, "nearly $30 million less than the next-closest bidder" and $50 million less than the initial proposal. The team consisted of developer Wright Runstad, Turner Construction, 360 Architecture for design, and MKA for structural and civil needs.

The primary design features included:

- Removing the track and lowering the field four feet and shifting the field about seven feet to optimize seat values and sightlines.

- Complete demolition and reconstruction of the lower bowl and the south deck.
- Building a Football Operations section under the west stands that would include team locker rooms, weight rooms, team meeting rooms, a hydrotherapy area, and player lounges.
- Building coaches' offices and a recruiting center above the stands on the west side, looking east to Lake Washington and the Cascade Mountains and west to the Olympic Mountains.

Architectural rendering of the new stadium, which opened in 2013.

- Permanent east end zone seating.
- Renovation of the Don James Center.
- Large landscaped plazas and grounds, with no perimeter fencing.
- Premium seating, including 25 suites, 30 patio suites, 2,555 seats in the Club Husky section, and 6,000 Tyee Heritage chairback seats in the lower bowl.
- Under the new south stands, a new state-of-the art UW Medicine Sports Medicine Clinic would be built. It would span 30,660 square feet, more than five times the size of the old clinic that was located in Hec Edmundson Pavilion. The clinic would provide a full range of outpatient services to UW student-athletes of all sports.

The new structure is being financed by donor contributions of $50 million and the issuance of $200 million worth of bonds to be paid off over 30 years. The debt service (principal and interest) will be funded with additional Tyee and season-ticket revenue and proceeds from the new premium seating areas.

Now fully realized and opened in the 2013 regular season, the stadium will provide a state-of-the-art home for Husky football for many, many years to come.

CHAPTER 11

"Mighty Are the Men Who Wear the Purple and the Gold"

The Husky fight song begins with these lyrics:

Bow down to Washington. Bow down to Washington.
Mighty are the men who wear the Purple and the Gold,
Joyfully we welcome them within the victor's fold.
We will carve their names in the Hall of Fame,
To preserve the memory of our devotion.

This chapter will focus on Washington's mighty football men. The Husky football program has been led by many players and coaches who have received awards and honors at the highest levels in collegiate football and the professional ranks.

Guy Flaherty Award

The Guy Flaherty Award is awarded annually to the player voted "most inspirational" by his teammates and is considered the top award given to a Washington football player. The medal was first awarded in 1908 to Guy Flaherty, whose sacrifices inspired the 1908 senior class to establish the award, with help from the former dean of faculty, Herbert Condon, and use up the $25 remaining in the class treasury.

Flaherty played every minute of every game during the 1906 and 1907 Washington seasons. A severe case of boils prevented him from playing in all but the first and last games of 1908. Despite being sidelined, Flaherty turned out every day with the squad and performed managerial duties for the team, a sacrifice acknowledged by each and every teammate.

National Football Foundation's College Hall of Fame Inductees

The National Football Foundation established the College Football Hall of Fame in 1951 and oversees its support, administration, and operations. The Hall of Fame recognizes the greatest achievements by players and coaches in college football. Of the nearly 5,000,000 players who have participated in college football since 1869, 829 have been inducted as of 2012. In addition, 178 coaches have been honored.

The College Football Hall of Fame was originally located in Kings Mills, Ohio (1972–94) before moving to South Bend, Indiana. In 2014, its doors will open in Atlanta, next to Centennial Olympic Park.

Eleven Husky players and five Washington coaches have been inducted into the Hall of Fame.

Guy Flaherty Award Winners

Year	Player
1908	Guy Flaherty
1909	Fred Tegtmeier
1910	Warren Grimm
1911	Tom Wand
1912	Tom Wand
1913	Wayne Sutton
1914	Herman Anderson
1915	Elmer Leader
1916	Elmer Noble
1917	Ernest Murphy
1918	No Award
1919	Sanford Wick
1920	Larry Smith
1921	Hanford Haynes
1922	John Wilson
1923	Leonard Ziel
1924	Chalmers Walters
1925	George Wilson
1926	Harold Patton
1927	Gene Cook
1928	Charles Carroll
1929	John Stombaugh
1930	Henry Wentworth
1931	Paul Schwegler
1932	John Cherberg
1933	Glenn Boyle
1934	Paul Sulkosky
1935	Abe Spear
1936	Byron Haines
1937	Everett Austin
1938	Jim Johnson
1939	Dan Yarr
1940	Dean McAdams
1941	Walt Harrison
1942	Thron Riggs

Year	Player
1943	Pete Susick
1944	Jim McCurdy
1945	Maurice Stacy
1946	Fred Provo
1947	Sam Robinson
1948	Mike Scanlan
1949	Joe Cloidt
1950	Roland Kirkby
1951	Jim Wiley
1952	Larry Smith
1953	Milt Bohart
1954	Larry Rhodes
1955	Earl Monlux
1956	Corky Lewis
1957	Dick Payseno
1958	Don Armstrong
1959	Don McKeta
1960	Don McKeta
1961	John Meyers
1962	Bob Monroe
1963	Chuck Bond
1964	Jim Lambright
1965	Ron Medved
1966	Jeff Jordan
1967	Cliff Coker
1968	Jim Cope
1969	Lee Brock
1970	Tom Failla
1971	Al Kravitz
1972	Calvin Jones
1973	Jim Andrilenas
1974	Dennis Fitzpatrick
1975	Dan Lloyd
1976	Mike Baldassin
1977	Warren Moon

Year	Player
1978	Michael Jackson
1979	Joe Steele, Chris Linnin
1980	Tom Flick
1981	Vince Coby
1982	Tim Cowan
1983	Steve Pelluer
1984	Jim Rodgers
1985	Joe Kelly
1986	Steve Alvord
1987	Darryl Franklin
1988	Jim Ferrell
1989	Andre Riley
1990	Greg Lewis
1991	Mark Brunell
1992	Dave Hoffmann
1993	Pete Kaligis
1994	Richard Thomas
1995	Leon Neal
1996	John Fiala
1997	Olin Kreutz
1998	Reggie Davis, Josh Smith
1999	Maurice Shaw
2000	Curtis Williams
2001	Willie Hurst
2002	Ben Mahdavi
2003	Owen Biddle
2004	Zach Tuiasosopo
2005	Joe Lobendahn
2006	Jordan Reffett
2007	Jordan Reffett
2008	Daniel Te'o-Nesheim
2009	Jake Locker
2010	Jake Locker
2011	Keith Price
2012	Desmond Trufant

Dave Hoffman was conference Defensive Player of the Year in 1992 and a two-time All-American linebacker.

Washington Players and Coaches in the College Football Hall of Fame

Name, Position	Years at Washington	Year of Induction
Gilmour Dobie, coach	1908–16	1951
George Wilson, HB	1923–25	1951
Chuck Carroll, HB	1926–28	1964
Paul Schwegler, T	1929–31	1967
James Phelan, coach	1930–41	1973
Vic Markov, T	1935–37	1976
Hugh McElhenny, HB	1949–51	1981
Jim Owens, coach	1957–74	1982
Darrell Royal , coach	1956	1983
Don Heinrich, QB	1949–50, 1952	1987
Bob Schloredt, QB	1958–60	1989
Max Starcevich, G	1934–36	1990
Rick Redman, G	1962–64	1995
Don James, coach	1975–92	1997
Don Coryell, DB	1947–49	1999
Steve Emtman, DT	1989–91	2007

All-Americans

The initial usage of the term "All-America" is reported to have been in 1889, when the 1889 College Football All-America Team was selected by Casper Whitney in *This Week's Sports*, in association with football pioneer Walter Camp. Camp took over the responsibility for picking the All-America team and was recognized as its official selector in the early years of the 20th century. The first Washington player to receive All-America recognition was Huber "Polly" Grimm, in 1910. Louis Seagraves was selected in 1916. Both were selected to the third team.

Before 1922, the most widely recognized All-America team selectors were Walter Camp for *Collier's Weekly Magazine*; *Athletic World Magazine* (for which 200 coaches contributed to the selection process), the *Chicago Tribune*, the *New York Tribune*, and the Central Press Association (for which 200 sportswriters contributed to the selection process).

It should be noted that coach Jim Owens was inducted into the Hall in recognition of his success as a player at the University of Oklahoma. Darrell Royal, a Husky coach in 1956, was honored for his overwhelming coaching success at Texas (1957–76) and for his many offensive innovations. Don Coryell, an undergraduate player from 1947 to 1949, was honored by the Hall for his coaching at Whittier College and San Diego State University.

In 1950, the NCAA's service bureau compiled its first list of All-Americans and continues to this day. Currently, the NCAA recognizes All-Americans selected by the Associated Press, the America Football Coaches Association, the Football Writers Association of America, *The Sporting News*, and the Walter Camp Football Foundation.

For a football player to be considered a unanimous All-American, he must be a first-team selection chosen by all of the above; for a player to be selected as consensus All-American, he must be named a first-team selection by a majority of the above.

Twenty-one Huskies have been recognized as consensus All-Americans and six as unanimous All-Americans. Below is a list of Husky All-Americans (unanimous selections are denoted by boldface).

Husky Unanimous and Consensus All-Americans

Player, Position	Year
George Wilson, HB	1925
Charles Carroll, HB	1928
Paul Schwegler, T	1930
Max Starcevich, G	1936
Vic Markov, T	1937
Rudy Mucha, C	1940
Ray Frankowski, G	1941
Roy McKasson, C	1960
Rick Redman, G	1963
Rick Redman, G	1964
Tom Greenlee, DL	1966
Al Worley, DB	1968
Chuck Nelson, K	1982
Mark Stewart, LB	1982
Ron Holmes, DL	1984
Jeff Jaeger, K	1986
Reggie Rogers, DL	1986
Mario Bailey, WR	1991
Steve Emtman, DL	1991
Lincoln Kennedy, OL	1992

Player, Position	Year
Lawyer Milloy, DB	1995
Benji Olson, OL	1996
Olin Kreutz, OL	1997
Reggie Williams, WR	2002

Other All-America Selections

The *2012 Washington Media Guide* lists almost 40 organizations that select an "All-America" team. Too many Husky players have been honored over the years by one or more of those unofficial selectors than can be listed here.

Below is a list of what I call "Other All-Americans": players who were chosen as a first-teamer by one or more of the official All-America voting bodies— Associated Press (AP), America Football Coaches Association (FC), Football Writers Association of America (FW), The Sporting News (SN), and the Walter Camp Football Foundation (WCF)— but who missed the mark of being a consensus choice.

Washington's Other All-Americans

Player, Position	Year	Voter
Paul Schwegler, T	1931	AP, FW
Dick Sprague, DB	1950	FW
Don Heinrich, QB	1950	AP
Hugh McElhenny, RB	1951	AP
Don Heinrich, QB	1952	AP
Milt Bohart, G	1953	FW
Bob Schloredt, QB	1959	AP
Calvin Jones, CB	1972	AP
Skip Boyd, P	1974	SN
Jeff Toews, OL	1978	SN
Tim Peoples, DB	1986	SN
Bern Brostek, C	1989	SN
Greg Lewis, RB	1990	SN, WCF
Dave Hoffmann, LB	1991	FW
Dave Hoffmann, LB	1992	FC
Jason Chorak, LB	1996	FN, SN

Player, Position	Year	Voter
Benji Olson, OL	1997	AP, WCF
Jerome Pathon, WR	1997	FC
Chad Ward, OL	2000	AP, SN
Larry Tripplett, DT	2001	FN
Reggie Williams, WR	2002	AP, FW

NCAA Postseason Awards

Two players in Husky history have received NCAA postseason awards. In 1990, tailback Greg Lewis was chosen as the recipient of the Doak Walker Award, one of the most prestigious honors bestowed by the NCAA. Doak Walker, who attended Southern Methodist University, was a three-time All-American halfback, kicker, punter, and a defensive back from 1946 to 1948. He received the Heisman Trophy in 1948. He graduated in 1949 and was selected in the first round (No. 3 pick) in the 1949 NFL Draft. He played for the Detroit Lions for six years.

Named after its original recipient, **the Doak Walker Award** is given annually to a Division I running back who has made extraordinary contributions to his team, maintains good academic standing and is on schedule to graduate, has a record of good citizenship within and beyond the athletic sphere, and demonstrates leadership, sportsmanship, and fair play.

The Rotary Lombardi Award is given annually to a Division I college football player who is a down lineman, end-to-end, either on offense or defense, setting up no further than 10 yards to the left or right of the ball at the time of the snap, or a defensive linebacker who shows leadership, courage, desire, and respect for authority and discipline. Husky defensive lineman Steve Emtman won the award in 1991.

The award was initiated in 1970, shortly after the death of Vince Lombardi, legendary coach of the Green Bay Packers and himself a standout football player who first made a name for himself as the smallest but toughest member of Fordham University's "Seven Blocks of Granite."

The Outland Trophy goes to the best college interior lineman in the nation, chosen by the Football Writers Association of America. The trophy is named after John H. Outland, one of only two players ever to be named All-American at two positions. From 1897 to 1899, Outland led the University of Pennsylvania to a 35–4–3 record. He contended that football tackles and guards deserved greater recognition and conceived the Outland Trophy as a means of providing such recognition. First awarded in 1946, Steve Emtman won the award in 1991.

PCC Offensive and Defensive Players of the Year

Five Washington players have been chosen as the Offensive Player of Year and three as the Defensive Player of the Year in the Pacific Coast Conference. They are:

Player, Position	Year
Warren Moon, QB (tie)	1977
Steve Pelluer, QB	1983
Steve Emtman, DT	1990
Greg Lewis, RB	1990
Steve Emtman, DT	1991
Mario Bailey, WR	1991
Dave Hoffmann, LB	1992
Jason Chorak, LB	1996
Marques Tuiasosopo, QB	2000

Morris Trophy

Ten players have received the Morris Trophy as the Pacific Coast Conference Lineman of the Year. The idea was conceived in 1980 by Traci Lee Morris, then married to Joe Sanford, Husky offensive tackle in 1975, 1978, and 1979. She wanted linemen in the conference to vote for the best opponent they faced in the trenches. She took her idea to Don James and Mike Lude, who solicited support for the award from other Pacific Coast Conference athletic directors. Her father, Husky booster Pat Morris, sponsored the award, first given in 1981.

Player, Position	Year
Fletcher Jenkins, DT	1981
Ron Holmes, DT	1984
Reggie Rogers, DT	1986
Bern Brostek, C	1989
Steve Emtman, DT	1990
Steve Emtman, DT	1991
Lincoln Kennedy, OT	1991
Lincoln Kennedy, OT	1992
D'Marco Farr, DT	1993
Bob Sapp, OT	1996
Olin Kreutz, C	1997
Chad Ward, OG	2000

Academic All-Americans

This award was started in 1952 and is conferred on male and female athletes in NCAA Divisions I, II, and III and NAIA athletes in all championship sports. Eleven Washington football players have received first-team Academic All-America honors.

Player, Position	Year
Jim Houston, TE	1955
Mike Crawford, G	1959
Bob Hivner, QB	1960
Mike Briggs, T	1963
Steve Bramwell, RB	1965
Mike Ryan, OG	1966
Bruce Harrell, LB	1979
Mark Jerue, LB	1981
Chuck Nelson, K	1981
Chuck Nelson, K	1982
David Rill, LB	1986
David Rill, LB	1987
Ed Cunningham, C	1991

Huskies and the Heisman

The Heisman Trophy is named after John W. Heisman, an accomplished college and club player who was a successful collegiate coach before becoming a sportswriter. He became the first athletic director of the Downtown Athletic Club (DAC) of New York City in 1930, where he started a structure and voting system to determine the best collegiate football player in the country. The DAC has given the award ever since, renaming it in Heisman's honor in 1936, after Heisman's death.

Six Huskies have finished in the top 10 in the balloting for the Heisman.

Player, Position	Finish	Year
Hugh McElhenny, RB	eighth	1951
Don Heinrich, QB	ninth	1952
Greg Lewis, RB	seventh	1990
Steve Emtman, DT	fourth	1991
Napoleon Kaufman, RB	ninth	1994
Marques Tuiasosopo, QB	eighth	2000

Husky Hall of Fame

In 1979, the Husky Hall of Fame began with 11 inductees. Two football players—running backs Chuck Carroll and Hugh McElhenny—and two coaches—Gil Dobie and Jim Owens—were among the honorees. Overall, 189 athletes, coaches, and teams have been admitted; 63 of them are football coaches and players.

Inductee	Years at Washington	Year Inducted
Charles Carroll	1926–28	1979
Gilmour Dobie	1908–16	1979
Hugh McElhenny	1949–51	1979
Jim Owens	1957–74	1979
Enoch Bagshaw	1903–07 (player), 1921–29 (coach)	1980
William Coyle	1908–11	1980
George Fleming	1958–60	1980

Inductee	Years at Washington	Year Inducted
Vic Markov	1935–37	1980
George Wilson	1923–25	1980
James Bryan	1920–23	1981
John Cherberg	1930–32 (player), 1953–55 (coach)	1981
Don Heinrich	1949–50, 1952	1981
Bob Schloredt	1958–60	1981
Alfred "Doc" Strauss	1902–03	1981
Ray Eckmann	1919–21	1982
Paul Jessup	1927–30	1982
Rick Redman	1962–64	1982
Arnie Weinmeister	1942, 1946–47	1982
Calvin Jones	1970–72	1983
Paul Schwegler	1929–31	1983
Don McKeta	1958–60	1984
Warren Moon	1975–77	1984
Sonny Sixkiller	1970–72	1985
Elmer Tesreau	1923–26	1985
Ray Frankowski	1939–41	1986
James Phelan, coach	1930–41	1986
Tom Greenlee	1964–66	1987
Roy McKasson	1958–60	1987
Dave Nisbet	1930–32	1988
George Strugar	1955–56	1988
Milt Bohart	1951–53	1989
Max Starcevich	1934–36	1989
Earl Clark, Trainer	1929–61	1990
Merle Hufford	1929–31	1990
Rudy Mucha	1938–40	1990
Jay MacDowell	1938–40	1991
William Smith	1931–33	1991
Charles Mitchell	1960–62	1992
Al Worley	1966–68	1992
Chuck Allen	1958–60	1994
Don James, coach	1975–92	1994

Inductee	Years at Washington	Year Inducted
1959 Football Team	1959	1994
Ray Mansfield	1960–62	1995
Dick Sprague	1950–52	1995
Joe Steele	1976–79	1996
1991 Football Team	1991	1997
Chuck Nelson	1979–82	1998
Steve Emtman	1989–91	1999
Walter Harrison	1940–42	1999
Ernest Steele	1939–41	1999
Don Coryell (for his college and NFL coaching success)	1949	2000
Michael Jackson	1975–78	2000
Nesby Glasgow	1975–78	2001
Ron Holmes	1982–84	2001
Jeff Jaeger	1983–86	2004
Napoleon Kaufman	1991–94	2004
Lincoln Kennedy	1989–92	2004
Jim Lambright	1961–64 (player), 1993–98 (coach)	2006
Greg Lewis	1987–90	2006
Blair Bush	1975–77	2008
Mark Stewart	1979–82	2008
Benji Olson	1995–97	2010
Dave Hoffmann	1989–92	2012
Lawyer Milloy	1993–95	2012

Pro Football Hall of Fame Inductees

In addition to exemplary play at the collegiate level, many Husky players have gone on to successful careers in the professional ranks. Three Washington players have been inducted into the Pro Football Hall of Fame.

Running back Hugh McElhenny was inducted in 1970. He played for the San Francisco 49ers (1952–60), Minnesota Vikings (1961–62), New York Giants (1963), and Detroit Lions (1964). Defensive tackle Arnie Weinmeister was inducted in 1984 and played for the New York

Yankees (All-America Football Conference, 1948–49) and the New York Giants (1950–53). Quarterback Warren Moon was inducted in 2006 and played for the Edmonton Eskimos (Canadian Football League, 1978–83), Houston Oilers (1984–93), Minnesota Vikings (1994–96), Seattle Seahawks (1997–98), and Kansas City Chiefs (1999–2000).

First-Round Picks

Among the many Husky players to enter the National Football League, 19 of them were chosen in the first round of the NFL Draft.

NFL Draft First-Round Selections

Player, Position	Team	Year	Overall Pick
Rudy Mucha, C	Cleveland Rams	1941	4
Dean McAdams, RB	Brooklyn Dodgers*	1941	8
Hugh McElhenny, RB	San Francisco 49ers	1952	9
Dave Williams, WR	St. Louis Cardinals	1967	16
Blair Bush, C	Cincinnati Bengals	1978	16
Doug Martin, DT	Minnesota Vikings	1980	9
Curt Marsh, OT	Oakland Raiders	1981	23
Ron Holmes, DT	Tampa Bay Buccaneers	1985	8
Joe Kelly, LB	Cincinnati Bengals	1986	11
Reggie Rogers, DT	Detroit Lions	1987	7
Bern Brostek, C	Los Angeles Rams	1990	23
Steve Emtman, DT	Indianapolis Colts	1992	1
Dana Hall, CB	San Francisco 49ers	1992	18
Lincoln Kennedy, OT	Atlanta Falcons	1993	9
Napoleon Kaufman, RB	Oakland Raiders	1995	17
Mark Bruener, TE	Pittsburgh Steelers	1995	27
Jerramy Stevens, TE	Seattle Seahawks	2002	28
Reggie Williams, WR	Jacksonville Jaguars	2004	9
Jake Locker, QB	Tennessee Titans	2011	8

* Yes, there was a Brooklyn Dodgers football team. In the NFL from 1930 to 1943, the team played their home games at Ebbets Field, home field of the baseball Dodgers.

Selected eighth overall by the Tennessee Titans in the 2011 NFL Draft, quarterback Jake Locker became the highest-drafted Husky since Steve Emtman.

All-Time Husky All-Star Teams

In 1989, a Huskies' All-Centennial Team was selected in celebration of 100 years of Husky football. The team was selected by alumni, members of the media, and longtime season ticket holders. (See page 124 for the full roster.)

Seattle Post-Intelligencer / Seattle Sports Council Sports Star of the Year

Created by Royal Brougham and the *Seattle Post-Intelligencer* in 1936, this event has celebrated the highest achievements of college and professional athletes and coaches in the state of Washington. Seventeen Husky football players—in addition to coaches Jim Owens and Don James—have received the award since its inception.

Honoree	Year
John Cherberg	1937
Dean McAdams	1939
Jim McCurdy	1944
Hugh McElhenny	1951
Arnie Weinmeister	1953
Jim Owens	1959
Don McKeta	1960
Rick Redman	1964
Calvin Jones	1973
Warren Moon	1977
Joe Steele	1979
Don James	1981
Chuck Nelson	1982
Greg Lewis	1990
Steve Emtman	1991
Napoleon Kaufman	1994
Marques Tuiasosopo	1999
Jake Locker	2009
Chris Polk	2011

Best of the Best

In this section, we integrate all of the awards presented up to now into the spreadsheet that follows. In order to be on the list, a Husky player had to be an All-Coast / All-Conference player. The other columns in the spreadsheet show which players have been honored with more selective awards during their college careers. These honors include:

- Conference Offensive/Defensive Player of the Year and other conference awards—shown in the spreadsheet

as OPOY (Offensive Player of the Year) and DPOY (Defensive Player of the Year)

- Other All-American: those players who received first-team selection by at least one the following organizations—Associated Press (AP), American Football Coaches Association (FC), Football Writers Association of America (FW), *The Sporting News* (SN), and the Walter Camp Football Foundation (WCF).
- Consensus All-American: those players who received first-team selection by a majority of the following organizations—Associated Press (AP), American Football Coaches Association (FC), Football Writers Association of America (FW), *The Sporting News* (SN), and the Walter Camp Football Foundation (WCF).
- Unanimous All-American: those players who received first-team selection from all of the following organizations—Associated Press (AP), American Football Coaches Association (FC), Football Writers Association of America (FW), *The Sporting News* (SN), and the Walter Camp Football Foundation (WCF).
- Other Awards and Records—e.g., Heisman balloting, national records, Most Valuable Player (MVP) in bowl games
- NFL first round draft pick
- Husky Hall of Fame selection
- College Football Hall of Fame selection

Now it is your turn. Who do you think is the best of the best? First, make a copy of the following chart. Then put an *X* in the last column, "Best of the Best," for the Husky players that you think are the very best at each position—maybe go two deep for every position. Invite your Husky friends to do the same thing, and then get together and discuss everyone's all-time team. See if you can argue until you reach a consensus (if you can't, that's okay). If you want, e-mail your list to me at *djoporter@msn.com*. I will compile all your votes and submit them to *Seattle Times* sportswriters and ask them to include it in the newspaper. Have fun!

Name of Player (by Position and Chronologically)	All-Conference / All-Coast	Conference Awards	All-Americans (Unanimous, Consensus, and Other)	Other Honors and Awards	NFL First-Round Draft Selection	Husky Hall of Fame Selection	College Football Hall of Fame Selection	Best of the Best
End or Tight End								
Dave Nisbet	1932					1988		
Bill Smith	1933					1991		
Jay McDowell	1940					1991		
Jack Tracy	1943							
Dick Hagen	1946							
Joe Cloidt	1950							
George Black	1952							
Jim Houston	1955							
Dave Williams	1965				16			
Rod Jones	1986							
Mark Bruener	1993–94				27			
Ernie Conwell	1995							
Cameron Cleeland	1997							
Offensive Lineman								
James Bryan	1923					1981		
Paul Schwegler	1930–31		Consensus, 1930; Other, 1931			1983	1967	
Max Starcevich	1935–36		Unanimous, 1936			1989	1990	
Vic Markov	1936–37		Consensus, 1937			1980	1976	
Ray Frankowski	1940–41		Consensus, 1941			1986		
Rudy Mucha	1940		Consensus, 1940		4	1990		
Walt Harrison	1942					1999		
Bill Ward	1943							
James McCurdy	1944							
John Zeger	1946							
Dick Hagen	1946							
Alf Hemsted	1948							
Bob Levenhagen	1948							
Ted Holzknecht	1950–51							
Mike Michael	1950							
Jim O'Brien	1951							
Lou Yourkowski	1952							
Milt Bohart	1953		Other, 1953			1989		
Duane Wardlow	1953							
Fred Robinson	1955							
George Strugar	1956					1988		
Marv Bergmann	1957							
Whitey Core	1957							
Chuck Allen	1959–60					1994		
Kurt Gegner	1959–60							
Roy McKasson	1960		Consensus, 1960			1987		
John Meyers	1961							

Name of Player (by Position and Chronologically)	All-Conference / All-Coast	Conference Awards	All-Americans (Unanimous, Consensus, and Other)	Other Honors and Awards	NFL First-Round Draft Selection	Husky Hall of Fame Selection	College Football Hall of Fame Selection	Best of the Best
Jim Skaggs	1961							
Ray Mansfield	1962					1995		
Rod Scheyer	1962							
Mike Briggs	1963							
Koll Hagen	1964							
Jim Norton	1964							
Fred Forsberg	1965							
Mike Ryan	1966							
Ernie Janet	1970							
Ray Pinney	1975							
Blair Bush	1977				16	2008		
Jeff Toews	1977–78		Other, 1978					
Tom Turnure	1979							
Rick Mallory	1983							
Mike Zandofsky	1986–87							
Bern Brostek	1989	Morris, 1989	Other, 1989		23			
Jeff Pahukoa	1990							
Dean Kirkland	1990							
Ed Cunningham	1991							
Lincoln Kennedy	1992	Morris, 1991–92	Unanimous, 1992		9	2004		
Tom Gallagher	1993							
Frank Garcia	1994							
Olin Kreutz	1996–97	Morris, 1997	Consensus, 1997					
Benji Olson	1996–97		Consensus, 1996; Other 1997			2010		
Chad Ward	2000	Morris, 2000	Other, 2000					
Elliot Silvers	2000							
Kyle Benn	2001							

Wide Receiver

Name of Player	All-Conf/All-Coast	Conf Awards	All-Americans	Other Honors	NFL First Round	Husky HOF	CFB HOF	Best
Tom Scott	1971							
Paul Skansi	1982			MVP Sun Bowl, 1979				
Lonzell Hill	1986							
Mario Bailey	1991	OPOY, 1991	Consensus, 1991					
Jerome Pathon	1997		Other, 1997					
Reggie Williams	2002–03		Consensus, 2002		9			

Running Back

Name of Player	All-Conf/All-Coast	Conf Awards	All-Americans	Other Honors	NFL First Round	Husky HOF	CFB HOF	Best
George Wilson	1923–25		Consensus, 1925	Co-MVP Rose Bowl, 1924, 1926; jersey retired		1980	1951	
Charles Carroll	1927-28		Consensus, 1928	Jersey retired		1979	1964	
Merle Hufford	1929					1990		

Name of Player (by Position and Chronologically)	All-Conference / All-Coast	Conference Awards	All-Americans (Unanimous, Consensus, and Other)	Other Honors and Awards	NFL First-Round Draft Selection	Husky Hall of Fame Selection	College Football Hall of Fame Selection	Best of the Best
Jim Cain	1936							
Sam Robinson	1943							
Keith DeCourcy	1944							
Roland Kirkby	1950			Jersey retired				
Hugh McElhnney	1950–51		Other, 1951	Heisman (8th), 1951		1979	1981	
Don McKeta	1959–60					1984		
George Fleming	1960			Co-MVP Rose Bowl, 1960		1980		
Charlie Mitchell	1961-62					1992		
Joe Steele	1979					1996		
Jacque Robinson	1982			Co-MVP Rose Bowl,1982; MCP Orange Bowl, 1985				
Greg Lewis	1990	OPOY, 1990	Other, 1990	Doak Waker Award,1990; Heisman (7th), 1990		2006		
Napoleon Kaufman	1992–94			Heisman (9th), 1994	17	2004		
Rashaan Shehee	1997			MVP Aloha Bowl, 1997				
Chris Polk	2011			MVP Holiday Bowl 2010				

Fullback

Jim Jones	1957							
Ray Jackson	1960							
Junior Coffey	1962–63							
Rick Fenney	1986							

Quarterback

Don Heinrich	1950–52		Other, 1950, 1952	Heisman (9th), 1952; National record for passes completed 1950, 1952		1981	1987	
Bob Schloredt	1959		Other, 1959	Co-MVP Rose Bowl 1960; MVP 1961		1981	1989	
Bill Douglas	1963							
Warren Moon	1977	Co-OPOY, 1977		MVP Rose Bowl 1978		1984		

Name of Player (by Position and Chronologically)	All-Conference / All-Coast	Conference Awards	All-Americans (Unanimous, Consensus, and Other)	Other Honors and Awards	NFL First-Round Draft Selection	Husky Hall of Fame Selection	College Football Hall of Fame Selection	Best of the Best
Steve Pelluer	1983	OPOY, 1983						
Marques Tuiasosopo	2000	OPOY, 2000		Heisman (8th) 2000; MVP Rose Bowl 2001				
Punter								
Skip Boyd	1973–74		Other, 1974					
Place-Kicker								
Chuck Nelson	1980–82		Unanimous, 1982			1998		
Jeff Jaeger	1986		Consensus, 1986			2004		
Defensive Lineman								
Jim Lambright	1964					2006		
Tom Greenlee	1965–66		Consensus, 1966			1987		
Steve Thompson	1966–67							
Dean Halverson	1967							
Lee Brock	1969							
Tom Failla	1970							
Gordy Guinn	1971–72							
Dave Pear	1973							
Charles Jackson	1976							
Dave Browning	1977							
Doug Martin	1978–79				9			
Fletcher Jenkins	1981	Morris, 1981						
Ron Holmes	1983–84	Morris, 1984	Consensus, 1984		8	2001		
Reggie Rogers	1985-86	Morris, 1986	Consensus, 1986		7			
Dennis Brown	1988							
Travis Richardson	1990							
Steve Emtman	1990–91	Morris, 1990–91; DPOY, 1990-91	Unanimous, 1991	Heisman (4th), 1991; Lombardi, Outland 1991; Co-MVP Rose Bowl 1992	1	1999	2007	
Jason Chorak	1996–97	DPOY, 1996	Other, 1996					
Jabari Issa	1998							
Larry Tripplett	2000–01		Other, 2001					
Linebacker								
Rick Redman	1963–64		Consensus, 1963, 1964			1982	1995	
George Jugum	1968							
Dan Lloyd	1975							
Michael Jackson	1977–78					2000		

Name of Player (by Position and Chronologically)	All-Conference / All-Coast	Conference Awards	All-Americans (Unanimous, Consensus, and Other)	Other Honors and Awards	NFL First-Round Draft Selection	Husky Hall of Fame Selection	College Football Hall of Fame Selection	Best of the Best
Bruce Harrell	1979							
Antowaine Richardson	1979							
Mark Jerue	1981							
Mark Stewart	1982		Consensus, 1982			2008		
Tim Meamber	1984							
Fred Small	1984							
Joe Kelly	1985				11			
Donald Jones	1990–91							
Chico Fraley	1991							
Dave Hoffmann	1991–92	DPOY, 1992	Other, 1991, 1992			2012		
Ink Aleaga	1995–96							
Jerry Jensen	1997							
Mason Foster	2010							

Defensive Back

Dick Sprague	1950		Other, 1950			1995		
Bob Pederson	1966							
Al Worley	1968		Consensus, 1968			1992		
Calvin Jones	1970–72		Other, 1972			1983		
Al Burleson	1975							
Nesby Glasgow	1977–78					2001		
Kyle Heinrich	1978							
Mark Lee	1979							
Ray Horton	1981							
Jim Rodgers	1984							
Vestee Jackson	1985							
Tim Peoples	1986		Other, 1986					
Charles Mincy	1990							
Dana Hall	1991				18			
Lawyer Milloy	1994–95		Unanimous, 1995		2	2012		
Tony Parrish	1996							
Hakim Akbar	2000							
C.J. Wallace	2006							

Kick Returner

Mark Lee	1979							
Anthony Allen	1981							
Beno Bryant	1990							
Joe Jarzynka	1998							
Charles Frederick	2003							

The Ten Best Teams in Husky History

In selecting my top 10 best teams, I have used three criteria. First, the team had to win the Pacific Coast Conference championship. If it did not, it had to be ranked in the top 10 in the national polls at the end of the bowl season. Second, the team had to play a full collegiate schedule. Third, the team had to play in one of the major bowl games.

10. 1936 Huskies

They won the conference title and finished the overall season with a 7–2–1 record but lost to Pittsburgh 21–0 in the 1937 Rose Bowl. They recorded six shutouts during the regular season, including "the perfect game": a 40–0 win over 20th-ranked Washington State. This team was ranked fifth in the final polls.

9. 1981 Huskies

The 1981 squad won the conference title, had a 10–2 record, and beat Iowa 28–0 in the 1982 Rose Bowl. The crucial games were the last two of the regular season: a 13–3 victory over third-ranked USC and a 23–10 win over No. 14 Washington State. This team was ranked 10th in the final polls.

8. 1977 Huskies

The 1977 team won the conference title, had a 10–2 record, and staged a 27–20 upset over fourth-ranked Michigan in the 1978 Rose Bowl. Its 54–0 thumping of Oregon in Eugene early in the season turned the season around, and two wins in November over USC and Washington State secured the first of many conference championships for head coach Don James. This team was also ranked 10th in the final polls.

7. 1990 Huskies

The team won the conference title, finished the overall season with a 10–2 record, and beat Iowa 46–34 in the 1991 Rose Bowl. The crucial games were in November—a 54–10 drubbing of Arizona that earned the Huskies a No. 2 ranking and a very convincing 55–10 road win over the Cougars. The team finished fifth in the final AP poll.

6. 1925 Huskies

The 1925 team won the conference title, finished the regular season with a 10–0–1 record, and went on to lose to Alabama 20–19 in the 1926 Rose Bowl—one of the most memorable in Rose Bowl history. This team recorded six shutouts, led the nation in regular-season scoring with 461 points, and gave up only 39 points during the regular season. This team ranked fifth in the final polls.

5. 1959 Huskies

The 1959 team won the conference title, finished the overall season with a 10–1 record, and staged a stunning 44–8 upset over sixth-ranked Wisconsin in the 1960 Rose Bowl—the first Rose Bowl victory in Husky history. This team recorded four shutouts in the regular season, holding opponents to just 65 points. The crucial games were a 13–6 win over Oregon State followed by 20–0 victories over Cal and Washington State. This team was ranked eighth in the final polls.

4. 2000 Huskies

This team won the conference title, finished the overall season with an 11–1 record, and beat Purdue 34–24 in the 2001 Rose Bowl for a No. 3 finish in the final AP poll. This team fought tooth and nail. It had an early season win over No. 4 Miami, won eight games by a touchdown or less, and trailed at one point in eight of its 10 regular-season victories. The crucial games were a 31–28 win at Stanford, a 35–32 last-minute win over Arizona, and a 35–28 victory over UCLA.

3. 1984 Huskies

The 1984 team finished second in the conference, posted an 11–1 record, and beat No. 2 Oklahoma in the Orange Bowl. The Huskies were ranked No. 1 for four weeks during the latter part of the season, before losing to USC 16–7. They were ranked second in the final AP poll, and three polls awarded this team the national championship.

2. 1960 Huskies

The 1960 team won the conference title, finished the overall season 10–1, and beat top-ranked Minnesota in the Rose Bowl 17–7. They were ranked sixth in the final regular-season poll. Remember, in those days, all but two

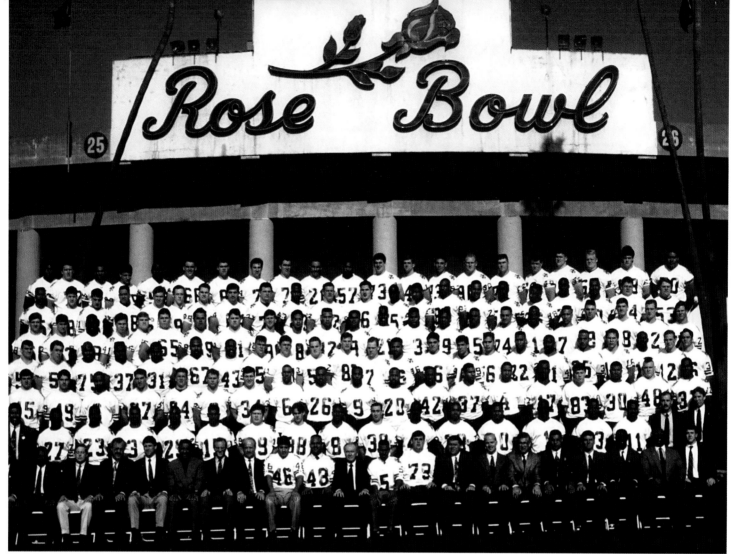

1991: the greatest team in Husky history.

polls completed their rankings before the bowl games were played. Of the two polls that waited until the bowl games were over to release their final rankings, one (the Helms Foundation) chose Washington; the other chose Mississippi. In an injury-riddled season, the Huskies lost only to fourth-ranked Navy (15–14. To clinch the conference title, they came from behind in Spokane to defeat the Cougars 8–7 with a late-game touchdown and two-point conversion.

1. 1991 Huskies

The 1991 team is the only team in Husky history other than those in the Gil Dobie era to post a perfect record

(12–0). They won a conference title, tied the 1925 team for most points scored in a season (461), gave up only 101 points to opponents, and won a share of the national title, with unbeaten Miami. Crucial wins along the way included a 36–21 win over ninth-ranked Nebraska in Lincoln and over seventh-ranked California (24–17) in Berkeley. In the last three games of the season, they had road wins over USC and Oregon State and topped off the season with a lopsided 56–21 victory over Washington State before more than 72,500 fans. They faced fourth-ranked Michigan in the 1992 Rose Bowl and dominated the Wolverines, beating them 34–14.

CHAPTER 12

The Greatest Comebacks and Bowl Victories in Husky History

In the history of Husky football, there have been 16 bowl victories and myriad comeback wins. This chapter details some amazing comeback wins when the Huskies faced a deficit of between 14 and 28 points. We previously discussed two of the greatest comeback victories: 30–29 over Oregon State in 1960 and 25–24 over Michigan in 1983. Here are the others. This chapter details some of the most unbelievable games in the team's history.

Two Seconds Left

November 12, 1988: Washington vs. Cal
The Bears ripped apart the Huskies in the first half by gaining a massive 263 yards. Defensive coordinator Jim Lambright let the Huskies have it during halftime. ("I don't think I can repeat what I said," he told the press after the game.) Whatever he said, it made an impression. The players came out of the tunnel with emotion, focused on shutting down the Cal offense. Early in the third quarter, the Huskies yielded a 47-yard field goal, putting them behind 27–3. But then Washington scored on four of their next six drives. Washington scored a touchdown and hit a successful two-point conversion, then followed with a field goal. Then, with seven seconds remaining in the third quarter, fullback Aaron Jenkins scored from nine yards out, ending a 70-yard march. The big play of the drive was a pass in the flat to Jenkins for a 25-yard gain. McCallum's successful kick cut the Cal lead to 27–18.

The score remained 27–18 for more than eight minutes, then Chico Fraley recovered a Cal fumble on the Bears 45. Seven plays later, Lewis found an opening off-tackle for the touchdown, and the conversion drew the Huskies within two with 4:20 to play. The Bears' next drive ended on their own 32, and their punt was returned to the Husky 43 with two minutes remaining. On fourth-and-2 from the Cal 49, Husky quarterback Cary Conklin ran for a first down on an option play. Then he found 6'4" flanker Brian Slater open downfield. Slater extended his arms skyward to make the catch at the Cal 14. After three more plays, McCallum trotted onto the field, confidently set up his line, and kicked the game-winning field goal.

Pelluer was conference Offensive Player of the Year in 1983.

He was mobbed by his teammates; the fans hugged each other and left Husky Stadium in disbelief and exclaiming, "Can you believe it?"

Chuck Nelson Nails It

October 10, 1981: Washington at Cal

The Bears led 14–0 at halftime and quickly increased the score to 21–0 in the first two and a half minutes of the third quarter. Then Husky quarterback Steve Pelluer took over, engineering several second-half drives and aided by the running of Ron "Cookie" Jackson. First, the Huskies drove downfield and fullback Chris Jones plunged over the goal line to get the Huskies on the scoreboard. A minute later, linebacker Ken Driscoll recovered a Cal fumble on the Bears 12. Pelluer then flipped the ball to Jones in the flat, and he outraced the Cal secondary to the pylon. Suddenly, it was 21–14. Near the end of the third quarter, Cal coughed the ball up again, at its own 25-yard line. The Husky drive stalled when Pelluer was sacked on third down. Nelson split the uprights from 37 yards out to get the Huskies within four.

In the fourth quarter, Washington almost gave the game away. Pelluer fumbled a center snap on third down, and then long snapper Doug Weston sent the ball high over the outstretched arms of punter Jeff Partridge and out of the end zone for a Bears safety. With nine minutes remaining, tailback Sterling Hinds, a world-class sprinter, finished a Husky drive by racing 16 yards to put Washington ahead 24–23. Cal wasted no time, kicking a 39-yard field goal and reclaiming the lead 26–24. Racing against the clock, the Huskies put together a drive and marched downfield. With 11 seconds to go, Nelson entered the game and kicked the game-winning field goal. The Huskies were on their way to a conference title and a 28–0 victory over Iowa in the 1982 Rose Bowl.

Boilermakers Burned

September 23, 1972: Washington at Purdue
In the previous season, the Huskies beat Purdue in a wild and wooly game in which the lead changed eight times. This time, the lead changed only once: after the Huskies overcame a 21–0 halftime deficit. Penalties killed the Huskies, who were flagged 11 times for 136 yards, including six clipping penalties. Throw in four interceptions, and you get some idea why the Huskies might have put their tails between their legs and gone quietly home to Seattle.

Led by quarterback Gary Danielson, who *rushed* for 213 yards, Purdue went into the locker room at halftime feeling pretty good about their chances. The Huskies came out after the intermission determined to stop giving away yards. When linebacker Bob Ferguson intercepted Danielson's pass at the Boilermakers 36, quarterback Sonny Sixkiller took the reins, engineering a scoring drive that culminated with a seven-yard touchdown from running back Pete Taggares.

The Huskies capitalized on another Purdue mistake in the fourth. Boilermaker Dick Rogers set up to punt, fumbled the snap, and fell on the ball at his own 34. Nine plays later, Sixkiller was in the end zone. The Huskies set up for the two-point conversion. Tight end John Brady came down with it, but the officials ruled offensive pass interference, and Purdue led 21–13. Then Husky defensive end Dave Worgan recovered a Purdue fumble at the Boilermakers 48 to set up another Husky touchdown. Unfortunately, the two-point conversion that would tie the game failed again.

On the ensuing drive, the Huskies forced Purdue to punt and then started on their own 15 with less than four minutes on the clock. Sixkiller was one cool and calm quarterback, completing four passes on the drive, including a 28-yard strike to Brady. With just more than two minutes left, the Huskies were on the Purdue 21. They gained another six yards and set up in the middle of the field for the winning field goal. Steve Wiezbowski split the uprights from 25 yards away with 2:04 remaining for the 22–21 victory.

Seattle Times reporter Dick Rockne quoted Owens, who received the game ball: "This has to be one of the most beautiful wins in my career."

McCallum Again, Same Score

October 28, 1989: Washington at UCLA
The Bruins blazed out of the locker room, quickly taking a 14–0 lead on their home field. By the end of the first quarter, they were ahead by 21. After place-kicker Alfredo Velasco missed a 34–yard field goal that would have extended UCLA's lead to 24 points, the Huskies started to recover. With almost 11 minutes left in the second quarter, Washington's free safety Eugene Burkhalter returned an interception to the Bruins 30. Four plays later, they had a touchdown. Then sophomore defensive tackle Steve Emtman recovered a fumble on the UCLA 24. Running back Greg Lewis did the rest to get the Huskies just seven back, 21–14.

Midway through the third period, Velasco put the Bruins up by 10 on a 37-yard field goal. The Huskies answered in the fourth with a touchdown, bringing them to within three at 24–21. Velasco then tacked on another field goal. But it was the Huskies that would have the last laugh. Conklin went to work, completing 5-of-7 passes on a 78-yard drive capped off by a 10-yard touchdown run by Lewis. It was up to McCallum, in to kick the extra point, to secure the victory. His kick hooked to the left but managed to go through the uprights—Washington 28, UCLA 27.

"Bedlam by the Bay"

October 9, 1993: Washington at California

That was the headline in the *Seattle Times* on October 10, 1993, the day after Washington beat California. California, coached by former Husky offensive coordinator Keith Gilbertson, had a 23–3 lead going deep into the third quarter.

The Huskies scored their first touchdown late in the third to cut the lead to 13. Then with 3:47 remaining in the game, they started a drive on their 24 and quickly got to the Cal 49. Then senior tight end D.J. McCarthy made a very key play, catching quarterback Damon Huard's pass in the corner of the end zone. With the conversion, the Huskies had closed to within six—23–17—with 2:06 to play.

Coach Jim Lambright called for an onside kick, and Jason Crabbe hit it perfectly. After it went the required 10 yards, sophomore cornerback Scott Greenlaw recovered it on the Cal 48. In a span of one minute and two seconds, Huard completed six of seven passes for all of the 48 yards and a touchdown to tie the score 23–23 with 45 seconds left. The extra point was good. With precious seconds on the clock, Cal still had a chance to win. The Bears reached the Husky 47 but were pushed back and out of field-goal range. The Huskies left Memorial Stadium with a very memorable 24–23 victory.

The Great Escape

September 22, 1979: Washington at Oregon

At the end of the third quarter, the Huskies found themselves down 17 against the Ducks in Eugene. Then with 41 seconds left in the period, Husky tailback Joe Steele dove into the end zone to cap a 36-yard drive. Steele scored another touchdown late in the fourth to close the gap to three.

Mike Lansford's ensuing kickoff was a boomer, and returned only to the Oregon 16. The Husky defense shut the Ducks down. Oregon's Mike Babb punted to the Husky 47, where Mark Lee cradled the ball and started to run laterally to elude a pursuing defender. He then broke loose from a potential tackler, turned the corner on the far side of the field, got a couple of key blocks, and sailed down the left sideline and into the end zone. Lansford's kick was good, and Washington upended Oregon 21–17.

A Drub for C-Dub

November 4, 2000: Washington vs. Arizona

On November 4, 2000, just one week after Curtis Williams' tragic accident, the Huskies met the Arizona Wildcats in Husky Stadium. Before the game, the Husky band marched into a C-DUB formation, and the fans applauded to show their respect and admiration for the injured player. Before the kickoff, the players of each team lined up on their 25-yard line and faced each other to honor Williams, who wore No. 25. Despite elevated feelings, Washington trailed 25–10 in the third quarter. Then John Anderson's 38-yard field goal cut the Arizona lead to 12.

In the fourth quarter, the Huskies found another level of play. In less than 11 minutes, they scored 22 points to win 35–32. First, junior tailback Willie Hurst took an option pitch that was almost a forward pass from quarterback Marques Tuiasosopo. He ran 65 yards for the score, and the extra point was good. On the next Arizona possession, the Huskies held the Wildcats to zero yards. A short punt gave Washington the ball on the Arizona 42. From the 23, Hurst was almost upended by defensive end Joe Tafoya, but made an exceptional move, turning over in midair, regaining his balance with an outstretched hand, and running for the touchdown. He got the two-point conversion against a Wildcats rush defense rated first in the conference. The Huskies took the lead for the first time, 28–25.

After giving up an Arizona touchdown on the ensuing possession, they quickly got to the Arizona 37 after a 25-yard pass to split end Todd Elstrom. After one more first down, Washington got a big break. Facing third-and-9 at the Wildcats 11, Tuiasosopo set up to pass and was almost sacked at the 20 when Tafoya grabbed his face mask—automatic first down. Two plays later Tuiasosopo ran in for the winning touchdown.

California Can't Hold a Lead against the Huskies

October 23, 1999: Washington at Cal

Taking on the Bears in their den, the Huskies found themselves down two touchdowns early in the third quarter. On third-and-13 at the Washington 17, Husky quarterback Marques Tuiasosopo had to make something happen. He lofted the ball deep for split end Todd Elstrom; the receiver was closely covered by Cal cornerback Chidi Iwuoma but managed to tear the ball away and then outrun everyone to the end zone.

Down 24–17 early in the fourth quarter, the Huskies struck again. On an 88-yard drive, the big play was a 36-yard pass to split end Dana Looker. Tailback Maurice Shaw ended the drive by charging nine yards to pay dirt.

The Bears responded; cornerback Deltha O'Neil intercepted Tuiasosopo's pass and ran to the Husky 24. On fourth-and-1 at the 4, Cal elected to kick a field goal and regained the lead.

With 2:53 left in the game, Washington took over on their 22 after a Cal punt. Tuiasosopo ran a quarterback draw for 14 and later passed to wide-open Looker for 39 yards, down to the Cal 21. After a few running plays, the Huskies had first-and-goal at the 10 with less than two minutes to go. Then Tuia handed off to Shaw, who bounced inside and got tangled up with Cal defenders. As he turned around to stay upright, he heard his quarterback calling for the ball. Shaw lateraled the ball back to Tuiasosopo, who fought for three yards. Then he ran for five more on an option play. On third-and-2, Shaw scored the winning touchdown for a 31–27 victory.

Cal Once More

September 29, 2001: Washington at California

Cal scored on its first two possessions, threatening to put the game out of reach in the early minutes. The Huskies desperately needed something and someone to turn the game around. Near the end of the first quarter, they got both. After Washington quarterback Cody Pickett got sacked near the Husky goal line, freshman punter Derek McLaughlin set up to kick from the back of Washington's end zone. He absolutely drilled it, sending the pigskin a school-record 74 yards. On the same play, Ray Carmel was flagged for an illegal block that put the ball on the Cal 15-yard line. Shortly after, Washington linebacker Jamaun Willis stripped the ball from Cal receiver Charon Arnold, and strong safety Greg Carothers recovered it on the Cal 42. Moments later, Pickett saw tailback Paul Arnold streaking toward the corner of the end zone and hit him

2002 All-American and two-time All-Conference wide receiver Reggie Williams takes off.

with a perfect pass, cutting the Huskies' deficit in half. Cal answered back, increasing their lead to 14. Washington's John Anderson's hit a 40-yard field goal and the teams went into the locker rooms for the half: Cal 21, Washington 10.

The second half was much different. First, Pickett teamed up with Arnold again for a 63-yard scoring strike. Then they put together a 70-yard drive that included a 44-yard pass to freshman wide receiver Reggie Williams.

Fullback Rich Alexis finished it with a one-yard run to put Washington ahead 24–21. Then with 5:26 to play, Alexis scored again and the Husky lead was increased to 10. The Bears were not yet in hibernation; they scored another touchdown to get within three, but the Huskies held on for a 31–28 comeback victory.

To the Top 10 in Tempe

September 5, 1998: Washington at Arizona State
Before a crowd of more than 72,000 at Sun Devil Stadium, Washington faced eighth-ranked Arizona State. It was the season opener for both teams. Both offenses looked solid—the teams scored a combined six touchdowns in the first half—but ASU had the edge going into the half, leading 28–14.

The Huskies came back and engineered two beautiful drives to take a 35–28 lead. The Sun Devils surged back and put 10 points on the board, regaining the lead at 38–35. Starting on their own 20, Washington started to put together a stunning drive. But after getting a first down, it looked rather bleak for the Huskies, facing fourth-and-17 at their own 33. Reggie Davis raced downfield to get behind cornerback Phillip Brown and caught Huard's pass at the Sun Devils 40. He shook off a tackler at the 10 and ran into the end zone for the game-winning touchdown with 28 seconds remaining in the nail-biter.

For the Apple Cup and a Return to the Rose Bowl

November 22, 1980: Washington at Washington State
Before a chilled crowd of almost 35,000 in Spokane's Joe Albi Stadium on November 22, 1980, the 16th-ranked Huskies got all they could handle from the Cougars. Washington entered the game 8–2–0 and tied for first in the conference with UCLA. Washington State was 4–6 and was led by quarterback Samoa Samoa. He got the Cougars off fast. They outgained the Huskies 176 yards to five to take a 14–0 lead with three minutes left in the third quarter.

Midway through the second quarter, Ricky Turner fumbled a Washington punt, which was recovered on the Cougars 28. Quarterback Tom Flick hit fullback Willie Rosborough for 11 yards and then for seven to tight end David Bayle. Rosborough scored from the 3 to make the score 14–7 with less than three minutes left in the half. On the next Cougars possession, Samoa attempted a quarterback draw, took a hard hit, and fumbled. Husky strong safety Ken Gardner recovered on the Washington State 32 with about 90 seconds left before the halftime break. It took only 35 seconds for Washington to score. On the scoring play, Flick passed over the middle to flanker Paul Skansi at the 6 and he darted into the end zone. The extra point was good, and the game was tied 14–14.

On the Huskies' first possession in the third quarter, Flick found split end Aaron Williams for a 41-yard touchdown. The play ended a 93-yard, 13-play drive. Again the kick was good, and the Huskies took their first lead, 21–14. The Cougars recovered a Husky fumble midway through the period. The play led to a 26-yard field goal to pull the Cougars within four. Early in the fourth quarter, Washington started a 64-yard drive. On second-and-9, Flick passed 16 yards to Bayle, followed by a 47-yard strike to split end Anthony Allen for the score. Nelson's kick was blocked, and the Huskies led 27–17. The lead was reduced to four with 5:48 left in the game when Samoa passed 33 yards to Pat Beach for a touchdown. Nose guard Mark Jerve blocked the extra point. The Huskies answered immediately with a 68-yard drive to the Cougars 12. On fourth-and-3, Nelson kicked a field goal. It was his 20th field goal for the season, a new Husky season record.

Huskies Overcome Many Mistakes to Beat the Beavers

October 24, 1970: Washington at Oregon State
The 3–4 Huskies found a very unusual way to beat the Beavers: throw six interceptions, give up two fumbles, and get penalized for 132 yards. Trailing by 14, the Huskies drove 49 yards to the Beavers 1-yard line. Electing to go for it on fourth down, fullback Bo Cornell dove high over the pile and scored the touchdown. Quarterback Sonny Sixkiller passed to halfback Darrell Downey for the two-point conversion. With just 81 seconds left in the half, Husky linebacker Ron Shepherd recovered a Beavers fumble on the Washington 36. Sixkiller then completed six

passes— the last one for five yards and a touchdown to flanker Jim Krieg. Steve Wiezbowski kicked the extra point, and Washington took a 15–14 lead into the locker room.

Early in the second half, Washington put the game away. After a fumble recovery at the Beavers 29, the Huskies scored in three plays. Less than a minute later, it was 29–14 when Husky tackle Gordy Guinn rushed into the Beavers backfield and pressured quarterback Jim Kilmartin to throw his pass into the stomach of defensive tackle Randy Coleman; Coleman rumbled 20 yards straight to the end zone. The lead was Washington's for the duration, and the game ended a 29–20 victory for the Huskies.

Washington's Bowl History

Washington has played in 33 bowl games. Perhaps surprisingly, only 14 of them were Rose Bowls—and two of those Rose Bowl victories (1961 and 1992) were national championships. Their overall record in bowl competition is 16–16–1. A full accounting of the Huskies' postseason matchups follows.

Two-time bowl MVP Chris Chandler.

Date	Bowl	Location	Opponent	Score	Husky MVP (if any)
1/1/1924	Rose	Pasadena, CA	Navy	14–14	
1/1/1926	Rose	Pasadena, CA	Alabama	19–20	George Wilson, Co-MVP
1/1/1937	Rose	Pasadena, CA	Pittsburgh	0–21	
1/1/1938	Pineapple	Honolulu, HI	Hawaii	53–13	
1/1/1944	Rose	Pasadena, CA	USC	0–29	
1/1/1960	Rose	Pasadena, CA	Wisconsin	44–8	George Fleming and Bob Schloredt
1/2/1961	Rose	Pasadena, CA	Minnesota	17–7	Bob Schloredt
1/1/1964	Rose	Pasadena, CA	Illinois	7–17	
1/2/1978	Rose	Pasadena, CA	Michigan	27–20	Warren Moon
12/22/1979	Sun	El Paso, TX	Texas	14–7	Paul Skansi
1/1/1981	Rose	Pasadena, CA	Michigan	6–23	
1/1/1982	Rose	Pasadena, CA	Iowa	28–0	Jacque Robinson
12/25/1982	Aloha	Honolulu, HI	Maryland	21–20	Tim Cowan
12/26/1983	Aloha	Honolulu, HI	Penn State	10–13	
1/1/1985	Orange	Miami, FL	Oklahoma	28–17	Jacque Robinson
12/30/1985	Freedom	Anaheim, CA	Colorado	20–17	Chris Chandler
12/25/1986	Sun	El Paso, TX	Alabama	6–28	
12/19/1987	Independence	Shreveport, LA	Tulane	24–12	Chris Chandler
12/30/1989	Freedom	Anaheim, CA	Florida	34–7	Cary Conklin
1/1/1991	Rose	Pasadena, CA	Iowa	46–34	Mark Brunell
1/1/1992	Rose	Pasadena, CA	Michigan	34–14	Steve Emtman and Billy Joe Hobert
1/1/1993	Rose	Pasadena, CA	Michigan	31–38	
12/29/1995	Sun	El Paso, TX	Iowa	18–38	
12/30/1996	Holiday	San Diego, CA	Colorado	21–33	
12/25/1997	Aloha	Honolulu, HI	Michigan State	51–23	Rashaan Shehee
12/25/1998	Oahu	Honolulu, HI	Air Force	25–45	
12/29/1999	Holiday	San Diego, CA	Kansas State	20–24	
1/1/2001	Rose	Pasadena, CA	Purdue	34–24	Marques Tuiasosopo
12/28/2001	Holiday	San Diego, CA	Texas	43–47	
12/31/2002	Sun	El Paso, TX	Purdue	24–34	
12/30/2010	Holiday	San Diego, CA	Nebraska	19–7	Chris Polk
12/29/2011	Alamo	San Antonio, TX	Baylor	56–67	
12/22/2012	Maaco	Las Vegas, NV	Boise State	26–28	Bishop Sankey

CHAPTER 13

Game Day
at Husky Stadium

Husky Stadium is the most recognized and recognizable football stadium in the Pacific Northwest and one of the most beautiful in the country. Visitors to the area see the stadium on city tours and are drawn to the size and design of the place. Commuters in and out of Seattle see Husky Stadium rise in the sky with the roofs of the upper decks reaching skyward like a giant jaw beginning to close. At the edge of Lake Washington, tens of thousands of fans descend on Husky Stadium and its grounds each game day, transforming the area into a midsized city unto itself. The venue is one of the most difficult places for opponents to play. Indeed, the fans, the students, and the architectural design help increase the crowd volume to deafening levels.

The leisure of summer is over, and autumn is just around the corner. Students resume classes. The pace of activity quickens. Alumni return to the campus to renew friendships. A new Husky football season begins.

Preparation for game day begins several days beforehand. Helmets are newly striped, the *W* affixed to each side. The Husky equipment manager and his assistants busy themselves, anticipating the requirements of ball boys, the sideline chain gang, the game clock operators, the officials, the visiting team, and Husky players and coaches.

The focus is football, but the event is nothing less than a major social happening. It is pageantry, bands, cheerleaders, tailgate parties, and legions of people. The staff of the Husky Facilities and Events Department has been on hand for hours already, making sure that everything runs safely and smoothly.

At the Marine Activities Center southeast of the stadium, a few boats are already tied up, and others are gliding in. They moor in Union Bay, their purple and gold pennants flapping in the breeze. Husky crews pull toward Laurelhurst Point, on an early morning workout. The first tailgaters arrive in the large parking lots north of the stadium to set up for their pregame parties. The aromas of hamburgers and sausages and salmon fill the air. Some people have brought radios with them, to listen to the Husky pregame show. A few among them mount portable satellite dishes so they can watch the games already being played in the Midwest and East.

Fans stream in from towns across the region, dressed in clothes that announce their allegiance to the Huskies. Some have pennants and pom-poms streaming from their cars.

Almost 500 come by small boats and seagoing yachts, and another 5,000 arrive on larger charter boats. Metro buses dedicated to serving the Husky faithful bring in another 20,000. Others drive, walk, cycle, and kayak. Kids weave in and out of the crowd walking to the stadium, imagining they are racing the length of the field for a touchdown. The fans will soon fill the stadium to capacity.

Several hours before kickoff, Husky band members arrive to rehearse. The sound systems are checked. The communications crew readies the miles of cable to tie together the stadium announcers and the video feeds for replays and promotions.

High above the field, rooms and suites are ready to welcome the press corps, the stadium announcers, the radio and television crews, NFL scouts, corporate sponsors, and donors. The Husky locker room under the west stands and the visiting team's locker room in the southeast corner of the venue are still quiet, though game uniforms and equipment are in each player's dressing area, just ready to be donned. Helmets hang nearby on a cart. Close by is the Husky team meeting room, soon populated with players and coaches making their final game preparations.

On the concourses, the concessionaires prepare. The smell of freshly brewed coffee, clam chowder, hot dogs, and

There are so many ways for Husky fans to experience game day. Here are just a few:

- Come to a game by boat—any boat! You can come by kayak or canoe and get some exercise to boot. The traffic should not be too bad, particularly if you come early and stay near the shores of Lake Washington and Lake Union and inside the Montlake Cut. Others come in small powerboats. Members of the UW crew team offer shuttles to anyone who wants to go to and from the boats and docks to the game. Or you can board one of the charter boats that bring large groups of fans from various watering holes around Lake Washington, Lake Union, and Portage Bay.
- Set up your own tailgating spot on the grassy knolls south of the stadium, along the Montlake Cut.
- Get a field pass from the Sports Publicity office. This may require a substantial donation to the program—and why not? Standing on the sideline during the game is a much different experience than sitting in the stands. You will be up close to all the action where you really feel, in addition to hear, the crowd noise during big Husky moments or a Washington touchdown.
- Enjoy brunch at one of the restaurants in the University Village or on Sand Point Way and then stroll past the Urban Horticulture Center and across the Wildlife Refuge to the

Conibear Crew House. Visit the Football Legends Center near the crew house. Bring along your granddaughter or grandson and toss a football back and forth as you cross the Refuge.
- Fly into Union Bay for a game on Kenmore Air after a flyover of Central Puget Sound and the Seattle area.
- Attend a current exhibition at the Burke Museum on the north part of the campus or the Henry Art Gallery, and then meander southeast to the stadium past the Gates Law School and PACCAR Hall, two of the newest buildings on campus, and Denny Hall, the oldest building on campus.
- Take a slow stroll through one of the most beautiful urban campuses in the country and admire the fall foliage and views of Mount Rainier. Start on the north side of campus on Memorial Way and go east through the Fine Arts Quadrangle. Find the gargoyles that adorn the buildings that form the quadrangle. Proceed south to Suzzallo Library. Enter the classic Gothic structure and go one story up to the magnificent reading room in the library, then look southeast into Rainier Vista to see the fountain framed by Mount Rainier. Take a little detour to the southwest part of the campus and enter the Sylvan Theatre area, on which the original columns of the first Territorial University building have been relocated. Imagine what it was like to attend the university in 1861.

Tailgaters gather on game day at Husky Stadium.

HUSKIES PARKING ONLY

teriyaki greets the fans as the gates are opened. Some walk to the "Zone" at the east end of the stadium to meet friends, eat food prepared by excellent Seattle restaurants, and get energized by the Husky band and cheerleaders. The Husky radio network, amid all the noise, broadcasts the pregame there, too.

The stadium scoreboard and sound system are checked. High above the stadium floor, the stadium announcer and his two associates review player names and numbers and rehearse the many announcements to be made during the game. Radio and television crews are preparing lead-in material.

A Washington State Highway Patrol escort clears the traffic lanes for the teams' buses, which arrive about three hours before the game. The coaches and players enter their locker rooms to begin the final phase of their pregame preparation. A staff of trainers begins taping ankles, applying heat packs, and helping athletes with their stretching routines.

At about 90 minutes before game time, place-kickers and punters from both teams come onto the field and execute their warm-up drills. Kicks boom, sailing end-over-end through both goal posts. Punters propel spiraling footballs high in the sky. Soon, other units emerge from the tunnel and begin their drills. Quarterbacks lob passes to receivers. Players start their agility drills, stretching and blocking drills, and run through a handful of offensive and defensive plays. Coaches move through the squads, exhorting the warriors to action. The intensity level is rising.

The scoreboard displays the names of the players and shows replays of the previous week's action. All television cameras are ready. The alumni band performs on the west side of the stadium. Split into two units, the Husky band serenades the fans in the north and south stands. Boats and buses continue to arrive and the stadium fills.

About 25 minutes before kickoff, the starting lineups are announced. The teams clear the field and head back inside for a final team meeting. Clad in purple-trimmed uniforms, Husky band members run to their first formation on the field. Husky cheerleaders pump up the fans with their gymnastic routines. "Bow Down to Washington" is heard for the first time, and the assembled fans sing loudly and enthusiastically. The band ends its routine with the formation of a flagpole and the unfurling of a large American flag to the strains of "America the Beautiful." With the flag completely unfurled, the assembled rise to sing the national anthem.

The cocaptains from each team come out and meet the officials in the center of the field for the coin toss. Then the band assembles in two lines from the Huskies' tunnel, out to about the 35-yard line. First, the visiting team emerges from the southeast tunnel. Then, led by the cheerleaders and the Alaskan malamute mascot, scores of purple-clad Huskies pour out of the northwest tunnel.

The ball is teed up. Amid the thunderous noise of the standing passionate Husky faithful, the men in purple and gold charge downfield to follow the football's lofty, spinning trajectory and to bring its receiver crashing to the ground. Husky Stadium: what a place to be!

There have been many football games played in the stadium, but this place is more than games and statistics. It is where indelible memories have been created. There are men in their eighties who remember, when they were youngsters, waiting with their friends for the right moment to crawl under a fence on the east end and dart past members of the Knights of the Hook to find a safe haven in some empty seats. There are longtime season-ticket holders who approach each season with great excitement and recognize that they may soon be seeing their last games. Most remember the Owens and James eras, the conference championships, Rose Bowl victories, and national championships. Each fan has his or her memories of big moments, big games, and extraordinary players. All of these memories combine to form the mystique of Husky Stadium and what it has meant to so many people.

CHAPTER 14

Timeline of Great Moments in Husky Football History

This chapter provides a chronological list of major events in the history of the University of Washington and Husky football, framed in the major periods of the history.

September 16, 1861: The Territorial University of Washington is opened. It is the first public university on the West Coast.

November 4, 1861: Classes begin, with Asa Mercer as the temporary president and the school's only instructor.

November 6, 1869: The first football game in the United States is played at Rutgers University in New Brunswick, New Jersey. Rutgers beats Princeton 6–4.

November 11, 1889: The Territory of Washington becomes the 42nd state in the United States of America.

November 28, 1889: The Eastern Colleges Alumni plays the University of Washington football team. Frank Griffiths is the captain for UW; there is no coach. The alumni team wins 20–0.

December 17, 1892: Washington wins its first football game, 14–0; Frank Atkins scores the school's first touchdown on a five-yard run. William Goodwin, a member of the Eastern Colleges Alumni team in 1889, becomes Washington's first coach in 1892. Also in 1892, the school colors of purple and gold are established.

December 29, 1893:, Stanford shuts out the home team 40–0. Stanford played three other Northwest schools and won all four matchups by an aggregate score of 156–0. Washington is admitted to its first conference, the Western Washington Intercollegiate Athletic Association, in this year.

November 22, 1894: Washington plays its first collegiate road game, in Walla Walla against Whitman College. Washington wins 46–0 and claims the first collegiate state championship.

September 4, 1895: The university moves to a new campus called the Interlaken site. A student athletic association is also formed.

October 19, 1895: Washington plays its first game on Denny Field, defeating the Seattle Athletic Club 12–0.

1895: Washington has its first unbeaten season. The team records four wins and one tie and outscores its opponents 98–8.

December 4, 1897: Washington plays its first out-of-state game against the Oregon Agricultural College in Corvallis, Oregon. Washington loses 16–0.

December 24, 1898: Running back Sterling Hill, one of four brothers to play football at Washington and a son of Eugene Hill, the fifth president of the University of Washington, records the then-longest touchdown in Husky history—94 yards—against the Puyallup Indian Reservation squad.

November 25, 1899: Washington beats Whitman 6–5 in a heavy rain- and windstorm to win the championship of Idaho and Washington.

September 1900: J. Sayre Dodge becomes the first paid Washington football coach.

November 30, 1900: Washington plays Washington Agricultural College (later renamed Washington State University) for the first time. The game ends in a 5–5 tie.

September 15, 1902: James Knight is hired as Washington's football coach and its first crew coach. He coaches football for three seasons and compiles a record of 15-4-1. His .775 winning percentage is still the second-best in Washington history.

November 27, 1902: Washington defeats Washington State 16–0 to win the first NIAA title.

November 20, 1903: By defeating Nevada 2–0, Washington claims the title of the Best Team in the West.

November 5, 1904: Royal Shaw records the longest run from scrimmage in Washington history. He ran 105 yards (the field was 110 yards long in those days) for a touchdown against Idaho.

November 24, 1904: Washington plays California for the first time. The game ends in a 6–6 tie. Shaw is the hero once again, with a 25-yard touchdown run to even the score. He later becomes the first Washington athlete to play Major League Baseball, joining Honus Wagner and the Pittsburgh Pirates in 1908.

November 28, 1907: Washington plays a scoreless tie with Idaho to start a 64-game unbeaten streak. From the last game of the 1907 season through the first game of the 1917 season, Washington never loses a game—winning 60 and recording four ties.

1908: The Pacific Northwest Intercollegiate Conference (PNWIC) is formed. Original conference members included Idaho, Oregon, Oregon State, Washington, Washington Sate, and Whitman.

1908: Robert Gilmore Dobie becomes Washington's head coach.

November 14, 1908: Washington defeats Oregon 15–0, beginning a 40-game winning streak.

1908: The Guy Flaherty Award is established.

June 1, 1909: The Alaska-Yukon-Pacific Exposition (AYPE) opens. The Olmstead Brothers' plan for the event orients the campus toward Mount Rainier. Rainier Vista becomes the most sacred space on campus.

Wee Coyle

October 18, 1913: Washington beats Whitworth 100–0 to break the school record of 99 points scored against Fort Worden in 1911.

November 15, 1913: Washington plays Oregon in Multnomah Stadium in Portland. It is the first time in Washington history that a group of men and women are allowed to make a trip away from campus to witness a Washington football game.

October 31, 1914: The 40-game winning streak ends when Oregon State and Washington battle to a scoreless tie in Albany, Oregon.

November 6, 1915: Washington crushes California in its first Pacific Coast Conference game—72–0 in Berkeley. In a much closer contest the next week, Washington defeats Cal 13–7 to record its first PCC home win.

December 2, 1915: The Pacific Coast Conference is formed. The initial members are California, Oregon, Oregon State, and Washington. Washington State joins the conference a year later.

September 30, 1916: Washington records win No. 100 against the Ballard Meteors. The score is 28–0.

November 30, 1916: After beating California in Berkeley two weeks before, Washington defeats the Bears at home 14–7, to win the first Pacific Coast Conference title. It is Gil Dobie's last game as Washington's coach.

December 8, 1916: Coach Dobie disagrees with the faculty athletic committee decision to suspend tackle Bill Grimm for cheating on a test, instead opting to keep his star in for the conference title game against California. University president Henry Suzzallo fires the coach, believing Dobie is more interested in winning football games than developing the character of student-athletes. Dobie leaves Washington with a 59–0–3 record and the highest winning percentage in school history.

October 25, 1919: Under coach Claude Hunt, Washington really beats up on Whitman College, winning 120–0—the biggest margin of victory in Washington history. Halfback Ervin Dailey scores seven touchdowns and amasses 350 rushing yards.

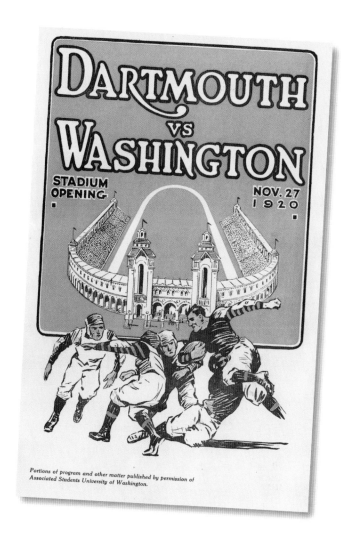

Portions of program and other matter published by permission of Associated Students University of Washington.

April 16, 1920: Ground is broken for a new stadium.

November 5, 1920: Stanford beats Washington 3–0 in the last game on Denny Field.

November 27, 1920: Dartmouth's football team journeys from Hanover, New Hampshire, to play Washington in the first game in Washington Field. The long journey does not seem to affect "the Green," who beat UW 28–7.

November 12, 1921: California avenges their 72–0 loss in 1915 by routing Washington 72–3 in Berkeley. It remains the worst defeat in Washington history. It is also the first year for head coach Enoch Bagshaw, a former UW player.

December 3, 1921: Washington plays Penn State for the first time and loses 21–7 in Husky Stadium.

February 3, 1922: The university officially accepts the nickname "Huskies" for its athletic teams. The nickname is announced during the halftime of a basketball game against Washington State. Football captain-elect Robert Ingram presents the name; it is enthusiastically adopted.

October 20, 1923: The Huskies play the University of Southern California for the first time and shut out the Trojans 22–0.

January 1, 1924: The Huskies play in their first bowl game. They tie Navy in the Rose Bowl, 14–14.

October 12, 1925: The Huskies travel to Lincoln, Nebraska, to play the Cornhuskers for the first time. The game ends in a 6–6 tie.

January 1, 1926: Washington makes its second Rose Bowl appearance and plays Alabama. In one of the greatest Rose Bowl games ever, Washington loses 30–29. Husky consensus All-American running back George Wilson is voted the co-MVP along with the Crimson Tide's Johnny Mack Brown.

October 23, 1926: Bonds had been issued to partially finance the stadium construction. They were repaid and burned during the halftime of the Washington State game. The Cougars ruin the rest of the day, beating UW 9–6.

November 3, 1928: Charles "Chuck" Carroll, the Huskies' second consensus All-American running back, scores six touchdowns in Washington's 40–0 win over the College of Puget Sound.

November 1, 1929: Washington plays the College of Puget Sound under the lights in Tacoma. The Huskies dim the Loggers 73–0.

October 27, 1934: Washington wins its 200th game, beating California 13–7.

October 14, 1935: Under head coach James Phelan, Washington beats the Cougars 21–0 to win the Governor's Trophy (later renamed the Apple Cup) for the first time.

November 26, 1936: Playing for the conference championship, the Huskies win 40–0 and hold Washington State to 61 total yards and intercept five Cougars passes. WSU never gets into Husky territory. Some call it the "perfect game."

January 1, 1937: After winning the conference title, the No. 5 Huskies face third-ranked Pittsburgh in the Rose Bowl and lose 21–0.

January 1, 1938: The Huskies win their first bowl game, beating the University of Hawaii in the Pineapple Bowl 53–13. Five days later, the Huskies defeat the Honolulu Townies 35–6.

September 29, 1942: Fritz Waskowitz, Washington's captain in 1937, is killed in action while serving with the U.S. Army Air Corps in the Pacific.

January 1, 1944: Because of wartime restrictions, two Pacific Coast Conference teams—USC and Washington—play in the 1944 Rose Bowl. The Trojans win 29–0.

November 27, 1948: Led by head coach Howard Odell, Washington plays No. 2 Notre Dame for the first time. The Huskies lose 46–0 in South Bend.

September 24, 1949: Before Minnesota fans have time to settle in their seats, sophomore running back Hugh McElhenny makes one of the fastest opening-play touchdowns ever. From his own 6-yard line, he speeds down the field completely untouched. It is one of the few Husky highlights in the 48–20 loss.

October 1, 1949: Notre Dame comes to Seattle for the first time, bringing a string of 29 wins with them. They beat the Huskies 27–7 on their way to another national championship.

September 23, 1950: The south-side upper deck is ready for the opening game of the 1950 season. It adds about 15,000 seats to the stadium, at a cost of $1.7 million.

October 7, 1950: The Huskies come from behind to beat coach Red Sanders' UCLA Bruins 21–20. As the final seconds ticks away, Jim Rosenzweig kicks an extra point for the victory.

November 4, 1950: The California Bears come to town, with the conference title at stake. With the Bears ahead 14–7, the Huskies have two chances to score in the last four minutes—one from the 2-yard line and another from the 9. Both times, the Bears defense thwarts the Huskies.

November 25, 1950: In Spokane's Memorial Stadium, the Huskies beat the Cougars 52–21. Quarterback Don

Heinrich and halfback Hugh McElhenny both establish very significant records. Heinrich breaks the national single-season passing record; McElhenny sets a Husky single-game rushing record and a new Pacific Coast Conference record for most rushing yards in a season. The King's single-game record of 296 yards remains the best in school history.

October 6, 1951: Hugh McElhenny catches a USC punt on his own goal line and turns up the north sideline of Husky Stadium with a clear path opened by his teammates. His punt return for the touchdown is still the longest in Husky history.

November 29, 1952: Inducted into the army a week before, quarterback Don Heinrich is given a weekend pass to play the Cougars in Spokane. He plays very well in the Husky victory and ends the game at the top of the nation in passes completed (137).

October 8, 1955: Facing 10th-ranked USC at home, the Huskies beat the Trojans 7–0. It is win No. 300 for the Huskies.

January 27, 1956: After a player revolt at the end of the 1955 season, coach John Cherberg is fired. He goes public about direct payments made to players by Husky boosters. As a result, athletic director Harvey Cassill resigns a few weeks later. After a Pacific Coast Conference investigation, the Huskies are put on probation for two years.

February 15, 1956: George Briggs, an assistant athletic director at California, is selected to be the new athletic director at Washington. He forms the Tyee Club to get boosters to pay funds for the athletic program to the university instead of directly to the players. He also goes looking for a new football coach, hiring Darrell Royal.

September 22, 1956: In the season opener, the Huskies score eight touchdowns and a total of 613 yards to beat Idaho 53–21, going on to a 5–5 regular-season record. In December, Royal gets his dream job: he becomes the head coach at Texas.

January 21, 1957: Twenty-nine-year-old Jim Owens, a teammate of Royal's at Oklahoma, becomes Washington's new head coach. He signs a three-year contract for $15,000 a year.

September 10, 1957: Coach Owens tests the physical limits of his players with a series of rigorous drills. One observing reporter calls it the "death march." Owens' expectations of phy sical toughness and conditioning become the hallmarks of his squads.

October 26, 1957: The Huskies win their first game in the Owens era, beating Oregon State 19–6 in Husky Stadium. For his excellent offensive and defensive play, the Associated Press selects fullback Jim Jones as the national "Back of the Week."

August 23, 1958: California, UCLA, USC, and Washington agree to establish the Association of Western Universities, beginning July 1, 1959. Stanford agrees to join the new conference in 1959. As a result, the Pacific Coast Conference is dissolved.

November 1, 1958: Washington beats Oregon 6–0. It is Owens' first shutout at Washington and the first Husky shutout in 33 games.

October 24, 1959: After a 22–15 loss to USC in Husky Stadium the week before, the Huskies stage a come-from-behind triumph over Oregon, 13–12. The win keeps their Rose Bowl hopes alive.

January 1, 1960: The Huskies face the sixth-ranked Wisconsin Badgers in the Rose Bowl. In the 13 years of Rose Bowl games played between Big Ten and PCC teams after World War II, the PCC had won just one. The Huskies crush the Badgers 44–8, giving Washington its first-ever Rose Bowl victory. George Fleming and Bob Schloredt are voted the game's co-MVPs.

October 3, 1960: Husky quarterback Bob Schloredt appears on the cover of the October 3 issue of *Sports Illustrated*, the first-ever Husky athlete to appear on *SI*'s cover.

October 22, 1960: In Multnomah Stadium in Portland, Oregon, the Huskies, down 15 at halftime, stage one of the greatest comebacks in their history, winning 30–29.

Sonny Sixkiller

November 19, 1960: The Huskies, unbeaten in the conference but trailing to Washington State late in the fourth quarter, start a 62-yard drive to score. A two-point conversion gives Washington the victory and another trip to the Rose Bowl.

January 2, 1961: Washington faces No. 1 Minnesota in the Rose Bowl. The Huskies win 17–7 and are declared national champions by one of the two polls that rank teams after postseason play (most others choose their national champions after the conclusion of the regular season).

November 18, 1961: Running back Charlie Mitchell returns a kickoff for 90 yards and a touchdown in an upset of UCLA, 17–13.

October 6, 1962: Sophomore quarterback Bill Douglas, from Wapato, Washington, passes for 86 yards and rushes for 34 in his first start. He leads the Huskies to a 41–0 win over Kansas State.

November 19, 1966: The Huskies win 19–7 over the Cougars in Pullman. Twelve of the 19 points—a school record—come from the kicking of Don Martin.

September 19, 1970: Sophomore quarterback Sonny Sixkiller leads the Huskies to a 42–16 win over Michigan State in the season opener. He is honored as National "Back of the Week" by Associated Press. It is his first-ever varsity game.

September 18, 1971: In one of the greatest games in Husky Stadium, Sonny Sixkiller and Purdue quarterback Gary Danielson duel it out right down to the final seconds. The Huskies win 38–35 on a 33-yard Sixkiller pass to wide receiver Tom Scott.

October 4, 1971: Sixkiller is featured on the cover of *Sports Illustrated*. He is the second Husky quarterback to be on the cover of *SI* and, to date, the last Washington player to be so honored.

November 10, 1973: Washington wins its 400th game with a 41–14 victory over Idaho.

October 26, 1974: The Huskies run all over the Ducks at home, 66–0, Washington's largest margin of victory since 1944.

November 23, 1974: In Jim Owens' last game as Husky head coach, quarterback Dennis Fitzpatrick sets a single-game record for rushing yards for a quarterback (249), which still stands today. He also sets a single-season record for rushing yards by a quarterback.

November 27, 1974: Jim Owens announces his retirement as head coach at the annual football banquet. He is 47.

December 23, 1974: Don James becomes the head coach at Washington.

November 22, 1975: Behind 27–14 with about three minutes left in the game, Husky defensive back Al Burleson intercepts a Cougars pass and goes 93 yards to pull the Huskies within six. The Huskies win the game on a 78-yard pass from quarterback Warren Moon to Spider Gaines. The ball is deflected off the hands of a Cougars defender into the hands of Gaines near midfield, and the Husky sprinter races the rest of the way to tie the score. Steve Robbins barely makes the extra point to win the game 28–27.

July 2, 1977: At the annual USA-USSR track meet in Sochi, Russia, Spider Gaines wins a gold medal, running the 110-meter hurdles in 13.69 seconds.

November 12, 1977: Warren Moon leads Washington to a 28–10 win over ninth-ranked USC on the Huskies' way to a conference title and a trip to the 1978 Rose Bowl. It is the Huskies' first conference title since 1963.

January 2, 1978: The Huskies beat fourth-ranked Michigan 27–20 in the Rose Bowl. It is the first bowl victory for James and the first Rose Bowl victory for the Huskies since 1961. Warren Moon receives the MVP Award.

December 22, 1979: After finishing second in the conference race to USC, the Huskies beat Texas 14–7 in the Sun Bowl. The MVP is awarded to Paul Skansi.

October 18, 1980: The Huskies beat Stanford 27–24 when Chuck Nelson kicks a 25-yard field goal on the final play of the game.

November 15, 1980: In a span of three minutes in the third quarter, Washington scores two touchdowns to help beat USC 20–10 in Los Angeles. It is the first Husky win over the Trojans in Los Angeles since 1964 and USC's first home loss since 1977.

November 14, 1981: After kicking his second field goal for a 6–3 lead over third-ranked USC, Chuck Nelson's kickoff bounces over the head of the Trojans' Fred Crutcher and is recovered in the end zone by Fred Small for the game-clinching touchdown.

November 21, 1981: The conference title comes down to the last regular-season game. The Huskies beat the Cougars and UCLA loses to USC, giving the Huskies the Rose Bowl bid.

January 1, 1982: Washington shuts out Iowa 28–0 in the Rose Bowl. Freshman running back Jacque Robinson is voted MVP.

November 6, 1982: Linebacker Mark Stewart makes 23 tackles and six sacks to help Washington beat UCLA 10–7.

Mark Stewart

December 25, 1982: Washington plays against the Maryland Terrapins for the only time in Husky history. The Huskies win the Aloha Bowl with a late-fourth-quarter drive. Quarterback Tim Cowan is named MVP.

September 17, 1983: Washington overcomes a 24–10 deficit in the fourth quarter to beat Michigan 25–24 in one of the biggest comebacks in Husky history.

October 8, 1983: Freshman kicker Jeff Jaeger boots a 52-yard field goal to help the Huskies beat the Beavers 34–7. It is the longest field goal during Don James' coaching career.

January 1, 1985: Washington beats second-ranked Oklahoma 28–17 in the Orange Bowl. Jacque Robinson is voted MVP for the second time in a major bowl game.

September 20, 1986: Washington records win No. 500 in a 52–21 rout of BYU.

November 8, 1986: By gaining his 100th win as Husky head coach, Don James becomes the winningest coach in Washington history when the Huskies beat the Beavers 28–12, eclipsing coach Jim Owens' 99 wins.

September 5, 1987: The north side upper deck and roof is added in time for the opening game of the 1987 season, adding 13,000 seats and costing $17.7 million. In the first game at the newly remodeled stadium, the Huskies defeat Stanford 31–21 before 73,676 fans.

December 19, 1987: The Huskies defeat Florida in the Freedom Bowl, 34–7, holding All-American running back Emmitt Smith to 17 rushing yards. Quarterback Cary Conklin is the MVP.

July 21, 1990: The opening ceremonies for the 1990 Goodwill Games are held in Husky Stadium before 70,000 people. The events span 17 days and involve more than 2,300 athletes from 54 countries.

September 22, 1990: The Huskies smother the No. 5 Trojans 31–0. After the game, USC quarterback Todd Marinovich says, "All I saw was purple."

November 3, 1990: The Huskies clinch the Pac-10 title by beating Arizona 54–10 and take their first trip to the Rose Bowl since 1982.

January 1, 1991: Washington beats Iowa in a 46–34 Rose Bowl shootout. Husky sophomore quarterback Mark Brunell is voted the MVP.

September 21, 1991: Down 21–9 in the third quarter, Washington comes from behind in Lincoln, Nebraska, to beat the Cornhuskers 36–21.

October 19, 1991: The Huskies beat seventh-ranked and undefeated California in Strawberry Canyon, 24–17. The Huskies remain unbeaten (6–0) and take over the top spot in the conference race.

November 23, 1991: Washington finishes the conference unbeaten after ending the regular season with a 56–21 victory over the Cougars.

January 1, 1992: Washington records a perfect season by defeating fourth-ranked Michigan 34–14 in the Rose Bowl,. They receive the No. 1 ranking from four major polls. (Unbeaten Miami is ranked No. 1 by only one poll.) Defensive lineman Steve Emtman and quarterback Billy Joe Hobert are voted co–Most Valuable Players.

September 19, 1992: It is a "night to remember." Before a national television audience on ESPN, Washington beats Nebraska 29–14 and jumps to No. 1 in the polls.

November 7, 1992: Washington loses 16–3 to 12th-ranked Arizona in Tucson, suffering its first loss of the season. Two days before the game, news that Billy Joe Hobert received a $50,000 loan from a wealthy Idaho scientist is reported. Hobert is suspended for the season, and his act spurs external and internal investigations of the Husky football program.

January 1, 1993: After winning their third-straight conference title, the Huskies play in the Rose Bowl and lose 38–31 to Michigan.

August 22, 1993: Don James resigns after 18 years of coaching the Huskies. Assistant head coach Jim Lambright becomes the new head coach.

September 4, 1993: Coached by Bill Walsh, Stanford comes to Husky Stadium for the season opener. Before the game starts, Husky players pay a surprise tribute to former coach Don James, who is in the stands.

September 24, 1994: The Huskies travel to Miami to play the fifth-ranked Hurricanes, who have won 58-straight home games. The 'Canes jump out to a 14–3 halftime lead, but in a span of about four minutes, the Huskies score 22 points on their way to a 38–20 comeback victory.

September 23, 1995: Before the largest crowd in Husky history (76,125), Washington beats Army 21–13.

November 18, 1995: The Huskies end the season with a share of the conference title, with USC. Based on the regular-season record, USC goes to the Rose Bowl and Washington goes to the Sum Bowl. Iowa defeats the Huskies 38–18.

September 20, 1997: Led by Brock Huard, the second-ranked Huskies lose 24–17 to No. 7 Nebraska in Husky Stadium. Huard is injured during the game and replaced by freshman quarterback Marques Tuiasosopo.

December 25, 1997: Washington faces coach Nick Saban's Michigan State Spartans in the Aloha Bowl. Husky running back Rashaan Shehee rushes for 193 yards on 29 carries to gain the MVP Award.

November 21, 1998: Washington beats the Cougars 16–9 to reach win No. 600.

December 25, 1998: After finishing fifth in the conference in a 6–5 regular season, the Huskies lose 45–25 to Air Force in the Oahu Bowl. Five days later, Coach Lambright is fired by AD Barbara Hedges. He is succeeded by Rich Neuheisel.

October 30, 1999: Husky quarterback Marques Tuiasosopo sets an NCAA single-game record of 207 rushing yards and 302 passing yards, leading the Huskies to a 35–30 win over Stanford.

September 9, 2000: The 15th-ranked Huskies beat fourth-ranked Miami 34–29 in Husky Stadium.

October 28, 2000: Washington beats the Cardinal in Palo Alto, 31–28, but there is no joy in the victory. Senior safety Curtis Williams is paralyzed while tackling Stanford running back Kerry Carter.

January 1, 2001: Washington beats Purdue 34–24 in the Rose Bowl. The Huskies' Marques Tuiasosopo outplays Purdue QB Drew Brees and is awarded MVP honors. The Huskies finish third in the national polls behind Oklahoma and Miami.

November 23, 2002: The Huskies face No. 3 Washington State in Pullman. The 9–1–0 Cougars, led by quarterback Jason Gesser, lead 20–10 late in the fourth quarter. A Husky touchdown and a field goal send the game into overtime. Husky kicker John Anderson splits the uprights in triple overtime, and the Huskies recover a Cougars lateral to win the game 29–26.

June 11, 2003: Coach Neuheisel is fired for twice lying to athletic director Barbara Hedges. Keith Gilbertson is subsequently appointed as the Husky head coach.

June 19, 2004: Todd Turner is named Washington's AD after Hedges' resignation.

December 13, 2004: Turner names Tyrone Willingham as the new Husky head football coach.

January 31, 2008: Todd Turner, who resigned in December 2007 as athletic director, is replaced by Scott Woodward.

December 8, 2008: Steve Sarkisian is appointed head football coach.

September 19, 2009: The Huskies upset third-ranked USC 16–13. With the last seconds ticking down, kicker Erik Folk drills a 22-yard field goal for the win.

December 5, 2009: In the final game of the season, the Huskies put together a great game plan and wallop 19th-ranked California 42–10. The Huskies rack up 463 yards to Cal's 296. Quarterback Jake Locker completes 19-of-23 passes for 248 yards and throws three touchdown passes. Defensive tackle Daniel Te'o-Nesheim has three sacks to increase his season total to 30, a new career record for sacks in school history.

October 2, 2010: The Huskies meet the Trojans in Los Angeles. Trailing 31–29, with three seconds on the clock, Erik Folk splits the uprights on a long field goal for the Washington win.

December 30, 2010: With a 6–6 bowl-eligible record, the Huskies face Nebraska in the Holiday Bowl. Washington holds Nebraska to 91 yards rushing and a total of 189 in the 19–7 win. UW running back Chris Polk is voted the MVP of the game. It is the last game of Jake Locker's outstanding collegiate career.

September 27, 2012: In a nationally televised game on Thursday night, the Huskies upset No. 8 Stanford 17–13.

October 27, 2012: For the second time in October, the Huskies face a top-10-ranked team. The Huskies beat No. 7 Oregon State 20–17.

November 23, 2012: The Cougars upset Washington after coming from 18 points down to tie the score at the end of regulation. The Cougars win 31–28 in overtime. It is only Washington State's third win of the season.

December 22, 2012: Washington plays Boise State in the Maaco Bowl. Despite losing 28–26, Husky running back Bishop Sankey is named MVP.

Bishop Sankey

Acknowledgments

I want to acknowledge the thousands of former athletes, coaches, students, faculty members, and Husky fans who have given their time, resources, passion, and loyalty to the Husky football program. I was motivated to write this book to chronicle the people and events that have shaped the history and traditions of Husky football.

Many helped me in the research and development of this book. First, I want to thank several members of the staff of the University of Washington Athletic Department. The Sports Publicity Section championed this project from the start. I greatly appreciate the time that Jeff Bechthold, director of communications for football, provided me, as well as the knowledge he shared with me about so many parts of Husky football history. Jeff was always available when I needed information.

I thank assistant athletic director Carter Henderson, who met with me several times to discuss the images that could be obtained from the athletic department for use in this book, and senior associate athletic director O.D. Vincent, who provided oversight of the process.

Thanks also to associate athletic director Chip Lydum for his considerable input on the renovation of Husky

Stadium, for giving me a tour of the stadium in December 2012, and for providing images of the stadium renovations.

Dave Torrell, the curator of the Husky Hall of Fame, also met with me several times, sharing his vast knowledge of Husky football and helping me to review the images collected in the Hall of Fame.

I greatly appreciate the people who met with me to share their knowledge and personal reflections on several eras and areas of Husky football history, including athletic director Scott Woodward, senior associate athletic director Paul King, Don James, Steve Sarkisian, Bob Rondeau, former Husky assistant coach Dick Baird, KJR's Dave Mahler, the *Seattle Times*' Bob Condotta, and former Husky quarterback Damon Huard. I also thank the players, coaches, and staff who talked with me during the course of my research for the previous books I've written, *Husky Stadium*, *Glory of Washington*, and *A Football Band of Brothers*.

A special thanks goes to former Washington governor Dan Evans, who chaired the Stadium Renovation Committee and who provided me a great summary of the work of the committee in making significant decisions

about the renovation process. Thanks also to Jon Runstad, the CEO of Wright Runstad and an original member of the committee. His leadership resulted in a significant reduction of the projected renovation costs.

The role of photographs in illustrating the Husky football tradition is crucial. Many thanks to the University of Washington Sports Publicity Department (UWSPD), the University of Washington Libraries' Manuscripts, Special Collections, and University Archives (UWMSSC), the Museum of History and Industry (MOHAI), and the University of Washington Athletic Department's Hall of Fame for providing archival materials for this book. Special thanks go to Carolyn Marr, Kristin Kinsey, Jeff Bechtold, and Dave Torrell.

Tom Bast, Adam Motin, and Katy Sprinkel of Triumph Books deserve special praise for making this book a reality. Tom began the discussion of publishing this book and its overall scope. Adam then helped me to finalize the content, the types and numbers of photographs, and the length of the book. Katy spent an inordinate amount of time in editing the manuscript and making it much more readable than when she first received it. She has a very special talent and is a joy to work with.

Finally, thanks to my wife, Dixie Jo Porter, who read drafts, provided wise counsel, and helped in a number of important ways. She is simply the most delightful and talented woman I know. She is also the most objective and charming critic of my writing.

Team and Individual Records

Each year, the University of Washington's Athletic Communications Department develops information on team and individual records established during the history of Husky football. Note that most of the team records are for teams that played at least 10 games in a regular season.

National Championship Teams
(Noted by Individual Polls)

Year	Voted By
1960	Helms Foundation
1984	*Football News*; Berryman; National Championship Foundation (which selected multiple national champions)
1990	FACT (selected multiple national champions)
1991	*USA Today* / CNN; UPI / National Football Foundation; Football Writers of America; *Sports Illustrated*; Berryman; Billingsley; DeVold; Dunkel; FACT; FB News; Matthews: National Championship Foundation; Sagarin.

Conference Championships

Year	Voted By
1916	Pacific Coast
1919	Pacific Coast (T)
1925	Pacific Coast
1936	Pacific Coast
1959	Athletic Association of Western Universities (T)
1960	AAWU
1963	AAWU
1977	Pacific-8
1980	Pacific-10
1981	Pacific-10
1990	Pacific-10
1991	Pacific-10
1992	Pacific-10 (T)
1995	Pacific-10 (T)
2000	Pacific-10 (T)

Unbeaten, Untied Teams

Season	Record
1909	7–0–0
1910	6–0–0
1911	7–0–0
1912	6–0–0
1913	7–0–0
1915	7–0–0
1991	12–0–0

Unbeaten Teams

Season	Record
1895	4–0–1
1908	6–0–1
1914	6–0–1
1916	6–0–1

Longest Winning Streaks

Games	Years
40	1908–14
22	1990–92
12	2000–01
12	1914–16
10	1981–82

Longest Unbeaten Streaks (Includes Ties)

Games	Overall Record	Years
64*	(60–0–4)	1907–17
22	(22–0–0)	1990–92
14	(12–0–2)	1924–25
12	(12–0)	2000–01
10	(9–0–1)	1922–23
10	(10–0–0)	1981–82

*NCAA Record

Most Points Scored in a Single Game: All-Time

Score	Opponent	Year
120–0	Whitman	1919
108–0	Willamette	1925
100–0	Whitworth	1913
99–0	Fort Worden	1911
96–0	College of Puget Sound	1924
81–0	Rainier Valley AC	1914
80–7	College of Puget Sound	1925
77–0	Whitman	1931
73–0	College of Puget Sound	1929
72–0	California	1915

Most Points Scored in a Single Game: Since 1945

Score	Opponent	Year
66–0	Oregon	1974
65–7	UC Santa Barbara	1971
63–6	Oregon	1951
58–6	Oregon State	1991
58–7	Montana	1951
58–28	Arizona	1997
56–67	Baylor	2011
56–3	Kansas State	1991
56–21	Washington State	1991
56–17	Oregon State	1981
56–7	Navy	1970

Most Points Scored in a Single Season (Since 1945)

Year	Total Points (Including Postseason)	Regular-Season Points
1991	495	461
1990	440	394
2011	434	378
1997	420	369
1984	412	384
2002	398	374
1996	391	370
2000	387	353
2007	380	380
1986	378	372
1971	357	357

Fewest Points Allowed in a Single Season (Since 1945)

Year	Total Points (Including Postseason)	Regular-Season Points
1945	54	54
1959	73	65
1962	83	83
1955	93	93
1961	98	98
1947	99	99
1960	107	100
1964	110	110
1991	115	101
1967	130	130

Individual Records

The Sports Communications Department posts many individual offense and defense records. With the counsel of a member of the department, I have provided those records in which fans are most interested.

Most Rushing Yards, Single Game

Player	Yards	Opponent, Year
Hugh McElhenny	296	Washington State, 1950
Chris Polk	284	Washington State, 2010
Corey Dillon	259	Oregon, 1996
Credell Green	258	Washington State, 1955
Louis Rankin	255	Stanford, 2007
Napoleon Kaufman	254	San Jose State, 1994
Dennis Fitzpatrick	249	Washington State, 1974
Napoleon Kaufman	227	UCLA, 1994
Louis Rankin	224	California, 2007
Corey Dillon	222	San Jose State, 1996

Most Rushing Yards, Single Season

Player	Yards	Year
Corey Dillon	1,695	1996
Chris Polk	1,488	2011
Bishop Sankey	1,439	2012
Chris Polk	1,415	2010
Greg Lewis	1,407	1990
Napoleon Kaufman	1,390	1994
Napoleon Kaufman	1,299	1993
Louis Rankin	1,294	2007
Greg Lewis	1,197	1989
Chris Polk	1,113	2009

Most Rushing Yards, Career

Player	Yards	Years
Napoleon Kaufman	4,106	1991–94
Chris Polk	4,049	2008–11
Joe Steele	3,168	1976–79
Greg Lewis	2,903	1987–90
Vince Weathersby	2,811	1985–88
Jacque Robinson	2,636	1981–84
Hugh McElhenny	2,499	1949–51
Louis Rankin	2,480	2004–07
Rich Alexis	2,455	2000–03
Rashaan Shehee	2,381	1994–97

Longest Touchdown Run

Yards	Player	Opponent, Year
105*	Royal Shaw	Idaho, 1904
94	Sterling Hill	Puyallup, 1898
92	Dean Derby	Illinois, 1956
91	Napoleon Kaufman	San Jose State, 1994
91	Hugh McElhenny	Kansas State, 1950
88	Ron Medved	Stanford, 1963
86	Rich Alexis	Arizona State, 2000
85	Rashaan Shehee	Washington State, 1995
85	Charlie Mitchell	Idaho, 1960
85	Ervin Dailey	Whitman, 1919

The field was 110 yards long in 1904.

Most Passing Yards, Single Game

Yards	Player	Opponent, Year
455	Cody Pickett	Arizona, 2001
438	Keith Price	Baylor, 2011 (Alamo Bowl)
438	Cody Pickett	Idaho, 2002
429	Cody Pickett	UCLA, 2002
428	Cary Conklin	Arizona State, 1989
404	Cody Pickett	Wyoming, 2002
399	Cody Pickett	California, 2002
387	Sonny Sixkiller	Purdue, 1971
371	Cody Pickett	Washington State, 2001
368	Cody Pickett	Washington State, 2002

Most Passing Yards, Single Season

Yards	Player	Year
4,458	Cody Pickett	2002
3,063	Keith Price	2011
3,043	Cody Pickett	2003
2,800	Jake Locker	2009
2,786	Cary Conklin	1989
2,728	Keith Price	2012
2,696	Cody Pickett	2001
2,609	Damon Huard	1995
2,463	Billy Joe Hobert	1991
2,460	Tom Flick	1980

Most Passing Yards, Career

Yards	Player	Years
10,220	Cody Pickett	1999–03
7,639	Jake Locker	2007–10
6,391	Brock Huard	1996–98
5,955*	Keith Price	2010–12
5,886	Damon Huard	1992–95
5,879	Marques Tuiasosopo	1997–2000
5,496	Sonny Sixkiller	1970–72
5,082	Cary Conklin	1986–89
4,917	Steve Pelluer	1980–83
4,735	Chris Chandler	1984–87

* Active

Longest Touchdown Passes

Yards	Quarterback to Receiver(s)	Opponent, Year
98	Jake Locker to Marcel Reece	Arizona, 2007
89	Cody Pickett to Reggie Williams	San Jose State, 2002
87	Cody Pickett to Charles Frederick	Oregon State, 2003
86	Carl Bonnell to Cody Ellis	Oregon State, 2007
84	Tom Flick to Willie Rosborough	Air Force, 1980
83	Jake Locker to Anthony Russo	Oregon, 2007
83	Marques Tuiasosopo to Todd Elstrom	California, 1999
83	Brock Huard to Corey Dillon	San Jose State, 1996
80	Keith Price to Jermaine Kearse	Baylor, 2011 Alamo Bowl
80	Jake Locker to D'Andre Goodwin	California, 2010
80	Cody Pickett to Reggie Williams	Arizona, 2002
80	Tom Manke to Harrison Wood	Air Force, 1967
80	Steve Roake to Jim Houston to Corky Lewis	USC, 1955
80	Don Heinrich to George Black	UCLA, 1952
80	Frank Waskowitz to Merle Miller	Washington State, 1937

Most Receptions, Single Game

Receptions	Player	Opponent, Year
15	Braxton Cleman	USC, 2002
14	Reggie Williams	Oregon, 2002
13	Reggie Williams	Arizona, 2003
12	Reggie Williams	Washington State, 2002
12	Dane Looker	USC, 1998
11	Reggie Williams	Washington State, 2001
11	Dane Looker	Arizona State, 1998
11	Jim King	USC, 1970
11	Jim Cope	USC, 1966
10	Reggie Williams	UCLA, 2003
10	Reggie Williams	Stanford, 2003
10	Reggie Williams	Ohio State, 2003
10	Patrick Reddick	California, 2002
10	Fred Coleman	UCLA, 1997
10	Anthony Allen	Oregon, 1982
10	Dave Williams	UCLA, 1965
10	Dave Williams	Stanford, 1965
10	Kasen Williams	Stanford, 2012

Most Receptions, Single Season

Receptions	Yards	Player	Year
94	1,454	Reggie Williams	2002
89	1,109	Reggie Williams	2003
77	878	Kasen Williams	2012
73	1,299	Jerome Pathon	1997
72	762	Dane Looker	1998
69	850	Austin Seferian-Jenkins	2012
68	1,163	Mario Bailey	1991
63	1,005	Jerome Kearse	2010
60	692	D'Andre Goodwin	2008
60	1,035	Reggie Williams	2001
60	718	Paul Skansi	1982

Most Receptions, Career

Receptions	Yards	Player	Years
243	3,598	Reggie Williams	2001–03
180	2,871	Jerome Kearse	2008–11
161	1,992	Paul Skansi	1979–82
143	1,048	Vince Weathersby	1985–88
141	2,306	Mario Bailey	1988–91
138	2,275	Jerome Pathon	1995–97
131	1,802	Devin Aguilar	2008–11
121	1,735	Charles Fredrick	2001–04
119	1,648	Sonny Shackelford	2003–06
118	1,693	Anthony Allen	1979–82

Most Receptions by a Tight End, Single Season

Receptions	Yards	Player	Year
69	852	Austin Seferian Jenkins	2012
43	651	Jerramy Stevens	2000
42	475	Kevin Ware	2002
38	795	Dave Williams	1965
36	360	David Bayle	1980
30	450	John Brady	1972
30	414	Mark Bruener	1993
30	366	Aaron Pierce	1991
24	414	Ernie Conwell	1995
21	361	John Brady	1971

Most Receptions by a Tight End, Single Game

Receptions	Player	Opponent, Year
10	Dave Williams	UCLA, 1965
10	Dave Williams	Stanford, 1965
9	Jerramy Stevens	Texas, 2001 (Holiday Bowl)
9	Austin Seferian-Jenkins	San Diego State, 2012
8	Jerramy Stevens	Arizona, 2000
7	Jerramy Stevens	Colorado, 2000
7	Jerramy Stevens	Miami, 2000
7	Mark Bruener	California, 1983
6	Austin Seferian-Jenkins	Oregon State, 2011
6	Joe Toledo	Arizona, 2004
6	Kevin Ware	Idaho, 2002
6	Jerramy Stevens	Washington State, 1999
6	Mark Bruener	USC, 1993

Most Receptions by a Tight End, Career

Receptions	Yards	Player
110*	1,390	Austin Seferian-Jenkins
95	1,102	Mark Bruener
88	1.113	Jerramy Stevens
81	743	Rod Jones
67	1,040	John Brady
62	1,133	Dave Williams
58	702	Aaron Pierce
55	824	Cameron Cleeland
51	802	Ernie Conwell
48	753	Scott Greenwood

*Active

Most Offensive Yards, Single Game

Yards	Player	Opponent, Year
509	Marques Tuiasosopo	Stanford, 1999
493	Jake Locker	Arizona, 2007
477	Keith Price	Baylor, 2011 Alamo Bowl
473	Cody Pickett	Arizona, 2001
430	Cody Pickett	Idaho, 2002
420	Jake Locker	USC, 2010
419	Cary Conklin	Arizona State, 1989
399	Cody Pickett	UCLA, 2002
396	Cody Pickett	California, 2002
391	Cody Pickett	Wyoming, 2002

Most Offensive Yards, Single Season

Yards	Player	Year
4,273	Cody Pickett	2002
3,188	Jake Locker	2009
3,073	Keith Price	2011
3,048	Jake Locker	2007
2,989	Marques Tuiasosopo	1999
2,982	Cody Pickett	2003
2,764	Cody Pickett	2001
2,753	Marques Tuiasosopo	2000
2,721	Cary Conklin	1989
2,692	Keith Price	2012

Most Offensive Yards, Career

Total Yards	Rushing Yards	Passing Yards	Player
10,103	−117	10,220	Cody Pickett
9,578	1,939	7,639	Jake Locker
7,374	1,495	5,879	Marques Tuiasosopo
6,330	−61	6,391	Brock Huard
6,004	118	5,886	Damon Huard
5,946*	−9	5,955	Keith Price
5,288	−208	5,496	Sonny Sixkiller
5,248	331	4,917	Steve Pelluer
5,178	96	5,082	Cary Conklin
5,093	358	4,735	Chris Chandler

Active

Most Kickoff Return Yards, Single Game

Yards	Player	Opponent, Year
176	Kevin Smith	USC, 2011
168	Kevin Smith	Stanford, 2011
166	Reggie Brown	Oregon, 1974
161	Jim Krieg	Stanford, 1970
155	Roc Alexander	Arizona, 2001
152	Buddy Kennamer	UCLA, 1969
150	Kevin Smith	Arizona, 2011
147	Quinton Richardson	Notre Dame, 2009
147	Louis Rankin	Arizona State, 2007
137	Jim Cope	Stanford, 1968

Most Kickoff Return Yards, Single Season

Yards	Player	Year
976	Louis Rankin	2007
958	Kevin Smith	2011
748	Toure Butler	1998
623	Roc Alexander	2001
601	Charles Frederick	2002
595	Jordan Polk	2008
576	Jesse Callier	2011
576	Jim Krieg	1970
573	Steve Bramwell	1965
565	Steve Bramwell	1963

Most Kickoff Return Yards, Career

Yards	Player	Years
1,532	Steve Bramwell	1963–65
1,397	Steve Jones	1986–88
1,373	Anthony Allen	1979–82
1,365*	Kevin Smith	2010–12
1,329	Charles Frederick	2001–04
1,309	Jesse Callier	2010–11
1,282	Kevin Smith	2010–11
1,206	Louis Rankin	2004–07
956	Roc Alexander	2000–03
931	Napoleon Kaufman	1991–94

Active

Most Punt Return Yards, Single Game

Yards	Player	Opponent, Year
166	Joe Jarzynka	California, 1998
134	Steve Bramwell	Baylor, 1964
131	Beno Bryant	Arizona State, 1990
130	Bill Cahill	TCU, 1971
122	George Fleming	Wisconsin, 1960 (Rose Bowl)
113	Steve Bramwell	Oregon State, 1963
109	Beno Bryant	Kansas State, 1991
109	Nesby Glasgow	Stanford, 1977
108	Anthony Allen	Stanford, 1981
106	Bill Cahill	Illinois, 1971

Most Punt Return Yards, Single Season

Yards	Player	Year
593	Beno Bryant	1990
460	Andre Riley	1986
425	Joe Jarzynka	1998
425	Ernie Steele	1940
421	Bill Cahill	1971
353	George Fleming	1959
340	Charles Frederick	2003
318	Ernie Steele	1941
318	Ernie Steele	1939
314	Steve Bramwell	1964

Most Punt Return Yards, Career

Yards	Player	Years
1,086	Beno Bryant	1989–93
1,061	Ernie Steele	1939–41
860	Joe Jarzynka	1996–99
723	Steve Bramwell	1963–65
699	Charles Frederick	2001–04
668	Bill Cahill	1970–72
642	Ray Horton	1979–82
627	Andre Riley	1986–89
619	George Fleming	1958–60
596	Calvin Jones	1970–72

Two players—John Anderson (2002) and Jeff Jaeger (1985)—have kicked five field goals in a single game, 14 have kicked four field goals in a game, and 27 have kicked three in a game. Following are the statistics for single-season and career superlatives.

Most Field Goals, Single Season

Field Goals	Player	Year
25	Chuck Nelson	1982
23	Jeff Jaeger	1985
22	John Anderson	2002
22	Jeff Jaeger	1984
21	Jeff Jaeger	1983
20	Chuck Nelson	1980
19	Jeff Jaeger	1986
19	Erik Folk	2009
18	John Wales	1984
17	John Anderson	2001

Most Field Goals, Career

Field Goals	Player	Years
85	Jeff Jaeger	1983–86
68	John Anderson	1999–02
61	Chuck Nelson	1980–82
42	Erik Folk	2009–10
40	Travis Hanson	1990–93
37	Steve Robbins	1974–77
36	John Wales	1984–96
28	Evan Knudson	2003–05
26	John McCallum	1988–89
24	Mile Lansford	1978–79

Longest Field Goals

Distance (Yards)	Player	Opponent, Year
56	John Anderson	UCLA, 1999
56	Don Martin	Air Force, 1967
54	Erik Folk	BYU, 2010
53	Erik Folk	Eastern Washington, 2011
52	Erik Folk	Oregon, 2010
52	John Anderson	Arizona, 2002
52	John Anderson	Oregon State, 2002
52	Jeff Jaeger	Oregon, 1983
52	Jeff Jaeger	Oregon State, 1983
51	John Anderson	California, 2002
51	Chuck Nelson	Kansas State, 1981
51	Ron Volbrecht	Rice, 1968

Chuck Nelson owns the longest kicking streak. He kicked 30 successful field goals from November 14, 1981 to November 20, 1982. Jeff Jaeger kicked 16-consecutive field goals during the 1983–84 seasons.

Most Tackles, Single Game

Tackles	Player	Opponent, Year
29	Michael Jackson	Washington State, 1977
29	Michael Jackson	Oregon State, 1977
28	Michael Jackson	Mississippi State, 1977
28	George Jugum	Oregon, 1966
27	Joe Krakoski	Washington State, 1983
26	Ken Driscoll	Oregon, 1980
25	Stan Walderhaug	Syracuse, 1977
25	George Jugum	California, 1968
24	Mark Jerue	Arizona State, 1981
24	Michael Jackson	Alabama, 1978

Most Tackles, Single Season

Tackles	Player	Year
219	Michael Jackson	1977
204	David Rill	1985
201	Dan Lloyd	1973
200	Mike Baldassin	1976
188	David Rill	1987
185	Dave Pear	1973
170	Ricky Andrews	1988
168	Michael Jackson	1978
168	James Clifford	1989
163	Mason Foster	2010

Includes both unassisted and assisted tackles.

Most Tackles, Career

Tackles*	Player	Years
578	Michael Jackson	1975–78
575	David Rill	1984–87
502	Dan Lloyd	1972–75
486	Ken Driscoll	1979–82
401	Joe Kelly	1982–85
389	Al Burleson	1973–75
386	Mike Baldassin	1974–76
378	Mason Foster	2007–10
376	Tim Meamber	1981–84
375	Bruce Harrell	1976–79

Includes both unassisted and assisted tackles.

Most Sacks, Single Season

Sacks	Player	Year
14.5	Jason Chorak	1996
13.0	Ron Holmes	1993
11.5	Donald Jones	1991
11.0	Daniel Te'o Nesheim	2009
11.0	Dennis Brown	1987
10.0	Terry Johnson	2003
10.0	Ray Catage	1982
10.0	Mark Stewart	1982
9.5	Richie Chambers	1994
9.0	Manase Hopoi	2004
9.0	Fred Small	1984
9.0	Ron Holmes	1982

Most Sacks, Career

Sacks	Player	Years
30.0	Daniel Te'o Nesheim	2006–09
28.0	Ron Holmes	1981–84
26.0	Donald Jones	1989–91
25.5	Jason Chorak	1994–97
24.0	Andy Mason	1990–93
20.0	Manase Hopoi	2002–04
20.0	Reggie Rogers	1984–86

Most Interceptions, Single Game

Interceptions	Player	Opponent, Year
4	Al Worley	Idaho, 1968
3	Russell Hairston	Oregon, 1993
3	Tim Meamber	Northwestern, 1984
3	Steve Lipe	Iowa State, 1974
3	Steve Wiezbowski	California, 1972
3	Al Worley	Wisconsin, 1968
3	Sam Mitchell	Oregon, 1952
3	Larry Hatch	California, 1946
3	William McGovern	Oregon State, 1947

Most Interceptions, Single Season

Interceptions	Player	Year
14	Al Worley	1968
12	Bill Albrecht	1951
8	Larry Hatch	1946
8	Walter Bailey	1991
7	Tony Bonwell	1972
7	Dick Sprague	1950
7	Jay Stoves	1943
6	Derrick Johnson	2003
6	Anthony Vontoure	1999
6	Tony Parrish	1997
6	Eric Briscoe	1990
6	Joe Kelly	1984
6	Roberto Jourdan	1972
6	Bob Schloredt	1959
6	George Fleming	1959

Most Interceptions, Career

Interceptions	Player	Years
18	Al Worley	1966–68
16	Larry Hatch	1946–48
13	Vestee Jackson	1983–85
13	Roberto Jourdan	1972–75
13	Bill Albrecht	1951–52, 1954
12	Walter Bailey	1990–92
11	Derrick Johnson	2000–04
11	Reggie Reser	1992–95
11	Calvin Jones	1970–72
10	Ray Horton	1979–82
10	George Fleming	1958–60
10	Dick Sprague	1950–52

Coaching Records

Since 1900, when J.S. Dodge became the first paid head coach of the University of Washington's football team, there have been 22 head coaches. Don James is the winningest coach in Husky history to date, but Gilmour Dobie's winning percentage of .976 is all but uncatchable. Below is a chronological listing of coaches, along with their tenures and overall records.

Coach	Year(s)	Overall Record	Winning Percentage
J.S. Dodge	1900	1–2–2	.400
Jack Wright	1901	3–3–0	.500
James Knight	1902–04	15–4–1	.775
Oliver Cutts	1905	4–2–2	.625
Victor Place	1906–07	8–5–6	.579
Gilmour Dobie	1908–16	59–0–3	.976
Claude Hunt	1917, 1919	6–3–1	.650
Tony Savage	1918	1–1–0	.500
Leonard Allison	1920	1–5–0	.167
Enoch Bagshaw	1921–29	63–22–6	.725
James Phelan	1930–41	65–37–8	.616
Ralph Welch	1942–47	27–20–3	.570

Coach	Year(s)	Overall Record	Winning Percentage
Howard Odell	1948–52	23–25–2	.483
John Cherberg	1953–55	10–18–2	.344
Darrell Royal	1956	5–5–0	.500
Jim Owens	1957–74	99–82–6	.545
Don James	1975–92	153–57–2	.726
Jim Lambright	1993–98	44–25–1	.664
Rick Neuheisel	1999–2002	33–16	.673
Keith Gilbertson	2003–04	7–16	.304
Tyrone Willingham	2005–08	11–37	.229
Steve Sarkisian*	2009–present	26–25	.510

*Active

University of Washington
Intercollegiate Athletics Financial Information
Major Operating Revenue and Operating Expenses (in millions)

	Actual 2011-2012	Percent
Operating Revenue		
Gate Revenues		
Football	$8.1	
Football Away Games and Other Sports	5.7	
Total Gate Revenue	23.8	28.8
Contributions		
Tyee Football Donor Seats	8.5	
Building Fund for Excellence (Football)	2.9	
Don James Center and Other Luxury Seating	6.2	
Non-Football Seat-Related, Scholarships, tec.	5.9	
Total Contributions	23.5	28.5
Other		
NCAA and Conference Distributions	16.2	
Multimedia (Signage, Radio, Local TV)	5.5	
Other sponsorships	5.5	
State Funded Tuition Waivers (Title IX)	3.1	
Other	5.0	
	35.3	42.7
TOTAL OPERATING REVENUE	**$82.6**	100.0%
Operating Expenses		
Salaries and Benefits	30.3	41.1
Financial Aid and Scholarships	10.1	13.7
Travel	6.5	8.8
Day of Game Expenses	4.6	6.2
Guarantees Paid to Visiting Teams	3.1	4.2
Donated Advertising and Supplies	3.9	5.3
Supplies and Equipment	2.3	3.1
UW Overhead, Utilities, Repairs, and Maintenance	3.9	5.3
Other Expenses	9.1	12.3
TOTAL OPERATING EXPENSES	**$ 73.8**	100.0%
NET OPERATING INCOME	**$ 8.8**	
PERCENT OF OPERATING INCOME	**10.6%**	

Notes on Above

1. Projected estimates of NCAA and conference distributions show significant increases due primarily to the revenue from the PAC-12 Conference.

2. The revenue from seating in the luxury suites, patio suites, and club seating start to significantly increase in increase in 2013–2014 and beyond.

3. The capital costs to renovate Husky Stadium and other athletic facilities are not reflected above but are included in a separate financial analysis and projections prepared by the athletic department. These projections also show the costs to service the debt incurred to renovate the statement. All estimated future operating profits are allocated to paying off the debt.

Economics of the University of Washington Athletic Program

In a recent study (January 2010), the Knight Commission on Intercollegiate Athletics Foundation reported that only 12 of 120 Division I athletic programs either broke even or made money in fiscal 2009. A *Seattle Times* article on December 23, 2012, reported that in the 120 schools in the top division of football, the median athletic budget in fiscal 2011 was $38 million. The richest programs generated almost $150 million. The article indicated that only 23 programs generated a profit in the 2011 year.

The University of Washington is one of the few schools in the nation that gets very little financial support from sources other than athletic activities. The university requires that the athletic program operates within its revenue base. In the academic year 2011–12, the latest year for which audited financial statements were available for this printing, the UW athletic department generated $82.6 million in revenue, had operating expenses of $73.8 million, and a profit of $8.8 million.

Other sources of information on the economics of Division I athletic programs indicate that football and men's basketball are the only sports to show a profit in most schools around the country—that is true of Washington as well. In the most recent detailed sport-by-sport financial analysis (for the 2010–11 academic year), football generated $39,405,237 of revenue. After allocation of all the related costs, the profit contribution was $16,995,057: 43 percent of the football revenue. Men's basketball had a 42 percent profit contribution, $4,458,317, on revenue of $10, 474,040.

The major revenue sources and operating expenses are shown, opposite.

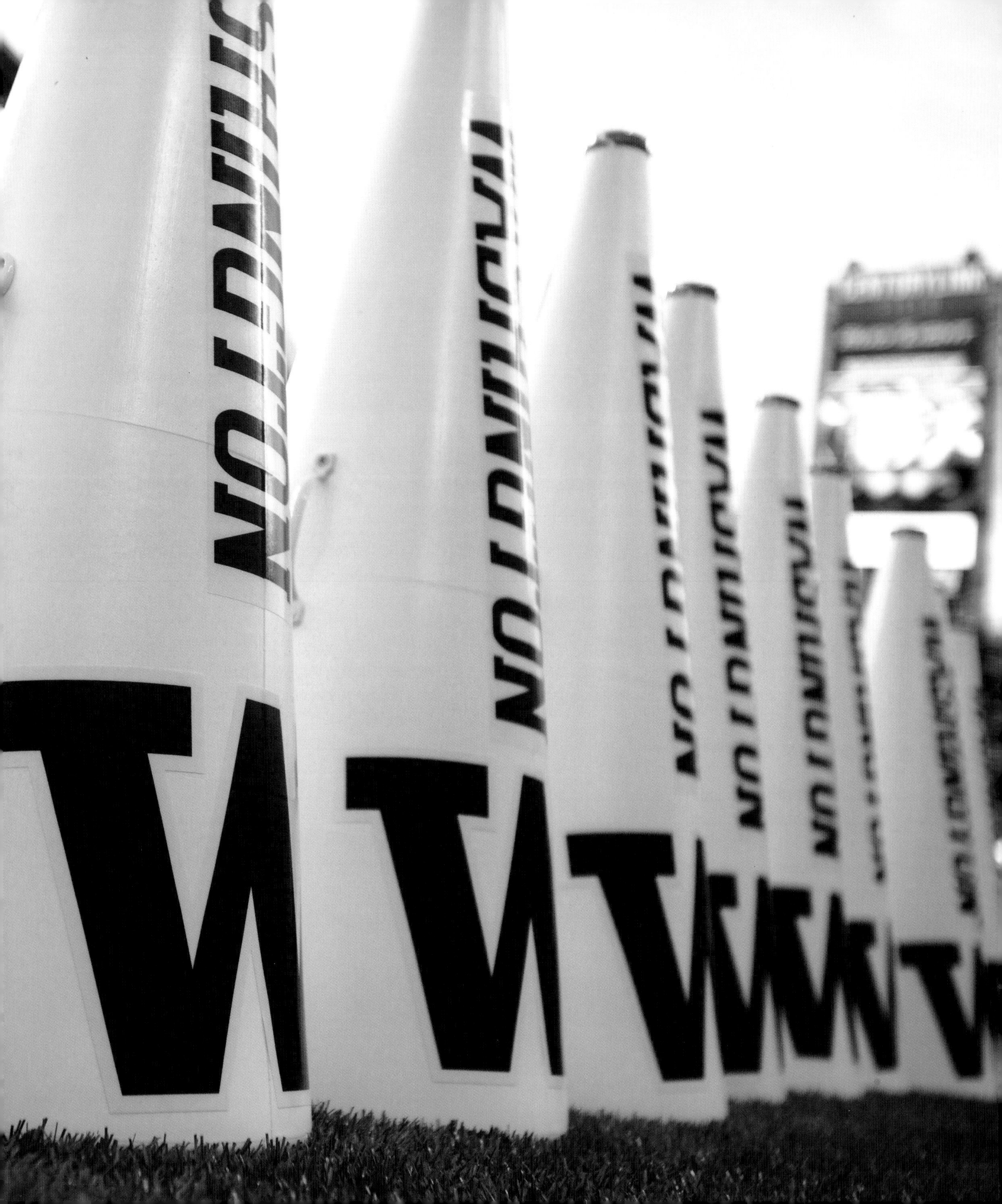

Research Methodology and Bibliography

I used many sources of information in the research for this book. In addition to the books listed below, there were four primary sources. One was the University of Washington Athletics Communications Department, located in the Graves Building. Another was the University Manuscripts, Special Collections, and University Archives Division (UWMssSCUA), located in Allen Library. The third was the Microfilm and Newspaper Collections Department in Suzzallo Library. The fourth was Seattle's Museum of History and Industry.

The Athletics Communications Department publishes annual football media guides and also has extensive references, including NCAA and Pac-10 publications. The Special Collections Department houses data related to early university and athletic history, including a complete set of the *Tyee* (the university yearbook), original copies of campus newspapers (the *Pacific Wave*, the *Wave*, and the *Daily*), and many photographs of early athletes and teams, some of which appear in this book. The Microfilm Department houses archives of many local newspapers, including the *Seattle Post-Intelligencer,* the *Seattle Times*, and the *University Daily*. Many of the quotes in the book—particularly game summaries—came from contemporaneous newspaper articles.

Finally, I interviewed and received correspondence from many of those listed in my acknowledgments.

Ambrose, Stephen, *Band of Brothers: E Company, 506th Regiment, 101st Airborne from Normandy to Hitler's Eagle Nest.* New York: Simon & Schuster, 1992.

Borland, Lynn, *Gilmour Dobie: Pursuit of Perfection.* Tribute Publishing, 2010.

Boyles, Bob and Paul Guide, *Fifty Years of College Football*, Wilmington, Delaware: Sideline Communications, Inc., 2005

Burke, Roger, *Once a Husky, Always a Husky*. Kennewick, Washington: Columbia River Book Co., 2005.

Chave, Karen and Steve Rudman, *100 Years of Husky Football*. New York: Professional Sports Publishing, 1990.

Daves, Jim and W. Thomas Porter, *The Glory of Washington: The People and Events That Shaped the Husky Athletic Tradition*. Champaign, Illinois: Sports Publishing, Inc., 2001.

Dent, Jim, *The Junction Boys*. New York: St. Martin's Press, 1999.

Dent, Jim, *The Undefeated: The Oklahoma Sooners and the Greatest Winning Streak in College Football*. New York: St. Martin's Press, 2001.

Egan, Timothy, *The Worst Hard Time: The Untold Story of Those Who Survived the Great American Dust Bowl*. New York: Houghton Mifflin Company, 2006.

Gates, Charles M., *The First Century at the University of Washington, 1861–1961*. Seattle: University of Washington Press, 1961.

Gayton, Carver. "Carver Gayton Reflects on the Jim Owens statue at Husky Stadium, University of Washington," http://www.historylink.org/index.cfm?DisplayPage=output.cfm&file_id=5745 (accessed October 5, 2012).

James, Don, as told to Virgil Parker, *James*. 1991

Johnson, Derek, *Husky Football in the Don James Era*. Seattle: Derek Johnson Books, 2007.

Johnson, Derek, *The Dawgs of War: A Remembrance*. Seattle: Derek Johnson Books, 2009.

Johnston, Norman J., *The Fountain & the Mountain*, Second Edition. Seattle: Documentary Book Publishers and the University of Washington, 2003.

Owen, John, *Press Pass*. Seattle: The Seattle Post-Intelligencer, 1994.

Quirk, James, *The Ultimate Guide to College Football: Rankings, Records, and Scores of the Major Teams and Conferences*. Champaign, Illinois: University of Illinois Press, 2004.

Porter, W. Thomas and Jim Daves, *Husky Stadium: Great Games and Golden Moments*. Chattanooga, Tennessee: Parker Hood Press, Inc. and Seattle: University of Washington Intercollegiate Athletic Department, 2004.

Porter, W. Thomas, *A Football Band of Brothers: Forging The University of Washington's First National Championship*. Victoria, British Columbia: Trafford Publishing, 2007.

Riffenburgh, Beau and Bill Barron, *The Official NFL Encyclopedia*. New York: New American Library, 1986.

Rockne, Dick. *Bow Down to Washington*. Huntsville, Alabama: The Strode Publishers, 1975.

Seaborg, Glenn T., with Ray Colvig, *Roses from the Ashes: Breakup and Rebirth in Pacific Coast Intercollegiate Athletics*. Berkeley, CA: Institute of Government Studies, 2000.

Sports Illustrated. "Boosters Mess It Up In Washington," *Sports Illustrated*, February 20, 1956.

Sports Illustrated. "One Eye on the Rose Bowl," *Sports Illustrated*, October 3, 1960.

Sports Illustrated. "The Wildest Rose," *Sports Illustrated*, January 9, 1961.

Torrance, Roscoe C., *Torchy!*. Mission Hill, SD: Dakota Homestead Publishers, 1973.

Hewitt, Lynn R., "The History of Intercollegiate Football at the University of Washington from its Origin through 1965," University of Washington, 1967.

Maurer, Bruce L., "A Compendium of Head Coaches of Intercollegiate Sports at the University of Washington, 1892 to 1970." University of Washington, 1970.

About the Author

W. Thomas Porter received his BA from Rutgers University, his MBA from the University of Washington, and his PhD from Columbia University. At Rutgers, he was selected to the All-East and All-America teams in baseball and was voted Rutgers' most outstanding athlete in his senior year.

After serving as an airborne officer and infantry company commander, he enjoyed three full-time careers. He was a professor of management planning and control systems at the University of Washington.

He was a partner of Touche Ross & Co., an international accounting and consulting firm, with several national responsibilities, including being the firm's national director for professional development, national director of strategic planning, and national director of executive financial planning.

His third career was in banking. He was vice chairman at Rainier Bank and Security Pacific Northwest and executive vice president at Seafirst and then Bank of America, where he was responsible for investment banking, investment management, retail investments, and financial-planning services. He was a member of Bank of America's Northwest Executive Committee.

He has authored 10 books on management planning and control and financial planning. In addition to this book, he has written three others on Husky athletics. All were regional best-sellers: *The Glory of Washington: The People and Events that Shaped the Husky Athletic Tradition*, *Husky Stadium: Great Games and Golden Moments,* and *A Football Band of Brothers: Forging the University of Washington's First National Championship*.

Porter has served on eight corporate boards of directors, some national and international in scope. He has been active in many community activities and chaired campaigns that have resulted in more than $100 million contributed. He was chair of the University of Washington's $54 million Capital Campaign for the Student Athlete, which provided funds to renovate Hec Edmundson Pavilion and build the Dempsey Indoor. For his community activities, he has received many awards, including the Volunteer of the Year Award from the National Association of College Athletic Directors and the Frank Orrico Distinguished Service Award, in recognition of his many contributions to Washington's athletic department; and he was a torchbearer for the 1996 Olympic Games, carrying the torch on a leg through Seattle.

Photo Credits

Robin Hood: xii

Museum of History & Industry: page xvi, 2, 4, 5, 8, 9, 10, 12, 15, 20, 28, 29, 34, 78, 194

Sky-Pix Aerial Photography: 163

University of Washington Athletic Department Hall of Fame: 27, 31, 32, 44, 46, 51, 52, 57, 62, 138

University of Washington, Special Collections: 7 (UW11589), 19 (UW19640), 26–27 (UW35580), 35 (UW29681z), 195 (PNW00751)

University of Washington Sports Publishing Department: ii–iii, vi, viii, x, xv, 17, 22, 24, 38, 40, 42, 44, 45, 47, 48, 49, 54, 56, 58, 61, 67, 71, 76, 81, 83, 87, 90, 92, 95, 97, 101, 102, 103, 108, 111, 112, 113, 117, 118, 121, 122, 124, 125, 128, 131, 133, 134, 135, 137, 141, 142, 146 (top), 146 (bottom), 148, 149, 151, 155, 157, 159, 161, 164, 167, 172, 180, 182, 185, 188, 191, 198, 199, 202, 204, 216, 220, 224